Managing Organizational Change During SAP® Implementations

 **PRESS**

SAP PRESS is issued by
Bernhard Hochlehnert, SAP AG

SAP PRESS is a joint initiative of SAP and Galileo Press. The know-how offered by SAP specialists combined with the expertise of the publishing house Galileo Press offers the reader expert books in the field. SAP PRESS features first-hand information and expert advice, and provides useful skills for professional decision-making.

SAP PRESS offers a variety of books on technical and business related topics for the SAP user. For further information, please visit our website: *www.sap-press.com*.

Gary Nolan
Efficient BW Implementation and Project Management
2007, app. 300 pp.
ISBN 978-1-59229-105-2

Ryan Leask and Mathias Pöhling
SAP xApp Analytics
2006, 408 pp.
ISBN 978-1-59229-102-1

Matthias Melich and Marc O. Schäfer
SAP Solution Manager
2007, app. 492 pp.
ISBN 978-1-59229-091-8

Ulrich Schmidt and Gerd Hartmann
Product Lifecycle Management with SAP
2006, 613 pp.
ISBN 978-1-59229-036-9

Luc Galoppin, Siegfried Caems

Managing Organizational Change During SAP® Implementations

Galileo Press

Bonn • Boston

ISBN   978-1-59229-104-5

1st edition 2007

Editor Jawahara Saidullah
Copy Editor John Parker, UCG, Inc., Boston, MA
Cover Design Silke Braun
Layout Design Vera Brauner
Production Iris Warkus
Typesetting SatzPro, Krefeld
Printed and bound in Germany

Contents at a Glance

Contents

PART II: UNFREEZING

8   Program Setup 159

PART III: CHANGING

9   Design 189

10 Build Phase 237

PART IV: REFREEZING

14   Life After SAP 331

Appendix 341

Foreword

They say that the most uncommon thing is common sense. They also say that change management is not rocket science. But if this is true, then why do so many projects fail or suffer the consequences of not practicing common sense?

Projects begin with the best of intentions. At the beginning of every project, the importance of change management and the "soft" side of the implementation is emphasized. This is particularly true for SAP implementations, as benefits of an SAP implementation do not come from implementing old processes into a new solution but by innovating and improving on those processes and using a software solution to realize the changes.

When these projects are launched, the focus is on team members who have the best skills and extensive experience in SAP but not who are the best change managers. The overall budget never seems to be sufficient, so the first thing to fall out is the change-management area (even if budget resources are committed to this in the beginning of the project).

I believe that these things happen because this area is often considered to be too "soft." It is difficult to properly describe or accept the results of the work as hard deliverables from the project team.

In this book, the authors share concepts and practices on change and project management during each phase of a program lifecycle. Obviously, no book can give the one and only solution to a change-management issue, but a more structural approach to change management will serve projects well. After all, the objective of any change-management program is to increase the probability of success and also—more importantly—increase the benefits of innovation and improvement. The contents of this book will help those embarking on projects and those in the middle of projects to more concretely identify and deliver against the needs of projects in this area.

Good luck!

Scott Park
Senior Vice President of Processes & Systems and CIO
Volvo Construction Equipment Group

Preface

Leading the organizational change that accompanies your SAP implementation is like driving across new territory. There may be a multitude of maps and travel guides with interesting stories, but they will not get you to your destination. If you want to get there, you will need to get in the car and start the engine. Weather conditions may require you to slow down and accidents may occur along your path. More often than not, your driving skills, experience, and sense of improvisation will determine how you get across safely. The same goes for SAP programs: the implementation matters. Managing organizational change means harmonizing the interaction between the hard stuff and the soft stuff in the context of your organization.

How does this book address all the facets of organizational change and at the same time deliver practical advice? We found the answer by taking a step back and looking below the surface at the fundaments of human behavior: emotions and perceptions. We found the patterns to codify, organize, and demystify the organizational change agenda, and we linked them to the program management approach and the chronology of an SAP implementation. To keep an overview, we linked some old and new concepts to provide diagnostics or "radars". That is how we translated the patterns we found into concrete actions at each stage of the program.

Organization of This Book

This book is logically organized into four Parts. These Parts make the book easier to navigate and read, and the sections are organized as follows:

Part I: Understanding SAP Organizational Change Management

This Part consists of six chapters, summarized here. The purpose of this first Part is to provide you with direct and pragmatic insight into the complex dimensions of organizational change during SAP implementations.

▸ **Chapter 1, Introduction: What is so Different About SAP Implementations**
The first chapter sets the stage for managing organizational change, and for this book. After reading this chapter, you are ready to start exploring the rest of the book.

▸ **Chapter 2, The Rollercoaster of Emotions**
This allows you to get a grip on the emotional dynamics that form the undercurrents of an organizational change. You will gain clarity about resistance and how it is best dealt with.

▸ **Chapter 3, Making Sense**
This chapter gives you a framework for creating a culture of change, based on the ingredients of change (skills, knowledge, and motivation). This chapter focuses on how you can use the resistance that occurs to make learning happen.

▸ **Chapter 4, Program and Project Management as Enablers of Change**
This chapter provides you with the context of SAP projects, but it does not stop there. This chapter introduces the concepts of benefits realization and program management along with the do's and don'ts of SAP program management.

▸ **Chapter 5, SAP Technology as a Co-Pilot**
In this chapter, you will see how the knowledge platform of SAP Solution Manager can help you manage the ingredients of change.

▸ **Chapter 6, Monitor Parameters of Change: A Radar View**
This chapter is revolutionary because it introduces marketing concepts with which to approach the internal organization. It sets out the basic dimensions for monitoring the hard stuff and the soft stuff during SAP implementations. More precisely, the concepts of "Hard Stuff Radar," "Soft Stuff Radar," and "Moments of Truth" provided in this chapter will enable you to better navigate through the remainder of the book.

The purpose of the next Part is to describe what should be addressed in each phase of the project lifecycle, proceeding according to the chronology of an SAP project. One of the things that makes this book stand out is the fact that we have blended this chronology into the change cycle. Thus, the remainder of the book falls down into Unfreezing, Changing, and Refreezing. Each chapter has a fixed structure. After discussing the phase specific characteristics and needs, and what happens at the level of the program, we discuss each of the four work streams of change management: Organization, Communication, Learning, and Performance Management. Finally, each chapter closes with a summary of the Moments of Truth and deliverables typical for that phase.

Part II: Unfreezing

This Part is titled Unfreezing, because all activities are aimed at the creation of an environment in which change can happen. It has the following two chapters:

▶ **Chapter 7, Program Initiation**
This chapter covers the biggest blind spot of all SAP implementations: Program Initiation.

▶ **Chapter 8, Program Setup**
In this chapter, we discuss the Program Setup. It extensively focuses on the basic deliverables that determine — to a large extent — the course and the success of an SAP implementation.

Part III: Changing

This part describes the implementation part of the SAP program lifecycle. During the four chapters in this Part, the SAP program will transfer your organization into the future state. It is made up of the following four chapters:

▶ **Chapter 9, Design**
In this phase, the system is blueprinted and the organizational change strategy is set out.

▶ **Chapter 10, Build**
As system prototypes get built, this is the time to translate the organizational change strategy into a concrete and tangible plan.

▶ **Chapter 11, Test**
Not only are systems tested, but organizational changes should also be reviewed and corrected.

▶ **Chapter 12, Deploy**
As the tension rises, the organizational change is now reaching a point of no return. This chapter shows you how to manage that stage.

Part IV: Refreezing

The program isn't over until this new balance has settled in. This Part discusses what you can do to facilitate this process:

▶ **Chapter 13, Post-Implementation**
This chapter closes the implementation loop by discussing the post-implementation phase and listing the topics that need to be taken into account when the program is closed.

▶ **Chapter 14, Life After SAP** ·
This final chapter discusses what you need to allow for when the implementation team has adjourned and it is up to the line managers to sustain the change.

The appendices include important supplementary information and examples to help you in your own change management process.

Acknowledgments

We would like to thank the people who have supported us while we were writing this book.

First, there are our families, who have shown a lot of patience and understanding. More than once, they must have felt abandoned, but nevertheless they were always there at difficult moments to give us the mental support we needed.

Secondly, we would like to thank Jawahara K. Saidullah and Chuck Toporek, editors at Galileo Press/SAP Press. Jawahara guided us through the whole writing process and has been very supportive throughout the book's development. We are also grateful to the people at Galileo Press/SAP Press who have helped us through the publishing process.

We would like to thank the people who have contributed greatly to this book, not only by taking the time to read and comment on drafts, but also by providing content to improve the quality of this book. In arbitrary order, they are:

▶ Christel Dehaes, Managing Partner at The Human Interface Group

▶ Daniel Devogelaer, Director Business Solutions and Project Management, Global Information and Business Services at InBev

- Guy Vander Eeckt, Industrial Director at Benelux at Air Liquide
- Herman De Bie, Project Engineer at BASF IT Services
- Ivan Mostien, Group Delivery Manager SAPHR at Arinso
- Luc Aerts, IS Solution Manager Global & WE, at InBev
- Marc Vermeir, Managing Director for Atlantic Consultants and former Vice President Information & Services at Cast and Lykes Lines LLC
- Marc-Oliver Schaefer, Senior Product Manager and SAP Solution Manager at SAP AG
- Mathias Melich, Director Product Management and SAP Solution Manager at SAP AG
- Peter Van Lier, Director at Deloitte & Touche Tohmatsu
- Sandra Hoeylaerts, EAME HR Process Manager at Huntsman
- Sandra Lizioli, Director at Bridge the Gap
- Tanya Lynn Larrydale, Change Control Coordinator at The Estée Lauder Companies
- Valerie l'Heureux, Project Coordinator at The Human Interface Group
- We extend our thanks to the people who have taken the time to read the drafts and give us comments, or who have supported us through their conversations on the topics of this book. In arbitrary order:
- Bob Boone, Global Roll-out Manager at Volvo IT
- Jan Manhaeve, Former HR Director of IBM Belgium
- Jeffer London, Director Learning & Development at Weber Shandwick, FutureBrand & Octagon, and partner at GreenHouse Group
- Johan Conix, Managing Director, Conix Solutions and former Vice President at Gartner
- John Sands, Vice President Change Integration at The Estée Lauder Companies
- Jonathan Manley, Senior Vice President and CIO at The Estée Lauder Companies
- Roger Leyssens, member of the executive committee and HR director at Dexia Bank
- Rohnny Van Calck, Vice President Risk and Asset Management at Volvo Construction Equipment

- ▸ Scott Park, Senior Vice President Processes and Systems & CIO at Volvo Construction Equipment
- ▸ Wolfgang Koehler, Project Manager at Deutsche Bank

And last but not least, we would like to thank all the people who have shown their interest and appreciation in our work. It has helped us to keep going for it.

PART I
Understanding SAP Organizational Change Management

In this chapter you will learn why SAP projects are not just technical software implementation efforts. SAP is process-oriented and integrated software. This has far-reaching consequences on the human side. It seriously alters the way we should approach projects, and it changes our notions of what an implementation should look like.

1 Introduction: What is so Different About SAP Implementations?

1.1 The Day I Got 10 Years Older

I remember that specific morning in 1997 when I arrived at our Philippines office. Three weeks earlier, we had popped the champagne bottles to celebrate the go-live of SAP. Our Manila site was the seventh rollout, so things had become pretty standard for us as Asia-Pacific (APAC) program leaders. The scope of our project was to implement the Sales and Distribution (SD), Materials Management (MM), Production Planning (PP) and Quality Management (QM) modules for all the production plants in the APAC region. By now, we were pretty sure that we tackled about every possible bump in the road towards a successful implementation, and this one was no different than all the others. However, from our progress monitoring a few days earlier we observed that the Philippines sales were down 40 % that month, while production was slow at 50 %. We were used to seeing a peak in sales and production before a go-live, followed by a drop of the same size the first weeks after. In previous rollouts, we had figured out that potential hiccups that could disrupt the day-to-day business were anticipated by building up stocks in production and with the customers. A 40 % drop was alarming, so I flew over to have a look.

Before I entered the building around 9 a.m., I bumped into Pedro, who told me that they had problems with the production orders, as raw materials could not be issued. The cause was in the Receiving department, where incoming goods were not processed properly and Planning had started to use wrong stock figures to forecast. We could expect things to go even worse if we didn't tackle the issues immediatly. In the project, the inbound process was well covered by Carlos from the Supply department. Unfortunately, he left because of a large-

scale reorganization that took place right after the go-live of SAP. I was puzzled to hear that because one month earlier Carlos was installed as the process lead for Supply.

While I had my coffee, I was told that the country manager Mr. Da Silva was in the plant fixing urgent matters. This didn't feel right. Mr. Da Silva was on the site to figure out the status of production orders? By the time I got there, I could sense that this was not the usual kind of urgency or hiccup. Key users were away from their desks, local process owners were no longer working for the company, and in their panic users switched back to paper documents if anything was registered at all.

Around noon I witnessed Mr. Da Silva receiving a call from corporate headquarters. Our Detroit-based Global Key Accountant complained that their Manila plant was receiving late and wrong shipments and their production line was going to halt in two days if the situation was not fixed immediately. I felt the adrenaline pumping in an awkward way. In the next few hours, I learned that Mr. Da Silva had accelerated the initiative to establish a centralized service platform for our three lines of business in the Philippines right after SAP went live. "Now that the new system is live, that will enable our service-center concept," he figured. "There is no need to wait to reduce our support staff headcount." Several of the newly installed process owners and the best-trained key users were made redundant; they had been on this systems project while business continued as usual.

At about 3 p.m., I reported my observations to my director in Hong Kong. I was surprised by the tone of my own voice: "Wayne, this company is coming to a grinding halt. Shipping to customers is almost at random, production is against plans that are based on wrong forecasts, material movements are not registered, documents are not printed, and we don't even know which orders have been shipped over the past month, so what shall we invoice?"

How could this ever get that bad? After six successful rollouts, the system was stable and reliable, we ran business processes that were world class, and we thought we understood what change was about. Could this be a people issue?

The above is a real situation that occurred in a large multinational organization. From our experience, we know that this happens more often than not. In the majority of SAP implementations—regardless of the version you may be installing—the system is rolled out with little or no knowledge about the organization and the changes that affect it. As you will learn in this book, the execution of a change can only go as fast as the ability of people to absorb and make sense of the changes. It is not the change from legacy systems to

SAP that causes disruption for people, but rather the change of processes that is necessary to make these systems work. More precisely, it is the *integration of processes*.

1.2   Integration of Processes

An organization's efficiency depends on the alignment of processes, systems, and people with each other. Therefore, like it or not, implementing SAP brings together three disciplines that seem at first glance to have nothing to do with one another: software engineering, business administration, and organizational psychology. If one of these three elements falls short, the remaining two cannot make up the difference. As Figure 1.1 points out, organizational change during SAP implementations is located at the intersection of people, technology, and processes. Implementing SAP not only requires a systems change (technology), but also a fundamental turnaround of the way things work (processes) and—as a result of that—a fundamental change of knowledge, skills, and behaviors (people).

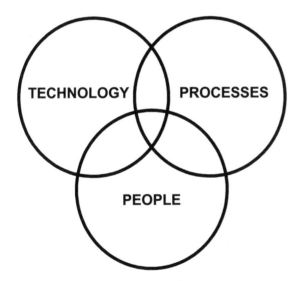

Figure 1.1 Cocktail of Three Disciplines

You may be aware that not all SAP projects are successful and that the return on investment is sometimes far from being sufficient. On the other hand, there are organizations that have tremendously increased their profits thanks to SAP. The logical question to ask is: "What is the difference between success and failure?"

When we look closer at what distinguishes the winners from the losers of SAP implementations, we soon find out that the losers mistakenly assumed that the scope is only that of a software installation. Even if the plain implementation is supported by some change-management activities, it is not sufficient to make an SAP implementation a success. Those who gain from SAP do so because they positioned the project as a fundamental business initiative that transforms the whole organization. Of course, the software installation is a part of it, but only a small part. In other words, successful organizations realize that the nature of the problem is organizational and not technical. In the following sections, we will have a closer look at what this means.

1.2.1 Process Fragmentation

Michael Hammer, the founder of business process reengineering, states that the root cause of SAP failures lies in disregarding some features of the functional organization, where each business function is a castle on its own. He calls this situation Process Fragmentation.

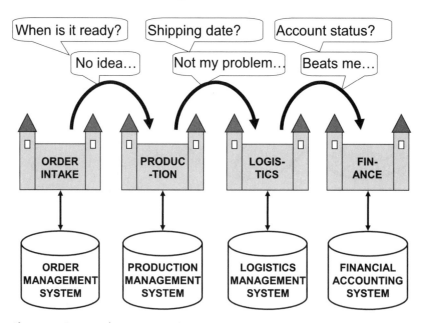

Figure 1.2 Functional Organization (Hammer, 1998)

As you can see in Figure 1.2, departments in the functional organization are separated from each other. Their knowledge about the end-to-end business process and the customer's needs are determined by the information that is captured in their own systems. In this organization, any sales representative would be glad to take a customer order, but when it comes to informing the customer about the production schedule, the sales representative is unable to answer. The production data is captured in the production-management system. The walls between the castles also make the production manager unable to say when the order will be shipped. In a functional organization, that's not his job. Nor will the sales representative be able to tell the customer when his last returned order would be refunded. That information is safely shielded within the accounting system.

1.2.2 Consequences of a Functional Organization

In a functional organization seen in the example in Section 1.2.1, the life of a customer order is fragmented by the information systems in which it is captured from step-to-step. At each step of the process, the functional information about the order is handed over to the next department, and this causes delays each time it sits on someone's desk. Moreover, misunderstandings and miscommunications arise because the incoming information is not always interpreted as it was packaged by the previous functional castle (see Figure 1.2). Each department applies its own terminology and codes its messages according to the customs of its own subculture.

Surprisingly, the factors that most keep the functional organization from being customer oriented are the very cornerstones of sound management, described as follows:

▸ **Competence**
Surely, our organizations wouldn't stand where they stand today if our people were not competent. However, competent people build boundaries around their domains of expertise and start to identify with those domains. Rather than saying "I work for Company ABC," people say "I am from Engineering/Production/Finance/Procurement." Competent people like being competent. That is what they are hired for and that is what they identify with.

▸ **Automation**
Administration and reporting should be automated as much as possible, and IT systems are there to support the business. However, in the past this meant that legacy information systems were castle-focused. Legacy systems are designed according to the specifications of the competent castle managers. They only process the data that is relevant to their departments and produce reports that confirm their competence. This reinforces the

fragmentaion of processes and makes the process even more invisible, cumbersome, and inefficient.

▶ **Performance-Based Reward**
Sound management dictates that rewards, incentives, and measures systems are designed to reward good performance. However, in a functional organization performance is not measured by the effectiveness of the process, but on the performance of the department. The Key Performance Indicators (KPIs) that are installed to reward functional efforts (e. g., maintain current headcount, reduce departmental costs by 10 %) may in fact punish the overall "end-to-end" process (e. g., order-to-cash) performance.

1.2.3 What Happens Once SAP is Implemented?

SAP is integrated software that addresses all castles of the organization and brings them together with shared data and seamless interfaces. The purpose of SAP is to integrate fragmented pieces of a process from end-to-end, be it account-to-report, procure-to-pay, order-to-cash, or hire-to-retire.

Integrating a fragmented process is a serious reengineering effort. The process becomes visible because transaction flows are the core elements on which the design of an SAP system is based. SAP also aligns the data flow to the transaction flow. This is a big deal, as it completely changes the way people work, and it changes the way information is distributed and who can access it. More specifically, you will be running into the following issues that will require you to rethink the current way of getting things done:

▶ Jobs are no longer narrowed by the information system of a specific department. Not only will you have access to the other castles' data, you also have to make sure that your input is adequate for further use. This means that you will have to better understand the job of the person who is next in the process flow.

▶ Organizational boundaries fade away as the seamless interfaces make it possible to peek right through the organizational functions. In reality, this produces a culture shock as different departments are suddenly exposed to each others' knowledge and nonsense. Certain vertical communication and information flows are eliminated and replaced by horizontal ones in function of the process.

▶ The authority moves to the people on the floor, as they get access to a universe of data. Information is power, so this shift is a big deal to managers who lose some of their authority because of that. However, there is no sense in granting power to frontline workers without requiring their accountability. Timely input of data of good quality is critical. Therefore, the biggest change is probably one in attitude: from controlled data processors to autonomous responsible persons with a broader awareness of the process. SAP only works when people take ownership of the information that they enter in the system.

▸ Processes become standardized, and the system forces you in a certain workflow. Invoices will not get paid without corresponding purchase orders, stock levels will not get updated without the proper production order confirmation, and products will not get shipped without delivery notes and a goods issues. Therefore, flexible heroic acts ("Let's fix it; we'll do the paperwork later") become impossible. This is quite a problem if your day-to-day work consists of ad hoc interventions. Standard processes also dramatically change the maintenance and support requirements. As all departments will be working on the same system with the same data, system availibility and response times are more critical than ever before.

1.2.4 What Implementing SAP Comes Down to: Managing the Soft Stuff

SAP holds the promise of increasing the performance of business processes. This can completely change the way you do business. Implementing SAP comes down to sharing data and increasing cross-functional communication. That is what you will get, whether or not you want it, so you might as well take control over it. When implementing any software, we pay attention to things such as the following:

▸ Requirements analysis

▸ Configuration/development

▸ Hardware requirements and system performance

▸ Capacity planning

▸ Data cleansing

▸ User training

▸ Unit and user acceptance testing

While these factors are necessary, they are far from sufficient for an SAP implementation. The success of your SAP implementation greatly depends on the management of non-technical issues: the *soft stuff*. According to

Michael Hammer (2005), the following are the keys to success of an SAP implementation:

- Positioning it as a strategic business issue
- Project teams with dedicated resources from across the organization
- Making the process owners the key decision makers (it's worth remarking that most organizations don't even have process owners). They must also be of the right level to be empowered to take decisions, and they must be trained so they understand their roles.
- Persistently working methodically and sticking to the project plan
- Using a system for rapid decision making and a refusal to reopen issues
- Concentrating the effort and keeping momentum
- Timeboxing and scheduling backwards from realistic unalterable dates
- Assuring the implementability of the design through extensive participation of the business
- Balancing the effort into realistic scopes and scales
- Program management that fits it all together
- Taking milestones seriously
- Not stinting on change management: the human dimension
- Executive commitment and leadership.

Please note that none of these critical success factors are technological in nature. They are all organizational issues. Hence, Michael Hammer's popular statement: "The soft stuff is the hard stuff."

1.2.5 Examples of Companies Serious About Processes

In the following examples, we briefly describe how organizations have radically changed their processes and structures before implementing SAP. The point is to make sure that people and structures get organized so they are capable of working in an integrated way. Only then should you be thinking about leveraging your organization's performance by means of SAP.

Company A: A Global Player in the Chemical Industry.

As a global player in the chemical industry, this company completely owns the vertical chain from production to consumer sales. Historically, its growing business resulted in a multitude of local sales offices, each with a small production and warehousing capacity. Each of these local sites had quite some independence, which brought along a high level of decentralization. Local sites started to invent their own best practices, producing and maintaining their own data, and they started to build on that. In the beginning, it was very difficult to convince people of the benefit of standardization and centralization. They had organized their worlds in a certain way and it was working well: local distribution centers with local customer support; local purchasing authority to a large extent; local planning and execution of transport; local billing, and local warehouses with spare parts for maintenance activities.

In the light of an increased competition and decreasing margins as a result of higher energy prices and increased raw materials prices, the company decided to launch a worldwide standardization. This resulted in an integrated SAP landscape with a geographical split-up into larger geographical regions comprising multiple sites.

Each site centralized a business function and executed it for its complete region. Each region now had a service center for each of the following functions:

▶ The distribution and warehousing is centralized on one site. There are still local stocks, but the stock situation of one region is centrally managed by one center.

▶ With regards to purchasing, approval workflows were installed for the whole region, and one single central catalogue ensures better purchasing conditions.

▶ There is a single point of contact for order management and customer support.

▶ As with distribution, transport planning was centralized.

▶ Control over the delivery of spare parts was controlled by consolidating it into one central warehouse that services the whole region.

Company B: Global Car Manufacturer

Within this company, which had entities around the globe, the whole of the accounting processes were supported by local systems, primarily focusing on meeting local legal requirements. On top of that, in most cases, these systems were installed on local servers. That resulted in the following:

- A fragmented accounting environment
- Accounting systems developed to meet local (legal) requirements only
- No standardized or common ways of working (accounting principles and rules)
- Consolidation on the group level taking too much time
- Fragmented information
- System fragmentation: a huge number of interfaces to other local systems (i. e., order-entry systems)

This entire situation caused a lot of inefficiency expressed in long process lead times. The technical infrastructure also cost the company a lot of money. This convinced the company to decide to implement SAP. The results were as follows:

- A more integrated landscape
- Global accounting environment
- Standardized ways of working, commonly used accounting systems across the group; one global chart of accounts
- Replaced legacy systems
- Better flow of information across the organization, facilitating improved consolidation

Furthermore, the new system allowed the company to improve the managerial accounting process by having a global structure in place.

1.3   Running Integrated Projects

The nature of SAP is that it brings together functions, integrates them into a process, and brings about the definition of joint benefits on the level of the organization. The most tangible examples can be found in production and logistics, where benefits can be defined in such terms as reduced lead time, or increased customer service. Realization of such benefits often has far-reaching consequences for the way organizations run their day-to-day operations. As a result, the specific characteristics of an SAP project inevitably affect the way we organize staff and run our projects.

1.3.1   Integration of Implementation Sub-Teams

Because the goal of an SAP project is process integration, the implementation should be organized around processes. The best implementation teams are staffed with the representatives of all organizational functions. They represent the needs of their departments, but these needs may conflict with the performance of the processes.

Another difficulty in working on integrated processes derives from the way organizations get things done. Projects are accomplished by fragmenting the work, dividing it among resources, and completing each of the fragmented pieces. Project sub-teams focus on doing their work and designing their solutions, but when it comes to bringing all the pieces back together and measuring how well the result improves the overall process, we often don't seem to be so successful.

The overall design is not completed when all the project sub-teams finish the designs of their fragments. In fact, the parts of the overall design need to fit together into a process, and this means that some sub-teams will need to re-do their work. For this reason, we need an integration team to make sure that the pieces fit together and that the sub-teams don't get stuck in positional fights that no one can win.

This is also where the integration test activities add major value. They ensure that processes work across functional domains. We have to make sure that enough time is reserved, not only to accomplish tests as such, but also to be sure that processes are really integrated into the organization and that SAP supports them smoothly.

1.3.2   Integration of Project and Organization

As we will discuss in Chapter 4, managing and running a project is very different from managing and running the day-to-day operations.

The organization must have a project culture. Project approaches must be integrated throughout the organization. A characteristic shared by organizations with project cultures is the fact that they have a permanent program office, which is responsible for starting up, monitoring, adjourning, and most of all synchronizing all the projects. This means that the organization must have resources with experience in managing and running large-scale projects and that SAP project expertise is permanently available in the organization. It also means that management supports a project culture and that managers behave accordingly.

If the organization does not have the adequate or appropriate resources internally, these must be hired externally, at least for the duration of the project.

Fostering SAP Ownership

Even when an integration team deals with internal conflicts, this does not guarantee success in implementing the design on the specific organization. The real test is yet to come. Just when all members of the project team think that the work is done, and they proudly hand off the project to the organization, the first thing they will hear is: "That's not going to work, because we are different." Most people with experience in multiple SAP projects have started to see patterns in the behavior after a while. They have been exposed to evergreens such as: "It is impossible to have a purchase order for this invoice," or, "There is no way our workers will confirm production data into the system."

The only way to prevent this from happening is by making the business responsible for the processes. That is the job of process owners. Process owners don't appear on stage just like rabbits out of a magician's hat; their presence is a carefully planned deliverable of the program management (see Chapter 3). By this we mean that most often process ownership does not exist in an organization before the start of the SAP implementation. Most of the time, functions prevail. Ensuring that the business takes ownership of the processes and the deliverables of the project requires contact throughout the lifecycle of the project.

For that same reason, the suggested budget in Figure 1.3 has a somewhat different structure than one would expect. Due to the disrupting effect of SAP projects, change-management activities and user training together should take up more than a third of the total budget. These figures only apply in terms of financial budget. In terms of effort, change management will even take more than 35 % of the total effort needed to implement SAP. Let's be clear, too, that change management is not limited to education and communication efforts.

Matching Ambitions and Capability Maturity

In 1997 (Jensen, 1997), a five-year research amongst 461 American companies revealed that complexity in teams and organizations is not an external factor, but rather an in-house creation. The researchers documented the four primary sources of work complexity, namely:

- ▶ Inadequate integration of initiatives in the organization
- ▶ Unclear goals
- ▶ How we communicate
- ▶ How we share knowledge and make it available

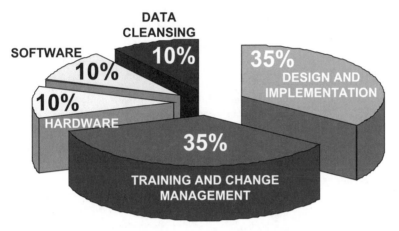

Figure 1.3 Pro-Forma SAP Implementation Budget: in Financial Terms (Hammer, 2005)

This list emphasizes the importance of the relationship between project teams and the organization for which they work. It is the primary task of the process owners to manage these relationships.

More precisely, to manage the complexity, process owners match the projects' ambitions with the capability maturity of the organization. As summarized in Table 1.1, the Capability Maturity Model (Carnegie Mellon SEI, 1996) indicates where an organization belongs in its evolution of productivity and quality. The Capability Maturity Model is a reliable indicator of how capable organizations are at reducing their own complexity.

Each level builds a foundation for succeeding levels. Process owners should keep in mind that an SAP project is not the solution for getting from Level 1 to Level 2. The dominant problems of a Level 1 organization are managerial. Other problems are masked by the difficulties in planning and managing projects. In Level 1 organizations, SAP projects are most likely labeled as software projects, and they fail under stress at the very point they are needed most.

Capability Maturity Level	Description
Level 1—The Initial Level	The level of heroic acts. Organizations on this level typically lack the discipline of good practices due to ineffective planning.
Level 2—The Repeatable Level	The level of individual initiatives. At this level, policies for managing a project and procedures to implement those policies are established.
Level 3—The Defined Level	The level of institutionalized processes. At this level, the standard processes across the organization are documented and integrated into a coherent whole.
Level 4—The Managed Level	The level of quantitative management. Productivity and quality are measured across all projects as part of an organizational measurement program. Organizations at this level measure their own processes to evaluate the projects' performances.
Level 5—The Optimizing Level	The level of continuous improvement. Honestly, we have never seen an organization that fully complies with this level of capability maturity. At the Optimizing Level, the entire organization is focused on continuous process improvement.

Table 1.1 Capability Maturity Model (Carnegie Mellon SEI, 1996)

A Level 1 organization that is trying to implement a defined process (Level 3) before it has established a repeatable process (Level 2) is usually unsuccessful because project managers are overwhelmed by schedule and cost pressures. This is the fundamental reason for focusing on change-management processes before engineering processes.

1.3.3 Don't Count on HR to do the Dirty Work

Whenever the human side is involved, engineering projects tend either to ignore it or to completely outsource it to the human resources (HR) department. Hopes, dreams, wishes, and expectations are never taken into account, and training, communication, and coaching are restricted to the minimum. The attitude in most projects is exemplified by this statement: "We'll take care of the process reengineering and the technical stuff; HR will do the soft stuff."

However, there are two fundamental reasons why you should not count on HR to do your dirty laundry.

HR is Not a Change Agent

HR safeguards continuity in the organization. Let's face it: By their very nature, the fundamental HR processes are aimed at safeguarding stability. However, when you ask HR managers about the core competencies of their departments, they will tell you that the management of organizational change is on the forefront. They are wrong. The basic processes of HR and their accompanying goals are as follows:

▶ **Recruiting and Selection**
  Goal: Employment Continuity

▶ **Training and Development**
  Goal: Knowledge and Skills Continuity

▶ **Performance Management and Appraisal**
  Goal: Performance Continuity

▶ **Compensation and Benefits**
  Goal: Stability in Personnel Costs

▶ **Work Organization and Communication Systems**
  Goal: Social Stability.

Therefore, HR should be approached as you would any other functional castle, and they should be the first target of your change-management efforts. But there is more.

HR is an Agent of Continuity

As a functional castle, HR will be impacted indirectly by the SAP reengineering effort and will most likely resist at first. Does that disqualify them from having any stake in the organizational change of the SAP implementation? Not at all. As we will discuss in the next chapter, change always happens in three phases: Unfreezing, Changing, and Refreezing. As the key strength of HR is to stabilize the human side of an organization around its technology, it is their role to lead the Refreezing stage. For the change to stick onto the organization, you are going to use the HR department's tools and methods.

Therefore, HR is one of the first targets to work with. The faster you can enlist them into becoming a continuity agent, the better. Just don't expect them to be on the same page from day one, as they—like everybody else—will resist the change in the beginning.

HR as a Co-Pilot in Long-Term Planning

From our experience, the only HR actions that have a positive impact take place at the beginning and at the end of the program lifecycle. This leads us to conclude that continuity and not change is HR's core business. Even when the organization is affected during the transition, HR should help you minimize the disruption of continuity.

As an example, program staffing of key people is a task that needs to be conducted in close alignment with HR as it should involve career perspectives and long-term accountability.

Gradually, as the program comes to a close, HR needs to become the owner of the deliverables regarding learning, performance, organization, and communication. The role of HR in this case is one of sustaining the change and integrating it into its standards and procedures. In other words: safeguarding stability and continuity of the new organization.

1.3.4 Don't Count on IS to do the Dirty Work

As mentioned at the beginning of this chapter, when an SAP implementation is labeled as a plain software installation, you start off on the wrong foot. Unwillingly, IS becomes owner of the effort and the attitude towards the initiative is often translated as follows: "SAP is complex software, so let the technical experts lead the way."

Again, there are two reasons why you should not count on IS to lead the project. Let's examine these reasons:

IS is Not a Change Agent

Ninety percent of the competent IS engineers are binary people: very competent at analyzing a program down to its bits and bytes and appreciating dimensions of algorithmic beauty that the outside world is unaware of.

The key strength of IS is automation and control, and its key processes, listed here, are designed to accomplish that purpose:

- **Incident Management**
  Goal: to control technical incidents
- **Problem Management**
  Goal: to control technical problems
- **Change Management**
  Goal: to control the software change management

▶ **Release Management**
Goal: to control major software releases

▶ **Configuration Management**
Goal: to gain control over every single object and to track it during its complete lifecycle.

Like the HR department, IS is there to bring stability to the organization through the support and control of current processes.

IS is an Agent of Stability

It is sometimes shocking to see how negligent some organizations are with regard to supporting their IS departments. During an SAP implementation, the pressures are extremely high on IS because of a combination of the following factors:

▶ We expect full support of legacy systems until cutover.

▶ We expect the techies to interface remaining legacy systems with SAP.

▶ We expect them to take the lead on data cleansing.

▶ At cutover, we expect them to be as competent in SAP as they were the day before in legacy systems.

In addition, the IS/IT department is responsible for maintenance and support, not only for the legacy systems as mentioned earlier, but also for the newly implemented SAP system. Maintenance and support is a service-oriented function that requires certain capabilities. Those responsible are expected to support the users in using the system properly. This requires that IS/IT has to be involved in the implementation from the very start. We get back to this in Part II.

The IS department does not deserve to be treated like this, and neither should it be behind the steering wheel. However, as its key strength is to automate and control processes, we should make use of that specific strength during and after the implementation.

IS is an Initiator of Change

Many times, IS/IT is the challenger of the status quo. We have often seen that it is not the business but the IS/IT department that encourages the organization to start the program. This remarkable fact goes against all theories and textbooks. However, in practice we see that IS managers are taking the lead and making innovative proposals in the earliest stage (program initiation).

In many organizations, it is the IS/IT department that persistently communicates the need to have certain systems replaced, to increase integration, to install new technology platforms, etc. These professionals initiate change by asking the business executives to think concretely about how this impacts the way they do business in the future. Most of the times, IS people are the first ones to ask: "Where do we want to go as an organization?" They know that the answer influences every single choice they will make system-wise, landscape-wise, configuration-wise, and procedure-wise.

The extent to which IS/IT can ignite the program initiation is directly linked to its level of capability maturity. At a certain maturity level, the IS/IT department normally has a very good look on how processes in the organization work, the extent to which processes are fragmented or integrated, the extent to which legacy systems are fragmented, etc.

This means that you have to remain open to initiatives or suggestions from the IS department. At the same time, you should be prepared to reframe its questions in the broader perspective of the future organization, linking them directly to clearly identified business benefits (we will return to this in Chapter 4).

1.4 Searching for Balance

In the following sections, we have listed some awkward dilemmas you will be confronted with once you start implementing SAP. Most of the time, they pop up as annoying problems or big question marks during the implementation, and more than often they are not thought of in the beginning.

1.4.1 Integrating Old and New

Most organizations are still using legacy systems designed for the needs of a specific (functional) part of the organization. Those systems typically run on technology that was purchased at the time that the system was developed and installed. Most probably, some functional and technical upgrades have happened over the time they have been used.

Also, when being used, the needs for integration with other systems have come to the surface. This has resulted in the development of interfaces. But even when interfaces strive towards integration, it will never be possible to realize seamless integration. Each system will still keep its own information (transactional as well as master data). So instead of having shared data, the same data is stored and managed multiple times in different databases.

It would be wishful thinking to believe that an SAP implementation will replace all existing legacy systems. So, even when using SAP, there is still a need for interfaces to other SAP or non-SAP environments.

But by applying the proper technology, integration of information and systems can be increased across the organization, even if systems are located in different geographical areas.

1.4.2 Drawing a Line

To make an SAP implementation successful, the system has to be integrated into the organization. The organization has to accept the system, and the system must support the newly implemented ways of working. We often see that organizations implementing SAP make a lot of changes to the standard package in order to meet the specific organizational requirements.

SAP is supposed to be an off-the-shelf product that supports best practices. It is designed to support best practice processes, and it functions at its best when not too many changes are made to the system. SAP is configurable to allow it to be customized to the specifics of the organization implementing SAP, but the objective can't be to redesign the system. When you understand this profound fact, you will understand that regularly the organization has to adapt to the system's way of working.

The art of successful implementation is to find a balance between integrating SAP into the organization and integrating the organization into SAP.

1.4.3 Balancing the Change and the Transition

Most SAP implementations start with lots of ambition and crystal-clear visions of the future. As the program progresses, gaps between the future state and the current state are analyzed. A strict plan is developed to implement the change. Clearly, there's nothing wrong with that approach, because it ensures that money and time will be best spent. However, most of the time these plans fail to cover the short and middle term. For example, consider the worldwide implementation of SAP for a company with 10 production plants, five distribution centers, and 20 sales offices. Let's say that it is phased over a period of three years with a pilot implementation in the first year that includes one production plant. In the first year, every individual is

100 % focused on delivering the pilot, as it is the first serious test for the implementation team. In doing so, inexperienced teams fail to plan for the transition period. This means that:

▶ One part of your organization will be running on the new SAP platform

▶ The rest of the organization will still need to interface with that part

▶ The SAP part will be growing chunk by chunk and you will continuously need to reshape the interfaces

▶ The supporting organizations will need to transition at the same speed and with the same proportions, more specifically the following:

  ▶ HR

  ▶ IS/IT

  ▶ Risk mitigation

  ▶ Process owners

In Part II, we will extensively cover the hard aspects of the change versus the transition, and we will argue that both can be nailed down into a *service level agreement* (SLA). In short, experienced teams know that the transition itself calls for separate rules of the game that are different from the final rules of the game.

1.4.4   A Contradiction in Terms

When talking about *change management*, we often encounter confusion regarding the terminology used. There is more than one possible interpretation. Here are some of misunderstandings that we came across:

▶ Confusing organizational change management with project-scope change management. The latter refers to a change in scope within a specific project context and how this affects the work done and the work ahead.

▶ Confusing organizational change management with software change management. The latter refers to the lifecycle of a change in a software system.

▶ Confusing organizational change management with a change of the management team. This example refers to a communication problem that a rollout manager had with a Taiwanese management team. Change management was a treated as not up for discussion. After a while, it became clear that the term "change management" may be clear in the US and Western Europe, but not so far beyond.

▸ We should note here that whenever we use the term *change management* in this book we are referring to organizational change management. We recommend you to be explicit about this in your communications as well.

1.5   Conclusion

As this chapter ends, you should realize that this is not going to be a technical book. We will focus on the transition from one paradigm to another. A paradigm is a view of how things work in the world: the set of beliefs that makes you blind to all other possibilities.

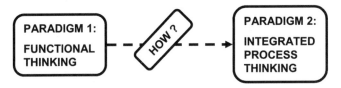

Figure 1.4 Paradigm Shift

As shown in Figure 1.4 and discussed throughout the following chapters, we take a closer look at what it takes to go from the paradigm of functional thinking to the paradigm of integrated process thinking. As a starting point, Chapter 2 explains in detail the dynamics that take place below the surface.

This chapter addresses what is going on below the surface in times of change. To successfully manage organizational change, you will need to spend some time below the surface of what is visible and explicit. The concepts in this chapter will be used as anchors throughout the rest of the book. So returning to this chapter from time to time may be helpful in understanding the dynamics of what is happening when you are managing organizational change.

2 The Rollercoaster of Emotions

2.1 Emotions Make a Difference

A recent survey conducted by the McKinsey Quarterly (2006) among 1,536 executives of publicly and privately held businesses across a full range of industries reveals the importance of emotions in the success of an organizational change. The respondents who experienced a performance transformation over the past five years were asked to rate it on a scale ranging from completely successful to completely unsuccessful.

Those who rated their transformation as Completely/Mostly Successful and Completely/Mostly Unsuccessful were asked what characterized the mood in the organization during the transformation. Figure 2.1 shows the responses to that question for both successful and unsuccessful organizations.

McKinsey concludes that negative and positive moods are reported in roughly equal proportions, with anxiety as the most common emotion, ahead of confusion, frustration, fatigue, and resistance. Among the positive moods, a sense of focus, enthusiasm, and feelings of momentum occur roughly equally. Finally, more of the top performers report positive moods, especially focus and enthusiasm.

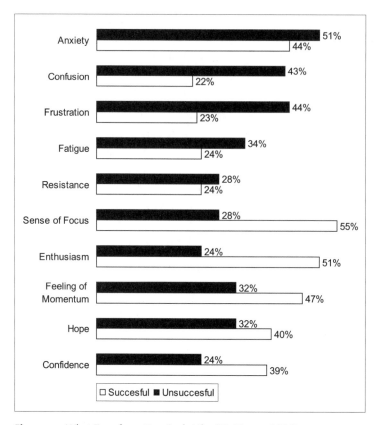

Figure 2.1 What Transformation Feels Like (McKinsey, 2006)

2.2 The Change Cycle

When people are confronted with change, they always go through specific phases. In each of these phases, people behave differently, as we will show in the upcoming subsections.

2.2.1 Two Sides to Every Change

There are always two sides to a change story: the visible and the invisible. As we point out in Figure 2.2, the visible is about what you know and do (the rational part), and the invisible is about how you feel (the emotional part).

It is fairly easy to tell people what they should know (Knowledge) or what they should be doing (Skills) in response to a certain change. But when it comes to Motivation, the $64 thousand question is: How will we make people want (Motivation) to change?

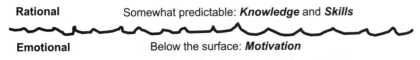

Rational   Somewhat predictable: **Knowledge** and **Skills**

Emotional   Below the surface: **Motivation**

Figure 2.2 The Rational and the Emotional Side of a Change

Have you already noticed how one and the same change, however small, causes a whole range of reactions depending on who is involved? A simple experiment is to observe how a small change (be it moving from one building to another one across the road or the change of your desktop PC) results in winners, losers, victims, rescuers, persecutors, and "us and them." Regardless of how neutral the change seems to be, the way it is perceived and reacted upon is always personal.

2.2.2   The Cycle of Life and the Denial of Death

It is striking how the major insights of the change cycle come from two angles that seem at first to be opposites: development psychology, and research on death and dying. Psychologists and biologists observed that we typically find children whining and being more difficult when they learn something new and it often takes a while before they adapt to and assimilate these new abilities. For human development "things will get worse before they get better" is almost a law of nature: A biological upgrade of our brain software leads to a drop in performance before we pick up and use our new-found abilities.

On the complete other side of the spectrum, Elisabeth Kuhbler Ross (1969) has described her work with terminally ill patients and found that they typically come to terms with their prognosis in five stages: denial, anger, bargaining, depression, and finally acceptance. In these cases, it is self-esteem that shows a serious drop-off and then picks up with acceptance in the same way as an infant coming to terms with its new abilities. Although most organizational change is not of a life-or-death nature, people may experience similar stages as they adjust to it, making Kuhbler Ross' advice highly applicable.

Looking at the change cycles in Figure 2.3, they seem quite logical and straightforward. Yet, when it comes to making a change happen in an organization, a team, or a project, we act as if a different logic applies. We somehow seem to think the natural cycle of change does not apply to our project. But it does.

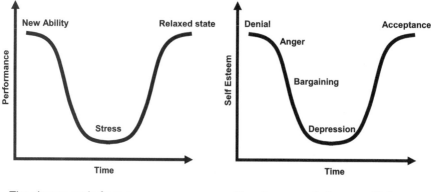

The change cycle from a developmental point of view

The change cycle from a palliative care point of view

Figure 2.3 Change Cycle

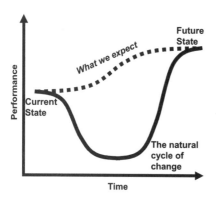

Figure 2.4 Denial of our Emotional Side Leads to False Expectations.

The dotted line in Figure 2.4 shows the expectation that people might have with regard to a transition from a current state to a future one. The fact that we perceive this transition in this way is caused by the fact that we look at organizational changes purely as a mathematical exercise. However, it is a false expectation because, when reality settles in, we are puzzled by the emotional responses to the change and terrified by the delays and the drops in performance. But we are only witnessing nature having its way.

Emotional and psychological factors ultimately decide the duration and success of the organizational change. Whenever people are involved, performance will drop and resistance will come. Either we ignore it until the last minute or we accept it as a given and incorporate it in our approach.

2.2.3   What is Going On? The Phases of Change

What is causing so many well-trained and educated managers and executives to ignore a phenomenon that is as old as humankind? The subsections that follow illustrate some observations in parallel with the Kuhbler Ross stages.

The Denial Phase

In this phase we often find expert teams planning the change and employees making up and hearing rumors about what is going on. Some typical observations follow:

▶ Top management sponsors are not visibly involved in the change.

▶ All the experts of the implementation team are working hard amongst themselves.

▶ Employees are very poorly involved and start to make up their own stories about what is going on.

The Anger Phase

In the anger phase, employees and managers cannot deny the fact that things are going to change. However, as they have not been involved, they feel helpless. The frustration builds up as long as they continue to be left out of the loop. Observations in this phase include:

▶ Middle managers are paralyzed by the gap between the present state and the future state.

▶ They feel inadequate to deal with the anger, the anxiety, and the sadness of their employees.

▶ Employees think their management is incompetent as they are confronted with contradictions between "future state" requirements and "present state" appraisals.

The Bargaining Phase

This is the most theatrical phase of the change, as people start to pull out all the stops in trying to get "back to normal." Here's what often happens in this phase:

▶ No room for negotiating agreements.

▸ Confusion about the negotiables and the non-negotiables.

▸ Lack of a concrete vision causes people to mix old stories with new realities.

The Depression Phase

In this phase it is clear to everyone that there is no turning back. The whole organization is impacted by the loss of an old world. Some people abandon at this stage, others deny sadness or become cynical about it. In this phase, we often observe the following:

▸ Instead of allowing for sadness, people keep a stiff upper lip, making it even harder (artificial enthusiasm and phony conversations).

▸ Some managers don't understand why it takes people so long to get over it.

▸ Managers don't allow a mourning ritual because they fear people will get stuck in the old ways.

The Acceptance Phase

This is when the first signs of success become visible. People learn to live with the new realities. In this phase, we often observe the following:

▸ No clear commmunication about the new reality and the successes that have been achieved.

▸ Projects and teams split up and people busy themselves in all sorts of ways. There is no shared story about what has been achieved.

▸ Managers are not present to confirm that what is happening is a series of small victories.

2.2.4 Why You Are Not the First to Make These Mistakes

It is not an easy thing to go through the dynamic of emotions and at the same time keep a clear perspective. Eventually, change gets personal, and in an organizational context, we are not used to this for the following reasons:

▸ We often don't know how to deal with strong emotions in our organization. We think they should be over and done with before they started.

▸ We don't trust one another to constructively deal with emotions.

▶ We know something must happen, but we don't know how.

▶ We are afraid of our own emotions because we are insecure about ourselves.

The bottom line is that we need to go through the rollercoaster of leading ourselves through our own changes to have the respect and authority to lead others through the organizational change.

2.2.5 Unfreezing—Changing—Refreezing

Kurt Lewin (1974) was the first to make active use of the cycle theory that things get worse before they get better in organizations. No change will occur unless the target organization is unfrozen, and no change will last unless it is refrozen.

Unfreezing

By far, the most difficult and important stage is that of unfreezing, the creation of a motivation to change. This is accomplished by changing the dynamics such that:

▶ The present state is somehow disconfirmed.

▶ Some anxiety or guilt is aroused because some goals will not be met or standards or ideals will not be maintained.

▶ Enough "psychological safety" is provided to make it unnecessary for the target individuals or groups to psychologically defend themselves.

Most efforts of unfreezing limit themselves to disconfirmation and the creation of pain. Those making such efforts fail to note that unless the pain is connected to something people care about, and unless they feel safe enough to do something about it, they have not really been unfrozen at all (Schein, 2002).

The effective manager acting as a change agent must try to convey the following ideas simultaneously (Schein, 2002):

▶ Your present behavior or attitude is unacceptable (disconfirmation).

▶ It is violating some of our standards or is causing us to fail in getting the job done (induction of guilt and/or anxiety), but ...

▶ I understand that learning something new is itself anxiety-producing, so I will help you to change and make you feel safe while you learn a new behavior or attitude (creation of psychological safety).

Changing

Once someone is unfrozen, he or she is more likely to pay attention to information, ideas, suggestions, or even orders that were previously ignored. People become active problem solvers because they are uncomfortable. They become motivated to change.

It is important to note that people may have had strong disconfirmation in the past but have not felt secure enough to do something about their situation. In practice, this comes down to a combination factors:

- **Identification**
  Behavioral patterns are offered which the subject can identify with (exemplary behavior of champions that becomes "OK" from now on).

- **Internalization**
  Eventually the change has to come from the individual. The change will only last when people find a motivation within themselves to make it last.

- **Obeying**
  When individuals are controlled from a position of power, their behavior tends to change. The disadvantage is that this often lasts as long as power is exerted or the person in power is present.

Refreezing

During this phase the new behavior becomes a habit. Research indicated that only internalized behavior can be permanent without outside validation (Schein 1980). Identification requires regular validation in the form of social support. Obeying, as mentioned earlier, requires continuous control.

Even if the change is being induced from a position of power, it is essential for the change agent to learn the even greater power of being helpful and supportive. People must be unfrozen to change; they must hurt somewhere. But that is not enough. Equally important is their sense of psychological safety: that it is OK to try something new and to give up something old and familiar. The smart change agent will make targets feel secure by finding a way to turn them into clients. Only then will their resistance genuinely give way.

2.2.6 Sponsors—Agents—Targets

We have been using the words "Agent" and "Target." Leading change involves building demand for change by managing three different groups:

sponsors, agents, and targets. According to Connor (1992) these groups are defined as follows:

▶ **Sponsor**
This is the individual or entity with responsibility for the success of a change initiative, and the necessary authority to commit required resources to the initiative. They possess sufficient organizational power to either initiate resource commitment (Authorizing Sponsor) or reinforce the change at the local level (Reinforcing Sponsor). Given the fact that an SAP implementation impacts much (if not all) of the organization, this would typically be the Chief Operating Officer (COO) or the Chief Executive Officer (CEO) to.

▶ **Agent**
This person is empowered by the sponsor to carry out specific tasks related to the change initiative.

▶ **Target**
This is an individual or entity that will be required to change behavior and actions. It is the scope of the SAP implementation that defines the targets. These are the most important people in the change process, because if the targets reject change, it will fail.

These definitions will serve as tags for labeling the different stakeholders we have to take into account. These tags determine how we approach each stakeholder in terms of communication and participation.

2.2.7   Operating Styles for Each Phase

Agents of change projects should adopt different styles according to the phase of the change. Initially, they take responsibility for breaking the fundamental structures that underpin the current context and beliefs. Cringely (1993) compares this destructive work to the job of commandos who prepare territory for the infantry:

> *"Commandos parachute behind enemy lines or quietly crawl ashore at night. Their job is to do lots of damage with surprise and teamwork, establishing a beachhead before the enemy is even aware that they exist."*

Whenever unfreezing is needed, agents take on a commando style to create the circumstances for change. Most times, the project leader gets the honor of preparing the territory. Whether it is to obtain commitment for blueprinting, design, testing, training or go-live, without the commando actions the efforts will be ignored by business as long as there is no pressure or hard evidence that things will change.

Once the path is cleared, changing can start. Now you will need an infantry of agents to get the job done: blueprinting, designing, testing, training, collecting and cleansing data, etc. The most important thing here is that an infantry takes on a structured approach. In the words of Cringely (1993):

> *"While the commandos make success possible, it's the infantry that makes success happen. These are the people who hit the beach en masse and slog out the early victory, building on the start given them by the commandos. [...] Because there are so many more of these soldiers and their duties are so varied, they require an infrastructure of rules and procedures for getting things done."*

Finally, the new structures are in place, and it is time to refreeze the new processes that have been installed by the infantry. This is the fragile process of handing over knowledge from project agents to the target users. You will find that there is still the need for a military presence by means of local coaching. These are the UN peacekeeping troops, a remainder of the infantry. Their only purpose is to stabilize the new order and eventually to hand over to the local peacekeepers: the police.

2.3   Resistance

Resistance is the emotion that occurs when our expectations of the way things are today are interrupted. Two words are important in this definition:

▶ **Emotion**
The essence of resistance is that it creates an emotion. That means not logical, not rational, and—most of all—not predictable.

▶ **Expectation**
Resistance does not only occur when things change, but when our expectations are interrupted, whether or not that makes rational sense.

2.3.1   Different Kinds of Interruptions

What exactly are we talking about when we talk about an interruption of our expectations about the way things are? In other words: How will you recognize a change when you see one? McKaskey (1982) summarized the characteristics of ambiguous, changing situations in Table 2.1.

Nature of the problem itself is in question	"What the problem is" is unclear and shifting. Managers only have vague or competing definitions of the problem. Often, any one "problem" is intertwined with other messy problems.
Information (amount and reliability) is problematical	Because the definition of the problem is in doubt, collecting and categorizing information becomes a problem. The information flow threatens either to become overwhelming or to be seriously insufficient. Data may be incomplete and of dubious reliability.
Multiple conflicting interpretations	For those data that do exist, players develop multiple and sometimes conflicting interpretations. The facts and their significance can be read in several different ways.
Different value orientations, political emotional clashes	Without objective criteria, players rely more on personal and/or professional values in order to make sense of the situation. The clash of different values often politically and emotionally charges the situation.
Goals are unclear, or multiple and conflicting	Either the goals are vague, or they are clearly defined and contradictory.
Time, money or attention are lacking	A difficult situation is made chaotic by severe shortages of one or more of these items.
Contradictions and paradoxes appear	The situation has seemingly inconsistent features, relationships, or demands.
Roles are vague, responsibilities are unclear	Players do not have a clearly defined set of activities they are expected to perform. On important issues, the locus of decision making and other responsibilities is vague or in dispute.
Success measures are lacking	People are unsure what success in resolving the situation would mean, and/or they have no way of assessing the degree to which they are successful.
Poor understanding of cause effect relationships	Players do not understand what causes what in the situation. Even if sure of the effects they desire, they are uncertain how to obtain them.
Symbols and metaphors used	In place of precise definitions or logical arguments, players use symbols or metaphors to express their point of view.
Participation in decision making fluid	The identities of the key decision makers and influence holders change as players enter and leave the decision arena.

Table 2.1 Characteristics of Ambiguous, Changing Situations (McKaskey, 1982)

Any of the characteristics in Table 2.1 may cause people to experience an interruption of their expectations about the way things are today, so it's fair to say that in today's world change is becoming the constant. This is exemplified by the observation that SAP projects are not over when the systems are live. As the business needs and aspirations evolve constantly, so must the supporting system.

2.3.2 Resistance is Necessary

A common misunderstanding about resistance is that it is a phenomenon that gets in the way, is something to avoid, something to prevent, etc. Resistance is emotion, and emotion contains the energy you need to move from the current state to the future state. The belief that resistance is a bad thing is caused by the fact that the emotion is interpreted as negative and the energy is mostly directed against the change.

What's more, emotions are infectious. When an outside event produces negative emotions for an individual in a close relationship, it easily sneaks into the team, the department, or even the whole organization. As a result, most of us will try to avoid emotions that get in the way.

The point is that you should not avoid the resistance or prevent this energy from being built up. Your job is to channel and redirect the emotional energy in such a way that it helps you achieve the goals of your project. To give you an idea of how to redirect energy, the key lies in suspecting yourself in the first place. We will come back to this point further in this chapter and later in Part III.

Nothing can ever be changed without the proper amount of energy. So resistance is not the problem but the means to achieve your goals. The real problem is indifference. Indifference means that the change is so flat, so generalized that it is not causing any interruption in people's expectations. Indifference means: no interruption, no emotion, no expectations, no fuel; full stop. Nothing is worse than people who don't care. Therefore, you need to be very explicit when communicating your change. Otherwise, you risk ending up in the dead-end street of indifference.

2.3.3 Four Basic Emotions

You need to know that there are four basic emotions at hand; i.e, four basic fuels that contain the energy we need to move from one state to another. Fear, anger, sadness, and happiness are the four basic emotions that can be experienced by every person in any culture. Just like the four basic tastes: bitter, sweet, sour, and salty.

Fear, anger, and sadness are not necessarily negative. Like salty, bitter, and sour they can be quite good. Whether we like the taste of something is an entirely subjective matter. It depends on our experiences, our education, and the company that we're in. Likewise, whether we experience change in a positive or negative manner also depends on our experiences, our education, and the company that we're in. This is a very valuable insight, because it proves that emotions follow beliefs (and not the other way around).

2.3.4 Reading Emotions

The problem with emotions is not their intensity, but rather the fact that they always come in disguise. You will almost never hear people saying that they are scared, angry, or sad because of a certain change. People communicate their emotions through "playing games." The analysis of these games is the study domain of Transactional Analysis (Stewart & Joines, 1987).

Transactional Analysis proposes a simple decoder for reading the emotions that occur as a result of change: it is called the Drama Triangle (Karpman, 1968). Fear, Anger, and Sadness hold the principal roles in this game. The associated roles are:

▶ The Persecutor role

▶ The Rescuer role

▶ The Victim role

A persecutor thinks of others as "not OK" and will use this against them by accusing them, belittling them, suppressing them, etc. A rescuer also thinks that others are "not OK" and helps them because he is convinced that they are not capable of helping themselves. A victim thinks of himself as not OK and therefore seeks out a persecutor for confirmation, or a rescuer because he or she "is incapable of dealing with it." The role of the victim is probably the most powerful of all three. A good victim can create a persecutor in every situation.

As Figure 2.5 illustrates, each role in the Drama Triangle is ruled by an emotion:

▶ **Persecutor (Anger)**
Only sees the errors of the SAP project, is critical; often in a bad mood.

▶ **Rescuer (Fear)**
Always goes that extra mile to "help" others; is always very busy, tired,

sometimes lonely; is completely sucked up by the SAP project and does not have five minutes to himself.

▶ **Victim (Sadness)**
Doesn't answer, doesn't help, never holds a point of view. I don't know/I can't/it's all the same to me. This whole SAP thing confuses him. It's killing us; we can't stand it any longer!

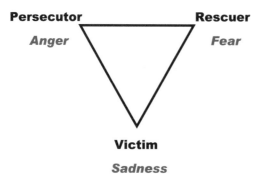

Figure 2.5 The Drama Triangle, based on Karpman (1968) and Callahan (2004)

After a while it is easy to see how people around us use these roles when interacting with one another, but individually we don't seem to be susceptible to this behavior. Nothing could befurther from the truth! It's almost impossible to see how we fall into the trap of this mechanical behavior.

2.3.5   Emotions are Data

Once you are able to disconnect the emotion and read the valuable information hiding behind it, you will soon find out that there is a positive use of these emotions. Most people unaware that their emotions can lead us forward. The key lies in our own ability and maturity to receive their communication.

▶ **Anger – Clarity**
When we are angry, we are often very aware of what we want or don't want. This leads us to clarity about our objective and the objective of our team. Anger helps us to make decisions, to stay alert, and to stop confusion.

There is a thin line between destructive anger and a vision that fuels a change. They both build on the same emotion but with a different sense of responsibility. When you allow frustrated people to find expression for their anger and you genuinely receive their communication, ask them what you could do to improve.

▸ **Fear—Courage**
When we are afraid, this means we are approaching unknown territory. New opportunities arise when we have the courage to take that direction. Fear often works as an indicator towards danger, but also towards new opportunities.

Often, the most frightened people are the closest to building the courage to deal with the unknown. Courage builds on the same emotion that can freak us out. Surprisingly, when you allow frightened people to put their anxiety into words, they tend to make room for courage to meet the challenges they are facing.

▸ **Sadness—Contact**
The essence of each relationship is contact. The measure in which we are in contact depends on the empathy and the self-confidence that we have. Cynicism, for instance, is a hidden form of sadness. Cynical people often are very good at sensing which relations are being left behind in a change project.

Again, there is thin line between cynical reactions and emotional intelligence. The underlying emotion is the same. Although cynical people are tough, they also know exactly who is left out. When they see the purpose behind the change, they may even be the best relationship builders.

2.3.6   Suspect Yourself First

How can we get the people who resist so hard to pull the cart with same amount of energy? You don't need to reduce the energy of the resistance, but instead you should change the underlying beliefs that guide it against the change.

The starting point for doing so is to offer yourself an alternative interpretation of resistance. For all the people that you labeled as "resistant," have a look at the following alternatives.

▸ I don't understand their point of view...yet.

▸ They did something I did not expect.

▸ They did something I did not want them to do.

▸ What they did does not fit into my model of how change happens.

▸ Either I know something they don't, or they know something I don't.

▸ Maybe I have made a mistake.

▸ I have created a problem for them.

▸ I am asking them to do something that feels unsafe.

The point is that when we label a person as "resistant," we stop the conversation, we map them on the Drama Triangle, and we place ourselves high above it. Rather than sitting in judgment, seek additional information that would help you understand the person's reactions (Karten, 2002).

2.4   Two Types of Change

You should be aware of the fact that there are two ways to make an organizational change (see Figure 2.6; IMA, 1997):

▸ The first one is going from the present state to the future state through a transition. Actually, this approach follows tha natural cycle of change as we discussed in the beginning of this chapter.

▸ A second approach goes from the Present State to the Future State with no preparation for the people undergoing the change. In this case, the transition is dealt with afterwards. The transition in this case is invisible, and the psychological, human, and financial costs are hidden in the organization.

APPROACH 1: ALLOW TRANSITION

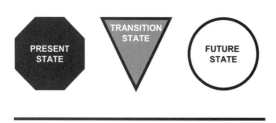

APPROACH 2: NO TRANSITION

Figure 2.6 Two types of Change (adapted from IMA, 1997)

We would not go so far as labeling the first approach as ethical and the second as unethical, but the differences are significant as we show in Table 2.2.

Transition Approaches	Approach 1: allow transition	Approach 2: no transition
Investment	High early	High later
Maintenance	Low	High
Time Frame	Slow	Fast
Motivation	Do it right	Do it
Commitment	Individual, "Ours"	Organizational, "Theirs'

Table 2.2 The Two Transition Approaches Compared (adapted from IMA, 1997)

Throughout this book we describe the first approach.

2.5   Conclusion: The Only Way Out

At the end of Chapter 1, we noted that the purpose of this book is to describe how to go from the paradigm of functional thinking to that of integrated process thinking.

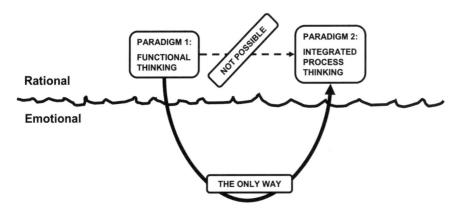

Figure 2.7 The Paradigm Shift

As we show in Figure 2.7, it takes more than textbooks to make a shift in paradigms. After reading this chapter, it should be clear to you that organizational change management has more to do with the emotional stuff below the surface than with the rational stuff above the surface.

Ignoring the emotional stuff that goes on below the surface is not an option if you want the organizational change to be a success. When you are dealing with emotions, the only way out is through.

But knowing this is not enough. You will need a strategy to orchestrate the maneuvers and a vision to guide you through the fog of emotions. The way to do that is by managing perceptions, which is the core of Chapter 3.

Because the emotional part of a change is the most difficult one, the purpose of this chapter is to give you a basic understanding of how to manage the perceptions that cause people to feel certain ways. Perceptions and expectations are going to be our two main tools for managing change.

3   Making Sense

3.1   The Three Basic Ingredients of Organizational Change

"I am well aware that I should be reporting my time on a weekly basis. But I don't do it. My job is to do market development and to acquire new customers. Filling out a timesheet is of no added value to me. Besides, nobody explained me why it is important to report my time on a weekly basis. And nobody asked for my input. So why should I care?"

(A successful private banker working for a major international bank.)

As you can see in Figure 3.1, every organizational change always has the same three ingredients:

- Motivation (the emotional stuff below the surface)
- Knowledge
- Skills

These three ingredients determine the domains of action for making change happen. They are the biggest needs during each cycle of change, as explained here:

- Questions and reactions, which fall into the knowledge category, often indicate a need for vision, a business case, or an overview. These refer to the "what" of the change.
- The skills category indicates a need for concrete and explicit knowledge, tools, and working instructions. In other words: People want to know "how" they will make the change happen.

▶ There is also an entire range of reactions that fall into the motivation category. These reactions reflect people's need for involvement and inspiration. Motivation determines whether people simply undergo the change or are active participants.

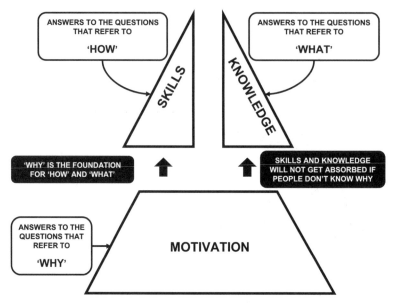

Figure 3.1 Three Ingredients of Change Management

3.2 The Why is Important

A frequent mistake in SAP projects is to postpone all contacts with the target group until the very last minute. Too much influence from the target group often has a delaying and disturbing impact. "Now we really need to provide information," is the usual statement. Your team isolates itself from the rest of the company (we call this *project cocooning*), and the communications department fires unidirectional communication (Knowledge) at the target group.

As illustrated in Figure 3.2, people feel as if a concept is being forced upon them and they aren't really given the time to fully comprehend it. The knowledge provided during training is so theoretical that it has nothing in common with practice. Many of the workers wonder why they have to spend all that time in training and are annoyed because their day-to-day work is piling up.

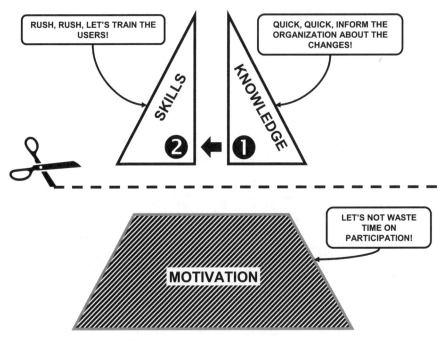

Figure 3.2 Where it Usually Goes Wrong

People have received all the explicit knowledge that is—strictly in rational terms–necessary to face the change. They have had the *know-what's* pushed down their throats. But the project grinds to a halt in the production phase because people have not been given the time to participate and build up *know-how*. As discussed in the previous chapter, you will be confronted with a performance drop in any case. Postponing participation to the very last minute will only make it worse.

Even before the change has really started, you are stuck in a negative, downward spiral because most target groups are not being motivated to take the project in hand. When reactions indicate that there is a need for involvement, an information session or training will have the wrong effect. It's important to know where the needs lie at what precise moment. The best way to find out is to involve the target group in the project in a timely manner. A change is always uncomfortable, and discomforts are easier to deal with when you participate in making them happen.

The inevitable truth is that people will need to build the *know-how* for the project to work, so it is better to do that during project preparation than to pay for it in terms of a sputtering go-live.

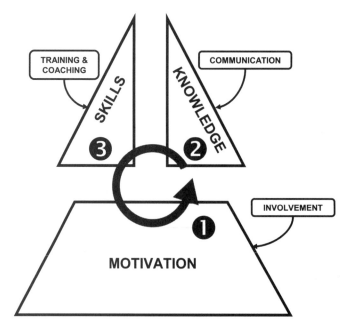

Figure 3.3 Building a Learning Relationship

As illustrated in Figure 3.3, people should be given the opportunity to be part of the creative process that is expected from them. That is why it's necessary to effectively involve your target group and your sponsors before, during, and after the change. Now that you have seen the three basic ingredients of organizational change, let's investigate in the next part of this chapter to see how they can be used to create a new culture.

3.3   What About Culture?

We'll explain the concept of culture and demonstrate how it is created. With this knowledge, you will be able to manage culture in the context of an SAP implementation.

3.3.1   Culture and SAP

When talking about culture in the context of this book, there are a few things to take into account:

▶ Culture is a sense-making mechanism. It determines how we perceive a situation; it shapes our attitudes, and it influences our behavior.

▶ A functional castle is a culture on its own. By definition, process integration inflicts culture shock. People from different castles speak different languages, so true communication is not evident when we bring them all together.

▶ According to Daryl Connor (1996) when facing an organizational culture that is different from that desired in making the change, there are three options:

1. Modify the change to bring it more in line with existing beliefs, behaviors, and assumptions.

2. Modify the beliefs, behaviors, and assumptions of the culture to be more supportive of the change.

3. Prepare for the change to fail.

When you look at the radical shift that is necessary to go from functional thinking to integrated process thinking, numbers 1 and 3 are not options. So the essential question is: "How do we modify the beliefs, behaviors, and assumptions of the culture to be more supportive of the change?"

3.3.2 The Creation of a Culture

A culture is like a pair of glasses you are wearing. Rose-colored glasses will make you feel happier than black-lensed glasses; that much is certain. What is less obvious, though, is that glasses of a certain color will make you see certain things more clearly and completely ignore other things; in other words, they determine the data you select.

In Figure 3.4, we illustrate how these glasses work when we are confronted with an interruption of our expectations. Our perception of what is going on in our organization follows the seven steps that are indicated. These seven steps are derived from Karl Weick's seven characteristics of Sense Making in organizations (1995).

If your purpose is to modify the beliefs, behaviors, and assumptions of the existing cultures, then these seven steps will be the foundation of your communication approach. In the following paragraphs, we have a closer look at each of the seven steps.

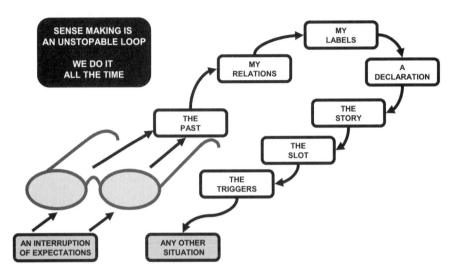

Figure 3.4 Sense Making Happens in Seven Steps

The Past

We make sense of our experiences by comparing them with previous experiences. The organizational past is an important indicator in predicting the reaction to the current organizational change. The past is something that comes walking in through the back door of emotions. People remember events that have the same emotional tone as what they currently feel. Past events are reconstructed in the present as explanations, not because they look the same but because they feel the same. Consider, for example, the site manager of a chemical plant who states:

> *"You know, we have been there before. This SAP project is just another hot-shot's program designed to launch him into the executive committee. We just need to wait until he gets promoted, and then things will settle down and return to normal. Once these project guys, return to the headquarters, we'll finally get things done over here."*

To describe this reaction in the words of Goss, Pascale & Athos (1993):

> *Statements of vision from chief executives have bewildered and even amused employees who just don't get why a CEO would describe a future that their experience says can never materialize.*

So people's experiences are a boundary to how much they can take about the current change, both emotionally and rationally. There is not much a leader can do about the organizational past. The past can be so persistent that you sometimes will need to break through the "been there, done that" syndrome the hard way.

My Relations

We make sense of changes in organizations while in conversation with others, while reading communications from others, and while exchanging ideas with others. That is how sense becomes organizational. So as a change leader, you do not necessarily want to change people's beliefs by brainwashing them one by one. Rather, you want to change the conversation so they can share conclusions and create joint beliefs.

Changing a conversation about what's going on requires different skills than just throwing slogans at people. That is why you need to make sure your SAP program is a topic on the agenda of regular meetings such as those of task forces or departments. People will need to get used to the fact that things will change in the near future, so you should make it the topic of their conversations in every possible way. This includes looking at your program from a marketing point of view. This marketing approach is discussed in more detail in Chapter 6.

My Labels

People are sense-making creatures. Whenever a change happens that affects us we give it a label and put it into a known category (dangerous, stupid, beautiful, etc.). Almost instinctively, we respond with familiar questions: *Who is behind this? What are the credentials of those people? Who said so? What will become of us after that change? Do they have the support of management?*

In the context of an SAP program, we can think of the struggle to collect data, to have data cleansed, or to get user acceptance tests completed by people who are not assigned to the project. Their depth of commitment and the time they spend outside of their working hours to the benefit of the project are determined by how they and their management have labeled the project, ranging from "of strategic importance" to "a pain in the butt."

The change will always be labeled. People will not rest until their soul-searching and conflicts have resulted in an identity. So why not help them in doing so? In Part III, we will extensively cover branding, communication style, and the use of symbols, all of which contribute to this step.

A Declaration

Words have consequences. We should never underestimate the power of words and conversations. A situation is "talked" into existence, and the basis is laid for action to deal with it. Declarations are the way we translate stuff from below the surface into explicit knowledge. As a simple example, when people constantly say that "this project stinks," they create a climate in which the observation of difficulties is stimulated and the observation of possibilities is constrained.

But the impact of negative declarations becomes even more of a problem when the messenger is supposed to be a sponsor. Take for example the finance director of a plant who openly questions the purpose of the SAP program during a training session and in presence of his complete staff. Some people's declarations are more powerful than others. Therefore, you should be really selective when you assign agents and make sure that you pick the opinion leaders. The same goes for assigning the project sponsors: Make sure you pick the most influential ones in rank and order.

The Real Story

People are interested in the truth, not the details. And people are not stupid. We construct the meanings of things based on reasonable explanations of what might be happening rather than through scientific discovery of "the real story." Here is a warning flag to heed at this point: *What is a simple truth for one group, such as managers, often proves implausible for another group, such as employees.* This is the most striking when talking about the benefits of an integrated system. Or, to put it in the words of one logistics supervisor:

> *"Please stop lying to me about how this SAP thing will make us work more efficiently. It may be true for my boss and my boss's boss, but for me it means five times more data input and mouse clicking before I get the transport documents out of this damn printer device!"*

Another proof that people are not stupid but are interested in the truth was witnessed by an HR manager who walked into the SAP project team's room one day. There, he discovered a drawing on the wall of a cliff and people falling from that cliff. When he asked the team members what that drawing meant, he got the following answer:

> *"The drawing was made once we found out what the hidden purpose was of this project: We are here to automate processes so that people can be fired.*

Management has not been honest about this up front, so at least here we can keep a visible score of what is going on."

In short, if your goal is to reduce headcount through the automation of processes, then be straightforward about it. Eventually people will find out anyway. And if they do, you have not only fired some people, but you also crushed the commitment of those who stay.

The Slot

Too many things are going on at the same time, and your SAP program is probably not the only initiative of strategic importance. Like an airplane waiting for takeoff, your program will only get a limited slot for takeoff in the attention span of an individual. Your program will not be the only one screaming for commitment and action. Take for example the large reorganization that took place in the middle of an implementation at a chemical company. Both teams (the SAP team and the reorganization team) were not keen on sharing information with one another. So people were left on their own to determine whether the two teams' messages were compatible.

Knowing exactly what people are in the middle of will help you to reformulate your communication at the level of the receiver. In the case of the reorganization of the chemical plant, this could have been done by having top management make sure that both project teams shared their essential information. Unfortunately they didn't, and this forced the SAP program team to have to make some substantial changes to the authorization concept at the last minute.

The Triggers

Nobody is capable of observing it all. Our observation is based on extracted cues. The cues that we observe depend on what we expect to observe, As a kind of self-fulfilling prophecy, we shape our reality according to how we expect it to be. When we think we are going to succeed at something, we will be triggered by every cue that confirms this reality and act upon it, and vice versa. The most obvious example is that of an SAP program steering committee whose sessions are only attended half the time by the executives who are supposed to participate in it. Unfortunately, these absences speak louder than words.

Another example is the irritation that is caused among the workers of a production plant when they see the SAP implementation team members arrive each morning much later than they do. Even if the SAP team members stay later, some production workers will perceive late arrival as a sign of disrespect.

The most common example is the disease of meetings that never start on time. This may be no problem in internal project-team meetings, but think about what cues you are sending out when you export that habit to meetings where users and key users are involved?

Finally, a positive example of this step: The executive who takes an unexpected walk around on the shop floor level to see what's cooking.

3.3.3   Diversity of National Cultures

When most people talk about cultural diversity, they mean the differences in national cultures. In the context of SAP implementations, this adds complexity to implementing SAP in multiple countries.

There are many authors, lists, and indices available that claim to answer all our questions on national cultural diversity. Among the most popular is the approach of Trompenaars and Hampden-Turner (1998). They describe the walls you may bump into when you travel from one country to another. According to them, this is how people's attitudes and behaviors differ from one country to another:

- ▸ **Universalism Versus Particularism**
  What is more important—rules or relationships?

- ▸ **Individualism Versus Communitarianism**
  Do we function in a group or as an individual?

- ▸ **Neutral Versus Affective**
  Do we display our emotions?

- ▸ **Specific Versus Diffused**
  To what extent do we get involved?

- ▸ **Achieved Status Versus Ascribed Status**
  Do we have to prove ourselves to receive status or is it given to us?

- ▸ **Internal Versus External Orientation**
  Do we control our environment or work with it?

Use this list as a reminder when hopping from one time zone to another, but never accept it as an excuse for not touching the functional castles.

3.3.4   A Culture of Change

Given that the introduction of integrated-process thinking provokes culture shock and that the diversity of national cultures adds to this complexity, organizational change efforts can get messy and chaotic at times.

Focusing on cultural differences, analyzing, and interpreting cultural indexes and theories will only get you paralyzed because there is no true or false when it comes to cultures. Instead, we advise to focus on a characteristic that all cultures have in common, be it cross-national, cross-functional, cross-gender, or cross-generational: Responsibility. This is a very simple, yet very essential insight of the book called *Who Moved My Cheese?* by Spencer Johnson (1998). According to Johnson, when something happens that interrupts our reality, we can do one of the following:

▶ Put all our energy in trying to get back to how it was before ("Why is this happening to me, it's unfair").

▶ Take it as a starting point and look for other available options ("Something interesting happened, let's see which options we have as a result of this change").

Responsibility is the specific ingredient that makes the difference here. Responsibility is a choice, not something that happens to you. Everything becomes clear when we study the English definition for "responsible": It literally means "able to respond" or "being capable of responding." When people choose to take responsibility in a situation, they co-own it. This insight is fundamental for change management. We always have the choice of becoming the owner or the victim of a situation. William Glasser (1998) calls this the *Choice Theory*. An owner will look for solutions; a victim will search for a persecutor or a rescuer.

However, we should not be too academic about responsibility, as one HR manager once put it:

> "If you want to see responsibility, don't go looking in the boardroom. Instead, have a look on the shop floor, in the production hall, and on the warehouse ramps. Sometimes it amazes me how these people can continue to deliver what the company promises, despite their management."

This quote clearly indicates that we should not let people participate just for the sake of controlling emotional mood swings. It gives us the insight that shop floor workers, logistics operators, purchasers, and invoice controllers may have a big influence on your earnings per share. So, for your company to be "able to respond" to future challenges, we suggest to include their points of view early on.

3.3.5 The Co-Creation of a Safe Place

As discussed in Chapter 2, the nature of all changes is: "Things will get worse before they get better." Another often-heard saying with regard to change is: "The only one who likes to change is a baby in a wet diaper." Not only is this is true for all changes (whether they are positive or negative), but it gets us to the heart of the matter: how people grow up. Just like the infant who returns into the safety of mother's arms, we are looking for a safe place when an upgrade of our awareness kicks in.

The point to remember in the context of organizational change is that human beings will only make the shift to the next level (the future state) when they have a safe place to return to. The best way to provide this safe place is through participation and interaction. Participation gives people the feeling of control over their own destinies, and that can make the difference between success and failure of the project. In practice, this means that you will need to build a learning relationship between the implementation program and the organization. This brings us to the next point: Learning.

3.4 Learning

Learning is something people do all the time. Most of the time, our learning takes place unconsciously, but things get stickier whenever our expectations get interrupted. Change is what makes learning interesting. But let's first look at the phases of learning.

3.4.1 The Four Phases of Learning

Our biggest task in an organizational change will be to take people by the hand and then, eventually, make sure they can help themselves. This is the domain of learning. A useful way to understanding what happens when we go through a change is to look at what happens when we learn something new. Learning always takes place in four stages, as shown in Figure 3.5 and listed below:

▸ Unconscious Incompetence

▸ Conscious Incompetence

- Conscious Competence

- Unconscious Competence

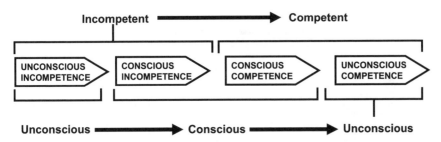

Figure 3.5 The Four Stages of Learning

Take, for example, the first time users are confronted with the SAP user interface. Until that moment, they have been unaware of it because they never tried it.

After getting into the driver seat for the first time and trying to find their way, they know enough to realize that they are incompetent at it. They are now the second phase of learning: Conscious Incompetence.

One day, they know their way around the favorites menu, they know what each button can do, and they even know some transaction codes by heart. At that point they are most probably in the third learning stage: Conscious Competence. They are skilled at using SAP, but it still demands a lot of their attention.

Finally, after a long while, they will be able to use SAP as an automatic response, and can take corrective actions in the course of doing their day-to-day job. They accomplished the fourth learning phase: Unconscious Competence. The skill by now has become a habit, which requires no extra attention.

3.4.2 Learning and Resistance

When we translate this dynamic to the context of an organization and start to wonder what this means in terms of resistance, we will find that these four steps are a reliable indicator in predicting when resistance will occur on a larger scale.

As shown in Figure 3.6, people will only start to react to the change from the moment that they become aware of their own incompetence in the face of change. What's even more important is that this resistance is actually the learning tension that is necessary to absorb knowledge. The frustration of my own incompetence is my best motivation to acquire new skills and knowledge.

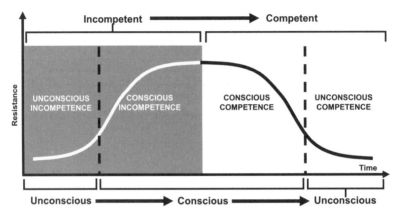

Figure 3.6 The Four Learning Phases and the Corresponding Resistance

3.4.3 The Coaching Dilemma

Once the person or group has achieved a new competence, and has begun to express these in new daily behavior, there remains the fragility of refreezing. For the new behaviors to last, they first must fit into the personality of the individual or the culture of the group that is being changed. Otherwise, the behavior will be only a temporary adaptation to the pressures of the change situation and will erode once the change agent has ceased to disconfirm the old behavior. New behaviors may not remain stable unless they also fit into the ongoing relationships and the work context of the person.

Finally, there is the coaching dilemma: "To what extent should I give them fish, and to what extent can I teach them how to fish?" We are very much in favor of learning that can be stimulated by the change agent's deliberate withholding of advice, suggestion, role models, or other cues of what to do. By forcing the learners to develop their own solutions, the change agent ensures that whatever is learned will, by definition, fit into the personality and the group. You will note that this is a slower and possibly more painful way to learn, but it increases the probability of successful refreezing.

3.4.4 Different Cycles Run at the Same Time

The members of executive team that decided to deploy the organizational change are the first to wrestle with their incompetence to shape a crystal clear future state. Next in line is the project team responsible for the implementation of the change. They will go through exactly the same cycle when they find out they are supposed to become ambassadors by the time they go-live with something they hardly know about right now.

By the time the user community is confronted with the end of the world as they know it (for key users, that is at the time of User Acceptance Testing; for other users, that is at the time of training), it may look like the whole organization is on fire. That is fine, as long as you are prepared for it.

Middle management is mostly the last group in line to be confronted with its incompetence. This occurs when they try to balance the continuity of their business against the upgrade and the performance dip of their most valuable resource: people. But the real hangover for them is yet to come; it happens when they are confronted with the fact that the frontline workers have more authority than before and have an ocean of information at hand.

In short, nobody escapes the resistance caused by this learning cycle, but knowing that learning occurs in four phases is very helpful in planning and preparing for the bumps in the road ahead.

3.5   Conclusion

Now we should be able to refine the drawing that we made at the end of Chapter 2. We suggested that the move from functional thinking to process thinking involves a journey below the surface.

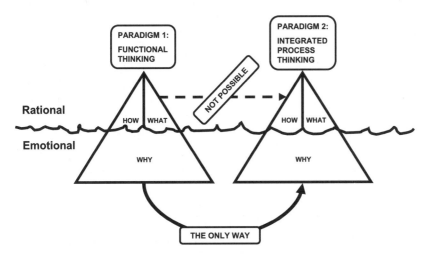

Figure 3.7 A Sharper View on the Paradigm Shift

Figure 3.7 gives a sharper view of this paradigm shift, based on what you have learned so far. We have seen that there are three ingredients of organizational change (knowledge, skills, and motivation) and that they need to be used throughout the seven steps of creating a culture. You learned that people will only adopt a new rational mindset if the underlying motivation has been addressed properly. Finally, we indicated that responsibility—the most important ingredient of all—can only be achieved through participation.

In Chapter 4, we will examine the context in which this all takes place: the context of program management.

This chapter illustrates how program- and project-management approaches enable the change triggered by an SAP implementation. You will learn why the technical part of the implementation is not sufficient for success. It must be supported by a program that integrates it with change management.

4 Program and Project Management as Enablers of Change

4.1 Vehicles of Change

A functional organization cannot change its own ways of working. The reasons for this are not necessarily to be found in the capabilities or the competences of the people, but in the fact that a functional organization is bound to execute its day-to-day jobs. Its people are focused on "getting the day-to-day work done;" e. g., taking orders, preparing deliveries, production, collecting money, etc. They don't have the time to question in depth the ways of working, or to come up with new ways of working to improve efficiency. Projects are the most suitable vehicles of change, as they are temporary undertakings with specific objectives. To manage a project is to manage the movement from one state to another (Reiss, 1992).

In contrast to ongoing, functional work, a project is a temporary journey undertaken to create a unique product or service. A project has specific resources (human and financial resources, time, and knowledge) during the period of its duration. This has to be seen as an investment made by the organization to realize the change.

However, in the case of SAP projects the end result is a different organization supported by an integrated software platform. Because of their complexity and their scale of impact on the organization, SAP projects differ from most other projects because they threaten the functional organization in its current form. That is why we will argue in this chapter that a project approach is necessary but not sufficient. To succeed with such a heavyweight change, we will need a program.

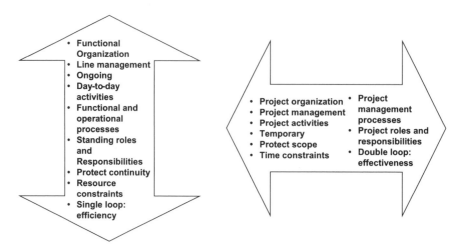

Figure 4.1 Operations vs. Projects

Figure 4.1 summarizes the main differences between day-to-day operations and projects. First, the objective of operations is to perform according to a frozen stable pattern, such as producing 500 electronic components per day with a scrap ratio of no more than 1%. Every investment of time and money is aimed at continuing to maintain this objective. The constraints of day-to-day operations are resources such as raw materials and people. The way these constraints are countered is through corrective actions of single-loop efficiency (Argyris and Schön, 1996). Single-loop efficiency is focused on maintaining stability of operations. It means that every deviation from a norm is immediately corrected.

Projects, on the other hand, are supposed to break up a specific context, in order to change it and to freeze the desired state. A critical success factor of projects is whether they are able to maintain and protect their scope. Constraints of projects consist of time and resources. The biggest difference though, lies in the presence of a double loop: The focus of projects is to question and change the frozen norm itself.

4.2 Delivery of Benefits

Each change must result in benefits to the organization. If that is not the case, there is no reason to go through the change, let alone to have it supported by implementing SAP. You should never be implementing SAP for the sake of SAP. The investment should be directly linked to the realization of business benefits over the course of a payback period.

4.2.1 Benefits Quantify Change Efforts

"Too often, project managers find themselves in the situation that their organization 'is going wall-to-wall SAP,' and they are then left to implement the chosen application without a clear understanding of the expected benefits and the organizational changes that will be required."

(Ward & Daniel, 2006)

SAP is integrated, process-oriented software supporting best-practice processes. It is also modular software, supporting functional domains such as Financials (FI), Controlling (CO), Production Planning (PP), Warehouse Management (WM), Materials Management (MM), and Sales and Distribution (SD).

As argued in Chapter 1, any SAP implementation should be embedded in a fundamental business initiative to transform the business. You are not implementing SAP for the sake of SAP or because of its features like multi-currency, the ability to define sales organizations, reporting, etc. You are doing so because you want to gain benefits that are essential for the survival of the organization. In *Managing Successful Programs* (2003), the U.K.'s Office of Government Commerce defines a benefit as follows:

> Change results in desired outcomes...Benefits are the quantification of these outcomes.

Benefits formulate the goal of a program in terms of the success of your organization. These are the beacons, guiding the program to develop in the right direction. Benefits are the basis of the business case to justify the cost of the SAP implementation as shown in Table 4.1.

Outcome	Benefit
Improved closing process	Closing process reduced from seven to three working days
Increased integration	Reduced number of databases from eight to three
Improved stock control	Stock rotation improved by 20%
Improved order management	Reduced average lead time order to delivery with four hours for parts sales

Table 4.1 Examples of Outcomes and Benefits

Realization of certain benefits can lead to the realization of other benefits. For example, the reduced average lead time for order intake-to-delivery may create more customer satisfaction.

You must be aware of how important the definition of benefits is for the success of the SAP implementation. Benefits can be identified in all functional areas, such as finance and controlling, customer relationship management, sales and distribution, profitability analysis, and materials management. Benefits can, for example, increase flexibility (agility), increase quality of service, reduce risks, reduce costs, or contribute to the realization of other benefits.

4.2.2 Reframe Features into Benefits

In an ideal world, the decision to implement SAP fits in an overall business strategic program derived from the company's business vision. As mentioned earlier, the implementation of that strategic program must realize benefits for the organization that are in line with the corporate goals. In many cases, however, the decision to implement SAP is based upon a combination of more or less compelling operational features, listed here:

- Legacy systems need to be replaced.
- More integration of information is required.
- Better integration of the IT landscape is needed.
- The current version of SAP will no longer be supported.
- Common ways of working need to be implemented.
- The supplier of current systems doesn't provide proper support, or worse, is no longer financially stable.

▶ Data integrity.

▶ System integration.

▶ Up-to-date software functionality meeting the needs of a modern organization.

▶ Up-to-date technological environment.

▶ Improved continuity and enhanced disaster-recovery planning.

Unless you are able to convert these reasons into benefits that serve the organizations strategy, you will not be able to win the hearts of your stakeholders. In short: If you are unable to come up with quantifiable benefits, you should consider not moving forward with the SAP implementation. If you do, you risk getting lost in the fog without a beacon to guide you.

4.2.3 A Program of Integrated Projects

Implementing SAP demands huge efforts and is very complex. Many organizations come to that conclusion when they are halfway through the implementation. These organizations lack a program that provides a framework in which the delivery of benefits can be managed and followed up (program performance management). Program management provides a management layer above project management, focusing on the following:

▶ Selecting the required set of projects, each of them delivering "products" needed to achieve identified benefits (end state).

▶ Defining these projects.

▶ Providing an infrastructure where projects can be run successfully.

A program is successful when it realizes the benefits that the organization identified, within timeline and within budget. Program success is also highly dependent on the successful execution of each of the projects within the program. Because projects are the building blocks of the program, if delivery fails at the project level, the overall program will eventually fail. Table 4.2 provides further insight in the differences between projects and programs.

Programs	Projects
Less well-defined end date; some continue until a defined organization state has been achieved.	Defined start and finish dates.
Focus is on delivering benefits; requires involvement after project end. Every program must directly benefit the organization in some way.	Focus is on delivering products. These products will be used by the operational parts of the organization, but not all of them will directly produce benefits.
More complex; interface with the strategy, contain many projects, drive operational change.	Simpler; only have to focus on delivering defined products.
Exist in a world that is constantly changing. These changes need to be constantly monitored and their impact on the program and its projects controlled and managed.	Projects are "ring-fenced." Change control is more structured and it is easier to control activity.
Macro view; have to consider the combined effect of a portfolio of projects, which should produce synergetic benefits, but sometimes conflict with each other. A balanced view is needed, which sometimes is detrimental to a few projects in the portfolio.	Micro view; only concerned with delivery of what has been defined, on time, in budget and to acceptable quality. Project managers are only concerned with other projects if their project is dependent on them. They will fight against any other project that threatens the success of their own project.

Table 4.2 Projects vs. Programs (Reiss & Leigh, 2004)

Additionally, in the context of SAP implementations, a program approach promotes a culture of integration. As the different projects practice the art of getting things done, the program ensures that all these defined and temporary projects synchronize and integrate with one another in terms of the benefits that the organization wants to achieve. Success in terms of the program is then formulated in relationship to the organization's strategic ambitions.

4.3 The SAP Implementation Program

The complexity of an SAP implementation demands a program approach. In this section, we explain what this means and how it alters your approach.

4.3.1 Program Lifecycle

Each program has a lifecycle. Figure 4.2 shows that each phase of the lifecycle is dominant at a particular time. It also shows how a program moves from one phase into the other. None of the phases are completely over until the full program is finished.

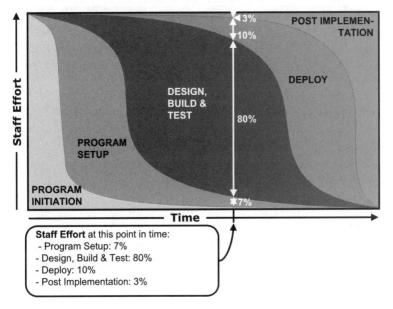

Figure 4.2 The SAP Program Lifecycle

As you can see in Figure 4.2, even when the program is officially in the design phase, some activities belonging to the previous and next phases, such as program setup and deployment, will be going on as well.

In Chapter 3, we distinguished three separate blocks of a change cycle: Unfreezing, Changing, and Refreezing. This insight allows us to manage the program lifecycle from a change point of view. It allows us to synchronize the user's learning phases with the program lifecycle and the project's moments of truth (i.e., critical success factors).

Throughout the rest of this book, Unfreezing, Changing, and Refreezing are used as a framework to guide any program-related action. As Figure 4.3 demonstrates, the change cycle only proves its usability in practice once we are able to map it to the lifecycle of a program.

Unfreezing, Changing, and Refreezing determine the tipping point from one phase to another. On the lower part of Figure 4.3, the learning phases are indicated from a user's point of view. You will note that the phase of unconscious competence does not appear. This is because this phase only settles in gradually and mostly long after the program has come to an end.

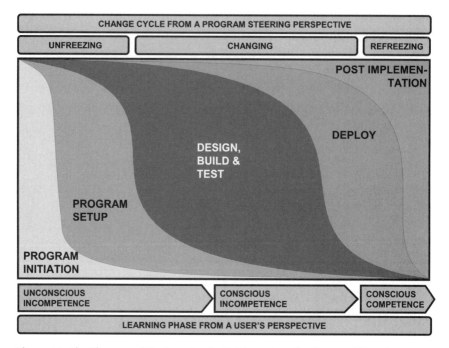

Figure 4.3 The Change and the Learning Cycle Mapped on the Program Lifecycle.

The program phases shown in Figure 4.3 provide the context of each project included in the program. Except for the program initiation and the program setup, it is important to note that these phases will be reflected in all the projects of the program.

Unfreezing

We will cover this more thoroughly in Part II of this book. The preparation of the program is the enabler to unfreeze the organization, preparing it for the intended change. Let's see what this involves:

▶ **Program Initiation**
   In this phase, the program manager is assigned, the business case is built for which the benefits need to be identified. A feasibility study is produced to make sure that the SAP implementation has an adequate chance of success. This fundamental phase sets the essential boundaries for the SAP implementation and the realization of underlying benefits.

▶ **Program Setup**
   Once the program has been approved based on the conclusion of the feasibility study and the program steering committee is installed, it is time to

take action. Until now, the program only existed on paper. The hardest part in this phase is to declare the program into existence. Therefore, activities in this phase typically include: program office installation, program charter definition, claiming resources from the organization, scope definition, project portfolio development, program structure definition, and timing and budgeting rituals.

Changing

This will be covered thoroughly in Part III. The execution of the program is about making the change in the organization happen. Let's get an idea of what this entails:

► **Design**
Once again, it is important to note that this is not only the design part of the technical software project but a phase that reappears in all underlying projects, such as the training and education project, and the data-cleansing project.

► **Build**
In a narrow project approach, this only includes the delivery of the prototype of the SAP tool. In a program approach, however, this is a phase that all projects have in common.

► **Test**
In the same way, this phase does not indicate the delivery of a fully tested, properly functioning system, but far more than that. Be aware that training, communication, performance management, and organization can be and need to be tested thoroughly.

► **Deployment**
Finally, deploying is far more than the technical go-live. Even in a "big-bang," single-instance, single-user community, the program has more than one go-live moment. This includes the technical delivery of the software pilot go-live, and the subsequent deployment of the solution across the global organization. But there are many more moments of truth that determine the success of the SAP implementation.

Refreeze

We will cover this in Part IV. Once all the changes are implemented, the organization must be frozen again, through the following phases:

- ▶ **Post Implementation**

  Post implementation is a broad term that covers more than you probably have budgeted for in terms of time and budget. We include it as a distinct phase to make sure that the post-implementation activities are aimed at making the change last and anchoring it within the organization.

- ▶ **Life after SAP**

  The program only truly closes when all benefits are realized, but in reality this only happens after the second wave of improvement projects. This is not a flaw; you just need to wait until the users have the same level of proficiency as those who delivered the solution. Only then will they be able to pinpoint the real areas of improvement.

4.3.2 Projects: the Building Blocks of the Program

A certain number of projects are needed to realize the benefits that the organization wants to achieve. All projects must be integrated into the program framework and positioned in the program-change lifecycle.

With the delivery of each project, the program progresses towards realization of its targets. This breakdown into projects allows close monitoring of progress.

The implementation program will consist of project streams, which aim at realizing specific outcomes. These projects are distributed across the program change lifecycle. Most of them will exist during the whole lifecycle, and a number of them only will exist during certain phases within the lifecycle. The most common project streams you will find within the SAP program are described here:

- ▶ **SAP Implementation Stream**

  The objective of this stream is to design, build (configure and develop), and implement SAP as a tool that supports the organization in its new ways of working, develops the interfaces, and migrates data.

- ▶ **IT/IS Stream**

  This stream includes all projects that are required to prepare the IT organization for the change, but also the installation of the infrastructure that is required for the SAP implementation.

- ▶ **Testing Stream**

  Testing is so crucial for an SAP implementation that it needs to be handled as a separate track. There are unit tests, integration tests, user acceptance tests, system performance tests, etc. The track also includes the preparation of the test activities.

▶ **Integration Stream**
The objective of this project stream is to ensure integration of processes, IT/IS, and organization. This stream is also responsible for re-integrating resources into the organization when the implementation is finished.

▶ **Program Management Stream**
Projects involving management of the program are launched within this stream. These projects would include risk management, quality follow-up, resource management, budget assignment and follow-up, progress follow-up, and performance management.

Finally, there are four specific streams that relate directly to managing organizational change during SAP implementations. These streams are outlined in Figure 4.4 and are described next:

Figure 4.4 Project Streams of Organizational Change Management

▶ **Organization Stream**
The purpose of this stream is to define and implement a new organization structure and to define and realize new ways of working. Within this stream, all the physical and logistical pains and inconveniences of restructuring are managed. The outcomes are new ways of working based on best-practice processes efficient realization of the corporate strategic goals. The overall objective in this stream is to refreeze a new workable organization structure.

▶ **Communication Stream**
The purpose of this stream is to support the program during its complete lifecycle in staying in touch with the organization. The main outcome of

this project track is the social construction of a new reality in the hearts and minds of employees. In this stream, you manage perceptions of what is going on.

▸ **Learning Stream**
This stream aims at upgrading the skills and knowledge of the organization. The main outcome of this project track is to preserve the quality of data input and the knowledge that will be shared across the organization.

▸ **Performance Stream**
The purpose of this stream is to alter the appraisal systems, reward mechanisms, and performance measurements so that they support the culture of integration. The outcome is a new psychological contract that rebuilds the commitment of the organization.

It is clear that each of these project streams has its own goals, but they will only reach their targets if we are able to integrate them properly. The outcomes realized by one of the streams will not lead to a benefit for the organization as long as all the other outcomes are not aligned.

4.3.3 Service Level Agreements: the Moments of Truth of a Program

As already discussed extensively, participation is the key element of user buy-in. The best way to measure participation is through moments of truth, such as training, user acceptance testing, breakout sessions with key users, department meetings, steering committees, and data-cleansing workshops. Moments of truth are contacts between the implementation team and the stakeholders of the program on occasions that are emotionally important for the stakeholder. Moments of truth are vital for the following two reasons:

▸ They provide a way to build a learning relationship with the organization.

▸ They provide you with the necessary feedback to keep you on track and prevent you from project cocooning (as explained later in this chapter).

We borrow the notion of "moments of truth" from Richard Normann (2001), who argues that a service company's overall performance is the sum of countless interactions between customers and employees, the so-called moments of truth that either help to retain a customer or send him to the competition.

To make the learning relationship within the organization a lasting one, we strongly suggest specifying the moments of truth into a bi-directional Service

Level Agreement (SLA). The SLA describes the level of service that both parties have to provide to each other. It allows formal follow-up of what the program delivers to the organization, but it also avoids users asking for additional functionality while you are rolling out the system.

We will cover how you should approach SLAs in the context of SAP implementations and how SLAs are used to pace an implementation throughout the complete program lifecycle.

4.3.4 Usability and the Second Wave

From a pure system-usability perspective, the majority of legacy systems are better than any of their SAP successors. Legacy systems were designed within the scope and the benefits of the functional castles. But even when implementing off-the-shelf software tools supporting best-practice processes, a basic degree of user friendliness is required to get acceptance from the user community. In all the implementations that we have been involved in, we have never seen an SAP implementation that meets all (user) expectations from the moment of go-live. Some examples are given below:

▶ Users complain that their day-to-day work has expanded with futile system interventions.

▶ Key users say that the system is too slow.

▶ Managers say they lack reports.

▶ During deployment across the organization, requests for changes to the system pop up. At best, these are requests that improve the system, but often they are requests to change the system so that it meets the current ways of working.

System-change management is therefore an important program process that safeguards and controls the core design of the system. This is also where SAP Solution Manager (see Chapter 5) adds value.

However, there is another reason users perceive the delivered solutions as not being user friendly, and that has to do with our own perception of a user. Here are some false assumptions that are emphasized by the illustration in Figure 4.5:

▶ They have the same technical interests and skills as any SAP project team member.

- They have lived through the same history we did, so they understand why a process or a transaction is designed and configured the way it is.
- They have been fully exposed and dedicated to the software as long as we have.

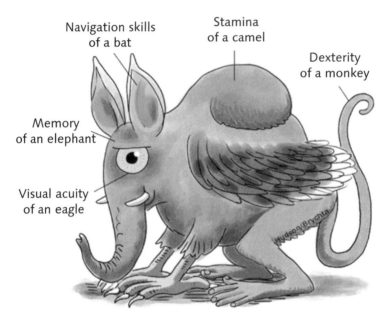

"The Perfect User"

Figure 4.5 The Perfect User (Taken from www.syntagm.co.uk)

Instead of complaining or blaming the users when our assumptions are proven wrong, we should instead look at the four phases of learning that we discussed in the previous chapter. We need to realize that different groups go through the learning cycle at different rates.

Remember that the majority of the user community tends to hit the wall of their conscience incompetence during the training sessions shortly before go-live. In organizational change, our job is to put every effort into bringing them over to a phase of conscious competence. That is the moment at which users will stop reporting inconveniences due to their lack of skills and start reporting on real shortcomings of the system. However, at that moment all shortcomings are still equally important to them.

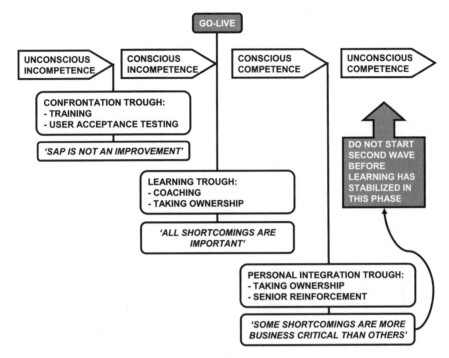

Figure 4.6 Learning Phases During SAP Implementations

As illustrated in Figure 4.6, we recommend waiting until the phase of unconscious competence before you start to set priorities for addressing all of the shortcomings. As the figure illustrates, the difference between conscious and unconscious competence for a user is precisely the fact that they can differentiate their own shortcomings from shortcomings of the system.

As a result, it is better to review your expectations of users and to accept that all of the users expectations will not be met at moment of go-live. That is why you should wait until refreezing has taken place by means of unconscious competence before launching the second-wave project to fine-tune and improve the current build.

4.4   Principles for Success

If you want to make your SAP implementation a success, some basic principles must apply. This section summarizes the basic principles you need to respect.

4.4.1 Commit to a Set of Common Rules

Most successful programs have sets of rules that are carved in stone. All sponsors should explicitly agree that these rules are treated as sacrosanct. Here are some examples of these holy rules:

▶ No other major initiatives run in parallel (e. g., installing a new organization structure independent of the program).

▶ Clear sponsorship of executive management (e. g., through the appointment of program directorship and steering committee membership).

▶ Business engagement (e. g., through the appointment of stream leaders and process owners and through the use of a business case).

▶ Declare holy standards (e. g., one global chart of accounts, global reporting process).

▶ Validation committees ensure business involvement and signoff (e. g., the steering committee and various validation workshops with business representatives).

▶ Safeguard continuity during the transition (e. g., by monitoring signoff criteria and benefits realization).

▶ Use a disciplined and structured approach (e. g., through the use a program approach and a choosing for and committing to a program management methodology).

▶ Know the business (e. g., through the use of business process mapping in swim lanes).

These are examples of fundamental agreements that can never be violated.

4.4.2 Autonomy and Accountability

Most of the time, your SAP program will change your organization; in fact, it will turn it upside down. Even in the case of an upgrade project, you will encounter situations where your stakes are opposed to those of the functional organization. Therefore, we recommend that the team be able to act and make decisions independently. This has to happen in a "protected environment" under the following conditions:

▶ Validation committees should be organized to ensure there are no surprises. Even if the program team takes a certain decision, the business owners must be informed properly, and they must confirm that they have been.

- Involving Internal Audit makes sure that there are as follows:

  - A minimal set of internal controls.

  - Proper delegation of duties.

  - Compliance with regulatory imperatives such as Sarbanes-Oxley for public companies, BASEL II in Europe, and FDA Part 11 for biotechnology and pharmaceutical organizations.

  - An independent view on the business case of the SAP implementation.

  - Support with regard to risk-management.

Autonomous also means that individuals in your project team are formally assigned, dedicated, and co-located in the project team. When we look at the strengths of autonomous teams, we see the following two major advantages:

- The fundamental strength of an autonomous team is focus. Everything the team members and the team leader are doing is concentrated on successful results.

- The second strength is the optimal cross-functional integration. Autonomous teams can attract and select the team participants more freely than can other program structures.

However, full autonomy calls for full accountability. Autonomy only works when your team will be held accountable for the final results of the program.

4.4.3 Requisite Variety

Requisite variety is the academic term used to indicate that the composition of your team should reflect the same complexity as the environment in which it must operate. Just as a chameleon is able to pick up the hues of its environment and adapt its colors to the surroundings, different project teams need to know the language of the organization they work for.

We borrow this idea from systems thinking (Ashby, 1956). For example, if your project team is assigned to design and implement an SAP landscape for the maintenance of a chemical plant, maintenance engineers of the plant should be dedicated to the project. The point is to make sure that every party that affects or that is affected by your project is represented in the program team.

4.4.4 Emotional Intelligence

By their very nature, SAP program teams are collections of extremely competent people. However, competence is not sufficient: We need experts with the ability to interact. As noted in the previous chapter, participation and interaction with the organization at every stage of the program lifecycle is essential for the success of SAP programs. To do so, every team member needs to be equipped with at least the minimal interaction skills needed. In fact, the interaction with the organization is best identified as a must-have competence. We have seen more than once that the involvement of one or more generalists with outstanding emotional intelligence to act as translators is not a luxury.

4.4.5 Automated Project Office

The complexity of leading an SAP team will soon lead you to scream for administrative support. All the simple tasks ranging from time registration to the logistics of running a proper meeting are hygiene factors for any large project. They do not influence the success positively, but when they fail they will soon become burdens and time consumers. We have had our best experiences with junior programmers who are lazy by nature, so that they want to automate just about everything that has to do with project administration to the benefit of every team member.

4.4.6 Teamwork

Generally speaking, we can say that program team members essentially have two basic responsibilities: their own functional responsibilities and the team responsibility.

Functional Responsibilities

Functional responsibilities are accepted by the individual core team member as a representative of his or her function (Clark & Wheelwright, 1992), as examined here:

▸ Ensuring the functional expertise of the program.

▸ Representing the functional perspective of the program.

▸ Ensuring that sub-objectives that depend on their function are met.

▸ Ensuring that functional issues impacting the team are raised proactively within the team.

Team Responsibilities

Core team members also wear team hats. The core team is accountable for the success of the program, and it can blame no one but itself if it fails to manage the program, execute its projects and its tasks, and deliver the performance agreed upon at the outset. The team has the following accountabilities (Clark & Wheelwright, 1992):

▶ Sharing responsibility for team results.

▶ Reconstituting task and content.

▶ Establishing reporting and other organizational relationships.

▶ Participating in monitoring and improving team performance.

▶ Sharing responsibility for ensuring effective team processes.

▶ Examining issues from an executive point of view (answering the question: "Is this the appropriate business response for the company?").

▶ Understanding, recognizing, and responsibly challenging the boundaries of the program and team process.

4.4.7   Proper Risk-Handling

You should be aware of the risks that might impact the success of the program at all times.

When examining risks, you need to assess what the impact of the risk would be on the program and the organization, and the probability of occurrence. The matrix in Figure 4.7 illustrates the distribution of these risks to evaluate how critical the situation is. Having one single risk in the upper right hand corner may be sufficient to jeopardize the entire program.

Figure 4.7 Risk Assessment and Risk Handling

Risks are not static. They evolve during the lifetime of the program. This means that you need a valid counterweight in the form of a credible risk mitigation plan. As obvious as it may seem, the distributed risk portfolio is not only there for information purposes, but as a guide in proper decision-making. This brings us to the next topic: the pitfalls you should be aware of when making decisions.

4.5 Pitfalls to Avoid

When you run an SAP implementation program, you must avoid pitfalls that might endanger the success of the program. To stimulate your awareness, we shall discuss some mistakes that we have experienced and that you are likely to make.

4.5.1 Project Cocooning

The fact that a program has its own objective(s), budget, organization, resources, and management is not a reason it should exist as a island within the company, having no contact with the rest of the organization. A remarkable phenomenon is that many teams isolate themselves in their own cocoons, having little contact as possible with what is—for them—outer space. This phenomenon is not surprising if you consider the following:

▸ The declaration and labeling of the program automatically creates the separate identity for the implementation team as opposed to the rest of the organization. Even though the organization needs to take ownership of the program and adopt its identity, this only happens long after go-live (assuming you are succesful).

▸ Competent implementation teams like being competent. They are not interested in moments of truth based on interactions because every sign of skepticism puts most of them at the edge of their comfort zones.

▸ Resistance is mostly countered with resistance. The implementation team will very soon state that it is not a charity initiative or a complaints desk. Project cocooning is a natural reaction in an atmosphere where you ask for feedback and all you get is complaints that have nothing to do with the subject. Due to a lack of interaction creativity or qualitative meeting techniques, a lot of teams close out and start designing by gut feeling. It should be obvious that this behavior only pushes the problem on to a phase where it will be even more painful.

4.5.2 One Size Fits All

SAP integrates processes, and this requires standardization. Standardization is required to strive towards more unity, but also to detect areas of performance improvements.

As an example, an invoice generated in the U.S. is not technically different from an invoice generated in Sudan. Nonetheless, certain processes and procedures must be customized to the local needs, depending on factors such as geographical location, type of business, historical way of working, payment behavior, cultural trade and business behavior, and legal requirements.

You should never ignore these kinds of local specific characteristics, because that will lead to unsuccessful SAP implementations. But they should at all times be limited to the strict minimum. Examples include:

▶ Imposing specific payment terms to be applied globally when these to not conform to market habits.

▶ Not allowing creation of accounts that are required for legal reporting

▶ Not allowing a pro forma invoice to accompany the goods, which is illegal in certain cases.

▶ Deployment standardization that is too strict and can damage performance.

Most of the time, SAP implementations are initiated in the company's global headquarters. We could call it global headquarter cocooning. To make things worse, if a plant, a distribution center, or a sales office is located in the physical neighborhood of the global headquarters, it automatically becomes the benchmark of all plants, distribution centers, or sales offices around the world.

4.5.3 Postponing Responsibility to the Second Wave

Closely related to the project cocooning pitfall is the NIHS attitude that is abundant in engineering environments. NIHS stands for *Not Invented Here Syndrome* and characterizes implementation teams who take nothing for granted. As stated earlier, competent people like being competent, and as a result their resistance strategies tend to be more sophisticated.

Their fear for committing to the unknown is hidden behind their incredible hunger for details. On the surface, they look like hard-working people making a lot of progress. However, when it comes to taking decisions and setting directions, these implementation teams start to over-intellectualize the circumstances to postpone any hard decision for the future. In the end, the program does not bring the fundamental business change it is supposed to. The end result is new software that is over-engineered to support the existing functional castles. Game over.

Our advice is to confront the competent risk avoiders with their behavior. At times like this, a bunch of pushy consultants can do no harm. It will be a learning experience for both sides.

4.5.4 Outsourcing the Driver's Seat

There is no greater insult for frontline workers than to receive the vision, the benefits, and the inspiration for the implementation from an outsider. By now you are aware that the SAP implementation is not a technical software installation effort but a fundamental business initiative that transforms your organization. The best way to kill it is to have it communicated and reinforced by consultants.

Many organizations are learning to use consultants, while not becoming dependent on them. This approach requires adapting, not adopting, the consultants' models. SAP implementations engage the heart, the mind, and the hands of the people, and this is the responsibility of the business leaders. After all, a program is just a midwife to deliver the benefits to the organization. After go-live, it depends on the organization for nurturing.

4.5.5 Ignorance of Organizational Maturity

The capability maturity model presented in Chapter 1 is a good indicator of organizational readiness for certain initiatives. We highly recommend matching the program ambitions to the maturity of the organization.

It should not surprise us that quality-measurement improvement processes or performance management processes turn out to be useless when the organization has not yet figured out a way to stabilize and put discipline into its processes. Each level of practices builds on the previous one, so it makes no sense to try to run before you can walk.

4.5.6 The Illusion of Full Control

Don't believe you can predict everything up front. The more precisely you plan, the more a coincidence will affect you. The success of your SAP implementation depends on the commitment, flexibility, and experience of your program sponsor, program owner, and program manager.

A program must provide infrastructure to manage the unpredictability of the change you are implementing. This translates into the need for creating buffers in time and resources whenever corrective measures must be taken. This also means that your project portfolio will change over the duration of the SAP implementation. Whenever necessary, you must initiate a new project to bring things back on track.

4.6   Conclusion

Without proper program and project management, it is impossible to make the change related to an SAP implementation happen. You will need a program approach to connect the software implementation to the realization of benefits. Then, you must be conscious about how each phase in the program lifecycle relates to the change cycle of the organization. And even then, success is not guaranteed. Our experience teaches us that to guarantee success, there are also some principles to follow and some pitfalls to avoid. It will take a large dose of perseverance, discipline, and empathy to succeed.

In Chapter 5, we will investigate how SAP technology supports the organizational changes as we explore the knowledge management features of SAP Solution Manager.

SAP technology is a facilitator of the change that your organization wants to realize. Without current technologies, a number of the benefits that accompany an SAP implementation wouldn't be so easy to achieve. In this chapter, we will briefly highlight SAP technologies that can support your change efforts.

5   SAP Technology as a Co-Pilot

5.1   SAP Solution Manager Manages Knowledge

Very soon after the start of an implementation program, knowledge and skills get built up which later on need to be absorbed by the organization. SAP Solution Manager can help you to administer and structure your change efforts.

5.1.1   From Information to Best Practice

When you want to manage the knowledge produced during the implementation and make sure it adds value to the organization, that knowledge needs to be structured properly and owned by the organization. According to Seely Brown (2000), knowledge has two dimensions, the explicit and the tacit. Figure 5.1 illustrates how the explicit dimension deals with facts and instructions (respectively the Know-What and the Know-How), whereas the tacit dimension is manifested in work practices and interaction (the Know-Why).

Knowledge comes alive in the process of doing things and in our participation with each other. In other words, explicit knowledge gets translated into tacit knowledge by our working together. Participation and collaboration between the implementation team and the rest of the organization is crucial in getting the knowledge anchored into practice.

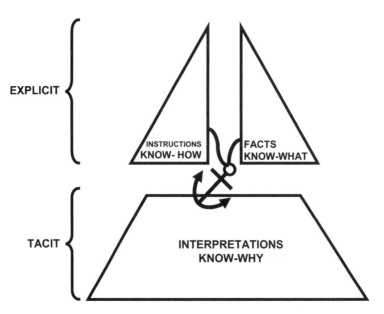

Figure 5.1 Three Types of Knowledge (adapted from Seely Brown, 2000)

5.1.2 Solution Manager Components

SAP Solution Manager supports you throughout the entire lifecycle of your solution, from the design to deployment. It provides central access to tools, methods and preconfigured content, which you can use during the evaluation, implementation, and productive operation of your systems.

The following description is a brief summary of the features of SAP Solution Manager. For a full description of its functionalities, we refer to the book *SAP Solution Manager* by Marc-Oliver Schaefer and Matthias Melich (2006, SAP PRESS).

Implementation of SAP solutions

When implementing SAP in your organization, SAP Solution Manager offers the following features that facilitate that process across the implementation lifecycle:

▶ SAP implementation methods and project management (ITIL).

▶ Customizing synchronization between the different environments (Transport Management, supported by workflow for approval).

▶ E-learning management.

▶ Test management.

The implementation lifecycle starts at the requirements-analysis stage. From a system-implementation perspective, this is fine. However, as noted in Chapter 4, program initiation and program setup are crucial elements from a change-management point of view. You may want to anchor the deliverables of these earlier phases in Solution Manager as well.

Solution Monitoring

The performance of the system is very important to how well it is accepted. As noted in Chapter 4, slow system performance may distort the perception of a user about the whole implementation effort. In such cases, from a user's point of view, the performance of the system equals the quality of the implementation. The better the system is monitored, the better the performance can be guaranteed. Some features of SAP Solution Manager in this area are:

▶ System monitoring.

▶ Business process monitoring.

▶ Central system administration.

▶ EarlyWatch Alert/SL reporting.

▶ Solution reporting.

Service Desk

Whenever issues are reported by users or by the implementation team members, support may be required by experts. SAP Solution Manager allows the organization of service desks and facilitates communication between user and service desk, whether it is internal or external (SAP or third party). The following components facilitate this process:

▶ Best practices for messaging.

▶ Integration of SAP or third-party help desks.

▶ Solution Manager Diagnostics.

▶ Service level agreement follow-up.

Delivery of SAP Services

During implementation of SAP—but also while supporting the live solution—communication with SAP is required for several reasons. Some bugs might need to be fixed, specific questions might need to be answered, or specific support to be delivered. SAP Solution Manager enables the following:

- Onsite/remote delivery of SAP services.
- SAP Safeguarding.

Change Request Management

Change request management is very important in managing the change of an SAP implementation. SAP Solution Manager offers features for tracking any (system) change request, approval path, and implementation follow-up.

As noted at the end of Chapter 1, you should bear in mind that change request management deals with controlling the software changes on development, quality, and productive systems. As such, it stands completely apart from the organizational change that is the subject of this book.

Nevertheless, to see the relevance of change requests that are raised, it is good to refer to the perspective offered in Chapter 4 about the learning phases. More precisely, as illustrated in Chapter 4, we recommend waiting until the phase of unconscious competence before you start to set priorities against all change requests. The difference between conscious and unconscious competence for a user is precisely the newfound ability to differentiate one's own shortcomings from shortcomings of the system, which can be solved by initiating change requests.

For this reason, it is better to review your expectations toward users and to accept that all of the users' expectations will not be met at go-live. That is why you should wait until refreezing has taken place by means of unconscious competence before launching the second-wave project of fine-tuning and improving the current build.

Upgrade of SAP Solutions

SAP Solution Manager facilitates system version management and supports your organization in the whole process of upgrading and maintaining your environment. In this context, SAP Solution Manager offers the following:

- SAP methods and tools that support you in the step-by-step realization of the upgrade or maintenance.
- E-learning management (Chapter 9 covers the use SAP Tutor).
- Test management.

5.1.3   Anchor Solution Manager into Practice

In the context of this book, we are predominantly interested in the features of SAP Solution Manager that support implementation. It is tempting to think that if the processes, procedures, and plans are mapped, using the solution would involve little more than following the map you are given and doing whatever it tells you to do. Unfortunately, that is mostly not the case in SAP implementations for the two following reasons:

► There is a large gap between what a task looks like in a process manual and what it looks like in reality.

► There is a gap between what people think they do and what they really do (Seely Brown & Diguid, 2000).

Clear Principles

The added value of SAP Solution Manager during the implementation phase is that it connects the team's documentation to practice. Each team member contributes to the pool of information, drawing from his or her own particular role, which the others recognize and rely on. In practice, this means that implementation teams are producing the bulk of programming documents, configuration documents, business processes descriptions, change requests, testing reports, etc.

However, all of these documents need to be retrievable, and clarity does not come without effort, so this requires you to specify basic principles for the storage of this knowledge before you start to use SAP Solution Manager. Examples include:

► Have a clear view of how you will structure SAP Solution Manager.

► Be clear on the approvals one must get in order to publish document.s

► Be clear on the nomenclature and level of detail of information.

Chunking

One of the main purposes of storing knowledge is to easily find and reuse it. Therefore, it is important to store knowledge in amounts that can easily be reused and recycled during other program phases and for other purposes. Examples of reusing and recycling are as follows:

▶ Process blueprints as inputs for test scenarios.

▶ Test scenarios as inputs for training exercises.

▶ Authorization profiles as inputs for communication planning and training design.

It is essential to start thinking about breaking knowledge down into information objects, the smallest useful chunks of information, which frees it to be used again. Think of this as creating and assembling Lego blocks. Whether you are assembling a bridge or a house or a spaceship, you use the same Lego pieces. Similarly, other project streams can use—and reuse—the same content or information objects.

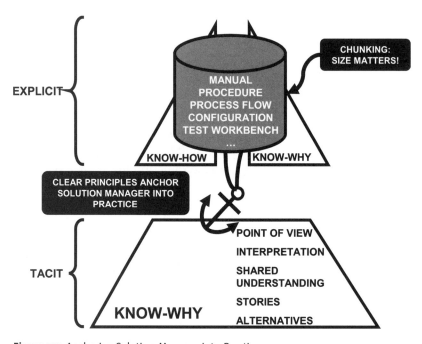

Figure 5.2 Anchoring Solution Manager into Practice

As Figure 5.2 illustrates, this knowledge chunking—if applied properly— creates interchangeable parts. That way, information is rendered reusable, interchangeable, durable, accessible, and affordable in terms of time spent during the most critical parts of your implementation.

5.2   SAP Technology Supports Integration

The newest SAP technologies support the realization of the benefits that your organization wants to achieve by implementing SAP. The most important benefit from this perspective is the integration of information into a single database.

Having a single database across a global organization was wishful thinking a number of years ago. That is why you will still find organizations that have implemented SAP but are using different SAP environments. In the latter case, integration becomes more difficult because of technical constraints. Also the total cost of ownership (TCO) will be higher for decentralized SAP setups.

Even more important is the integration of information flows underlying the integrated processes. SAP is a huge system that needs high-performance hardware environments to achieve acceptable response times. Earlier in this chapter, we noted that system performance of business applications such as SAP is very important in nurturing user acceptance because it influences the perception of the complete implementation effort. If users have to stare at a screen too long after they push a button before something happens, they get very irritated. In turn, this influences their perception of whether the implementation was successful.

Even though your organization may have decided for strategic reasons that SAP is your standard, there will always be other legacy systems in use. In that case, SAP Exchange Infrastructure (SAP XI) enables integration between SAP and other SAP or non-SAP environments. The main features of SAP XI that enhance integration and transparency of information flows are, as follows:

▶ It connects SAP and non-SAP applications.

▶ It connects applications to applications (A2A) and businesses to businesses (B2B).

▶ It enables asynchronous and synchronous communication.

▶ It delivers pre-defined integration knowledge based on standards.

▶ It provides pre-delivered integration contents for connecting SAP to SAP solutions.

▶ It allows design, execution and monitoring of automated processes across applications and systems.

▶ It offers industry-standard contents.

SAP XI is an integral part of SAP NetWeaver. So is SAP Solution Manager. SAP NetWeaver also offers functionality that helps achieve the underlying benefits of an SAP implementation. The mission of SAP NetWeaver is to provide an answer for the following process integration challenges:

▶ **Integration of System Landscapes**
Separate business units with independent IT systems in heterogeneous landscapes.

▶ **End-user Integration**
Role-based access to actions and interaction (collaborative processes).

▶ **Enterprise Application Integration**
Interacting business applications within and across the enterprise boundaries.

▶ **B2B Integration**
Interacting organisations, business partners, customers, vendors, and suppliers across the value chain.

SAP NetWeaver offers business process management functionality that is integrated with the ARIS Process Platform. Business process management within SAP NetWeaver offers solutions to integrate the following:

▶ People (SAP Enterprise Portal):

  ▶ Multi-channel access.

  ▶ Portal.

  ▶ Collaboration.

▶ Information (SAP Business Intelligence):

  ▶ Knowledge management.

  ▶ Business intelligence.

  ▶ Master data management.

▶ Process (SAP XI):

  ▶ Integration Broker. (Offers standards that make it easier to set up and maintain collaborative business scenarios. These include integration scenarios, industry processes, integration process patterns, message interfaces, mapping programs, and workflow templates.)

  ▶ Business process management.

▶ Application

5.3   Conclusion: Integration on Two Levels

In summarizing this chapter, we want you to be aware that SAP supports integration on two different levels:

- ▶ SAP Solution Manger integrates the skills and knowledge of your program into practice during the implementation and facilitates the maintenance and support of the SAP environment within the system and within the organization.
- ▶ SAP XI facilitates the integration of data, information flows and business processes.

The shift from functional thinking to integrated process thinking occurs from more than an organizational-change perspective. SAP will also facilitate the integration on the level of its technology. Chapter 6 will discuss how to monitor parameters of change.

You must move an entire community from the paradigm of functional thinking to the paradigm of integrated process thinking. Marketers face a similar kind of change challenge when they want to introduce new products into a market. They manage their efforts based on soft elements like the customer relationship as well as the hard stuff. In this chapter, we underscore that need to build radars so you can monitor the parameters of change properly.

6 Monitor Parameters of Change: A Radar View

6.1 Implementation Marketing

In our opinion, marketers know more about how to cope with a changing environment than any other people inside an organization. In fact, the survival of most organizations depends on their marketers' ability to respond to the "more-better-faster-now" changes in customer environment. Changing is what marketers are good at, and that is why their insights are valuable when making change happen inside a company.

6.1.1 Population Analysis

For starters, in a 1962 book called *Diffusion of Innovations*, Everett Rogers stated that adopters of any new innovation or idea could be categorized on a classic bell-shaped curve, as described in Table 6.1.

Group	Characteristics
Innovators (2.5 %)	Venturesome, educated, multiple information sources, greater propensity to take risk
Early Adopters (13.5 %)	Social leaders, popular, educated
Early Majority (34 %)	Deliberate, many informal social contacts

Table 6.1 Segments of a Consumer Population (Rogers, 1962)

Group	Characteristics
Late Majority (34 %)	Skeptical, traditional, lower socio-economic status
Laggards (16 %)	Neighbors and friends are main information sources, fear of debt

Table 6.1 Segments of a Consumer Population (Rogers, 1962) (cont.)

Building further on Rogers' observations, Geoffrey Moore's (1991) key insight is that the groups adopt innovations for different reasons. According to Moore, early adopters are technology enthusiasts looking for a radical shift, while the early majority wants a productivity improvement. Both groups are divided by a chasm.

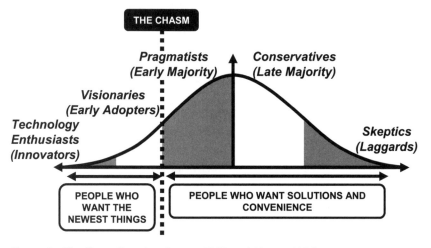

Figure 6.1 The Chasm (based on Rogers, 1962; and Moore, 1999)

Moore's observations come close to what you can expect when introducing a shift from the paradigm of functional thinking to one of process thinking. These are examined below:

▸ **Technology Enthusiasts (Innovators)** are explorers.

▸ **Visionaries (Early Adopters)** are more geared towards exploitation. They are not especially bothered by the fact that the product doesn't work. They are willing to make it work.

▸ **Pragmatists (Early Majority)** want a product that works. They want a 100 % solution to their business problem. If they get the 80 % that delighted the visionary, they feel cheated, and they tell their pragmatist friends.

▶ **Conservatives (Late Majority)** buy products because they really have no choice. They are not reassured by having books about the product, because the existence of books implies the product isn't simple enough to use. Conservatives will not tolerate complexity.

▶ **Skeptics (Laggards)** are not going to buy, though they may talk other people out of buying.

The problem in crossing the chasm is that the visionaries aren't good references for the pragmatists. They provide tales of heroics. Pragmatists want references from other pragmatists. This brings us to the basic insight that it is going to take strong marketing and employee relationship management (i. e., customer relationship management from the implementation team towards the organization) to reach the majority.

6.1.2 Lessons from Customer Relationship Management

Customer relationship management (CRM) is the art of building learning relationships with your target public. In Chapter 3, we described the importance of building a learning relationship between the implementation team and the organization. CRM tells us how to do that if we are willing to replace the "c" of customer with the "e" of employee.

Seth Godin, one of the pioneers of CRM, introduced the concept of Permission Marketing in 1999. Table 6.2 mentions the six levels of permission that can depict the relationship with a customer, according to Godin.

Level	Description
Intravenous Treatment	The doctor treating you in the emergency room doesn't have to sell you very hard on administering a drug.
Green Stamps	Executives suffer through long layovers to gain frequent-flyer miles. Here, the company rewards customers in currency they care about.
Personal Relationships	The corner dry cleaner enjoys implicit permission to act in your best interest. A favorite retailer can "upscale" you (recommend something more expensive) without offending you.
Branding	Given a choice between the known and the unknown, most people choose the known.
Situational Selling	If you're in a store and you're about to make a purchase, you often welcome unsolicited marketing advice.

Table 6.2 The Six Levels of Permission (Godin, 1999).

Level	Description
Spam	Where most marketers live most of the time: calling a stranger at home, during dinner, without permission. You wouldn't do it in your personal life. Why do it to potential customers?

Table 6.2 The Six Levels of Permission (Godin, 1999). (cont.)

6.1.3 Pushing and Pulling

The six levels of permission can help us to get more clarity about our position in relationship with the organization. It becomes even more interesting when we start weaving in the insights of Malcolm Gladwell (2000), who investigated what determines the moment of critical mass, the threshold, or even the boiling point of a marketing effort. He calls it the *Tipping Point*.

From an SAP Implementation point of view, the combination of Gladwell's and Godin's observations are illustrated in Figure 6.2.

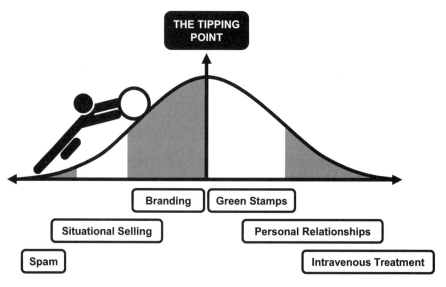

Figure 6.2 The Tipping Point (Gladwell, 2000 and Godin, 1999)

Starting an SAP Implementation program may at times resemble pushing a boulder up a hill. You seem to be making an 80 % selling effort for barely a 20 % response. Your learning relationship with the organization hinges on the lower levels of permission, as you are in the beginning of a relationship.

You soon find out that as the permission level evolves, you will get buy-in from pragmatists and conservatives. Before you know it, the boulder starts rolling as a result of the people going through the change cycle. Instead of you pushing a boulder alone, the organization is now pulling at your sleeves to move it forward. At that moment, you need a different set of relationship skills to pace the implementation. That is also when you will realize that a new type of team participation is required: the phasing in of the UN Peace-keeping Troops.

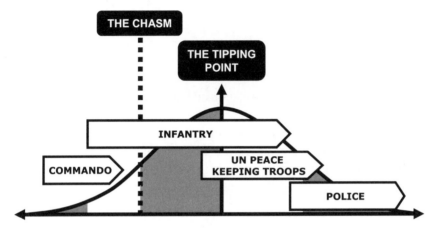

Figure 6.3 Different Change Agents at Different Stages (adapted from Cringely, 1993; Moore, 1999; and Gladwell, 2000)

Looking back at Cringely's team styles that we used in Chapter 2, the commandos are the change agents that make success possible, and the infantry make success happen by pushing the boulder past the **Chasm** to the **Tipping Point**. Figure 6.3 illustrates that a new team operating style is necessary as the organization lifts the project out of its cocoon.

6.2   Building a Soft-Stuff Radar

In each of the chapters of this book where we describe the key considerations for each phase of the program lifecycle, we will be using a radar view to indicate which of the soft-stuff parameters matter the most. Now let's get an idea of the components of the soft-stuff radar.

6.2.1   Learning Relationship Radar

The first soft-stuff radar that you need is the one describing the learning relationship between the implementation team and the organization. The learning-relationship radar has two parts: what you will do and what you will experience. What you do clearly needs to be in line with what you will experience.

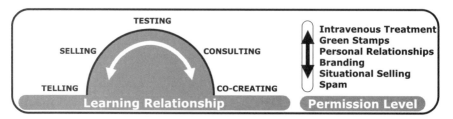

Figure 6.4 The Learning-Relationship Radar (based on Senge et al., 1994, and Godin, 1999)

On the action part of the learning-relationship radar in Figure 6.4, we recommend the level of participation you should allow in the specific phase you are in: Telling, Selling, Testing, Consulting, or Co-creating. The experience section of this radar refers to one of the six levels of permission, discussed earlier in this chapter.

6.2.2 Change-Agent Radar

The second soft-stuff radar focuses on you and your team as a change agent. As with the previous radar, the change-agent radar has an action part and an experience part.

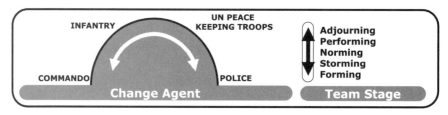

Figure 6.5 The Change Agent Radar (Cringely, 1993 and Tuckman, 1965)

As you can see in Figure 6.5, we recommend specific team staffing and styles according to the phase of the implementation. However, while you are stirring up the organization, you will notice significant changes going on in the dynamics of your own change-agent team. To keep track of that dynamic, we included in the radar the team development stages as described by Bruce Tuckman (1965). Table 6.3 describes these team-development stages.

Team Stage	Description
Forming	▶ Uncertainty ▶ Feelings not dealt with ▶ Poor listening ▶ Weaknesses covered up ▶ Unclear objectives ▶ Low involvement in planning ▶ Boss makes most decisions
Storming	▶ Experimentation ▶ Risky issues debated ▶ Wider options considered ▶ Personal feelings raised ▶ Intra-group conflicts ▶ More listening
Norming	▶ Methodical working ▶ Agreed procedures ▶ Established ground rules ▶ Close relationships start to develop
Performing	▶ High flexibility/ability to lead process ▶ Maximum use of energy and ability ▶ Needs of all met ▶ Development is a priority ▶ High commitment ▶ Balanced team roles ▶ Shared leadership

Table 6.3 Team Development Stages (based on Tuckman, 1965)

6.2.3 Change-Target Radar

Finally, we definitely want to track the target groups of our organizational change. The radars that we offer are only partially action radars. This means that the learning stages can be stimulated at certain times during the program lifecycle, but we have no precise control over how long they will take.

The second part of the change-target radar in Figure 6.6 refers to the segment of the target group you are most likely to get in touch with in each stage. We call it target segment. Marketers would be talking about market penetration level.

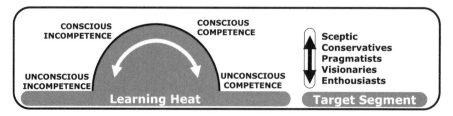

Figure 6.6 The Change-Target Radar (based on Moore, 1999)

6.3   Build a Hard-Stuff Radar

As indicated in Chapter 4, we recommend a program approach combining multiple project streams to realize the benefits of integrated processes. It almost goes without saying that a soft-stuff radar will not give you all the necessary indications you need to navigate each project stream.

Throughout the program lifecycle, the organizational change streams (Learning, Communication, Performance, and Organization) need to be monitored from the hard side as well. This means monitoring the basics: time, headcount, and money.

Just as we have with the soft-stuff radar, in each of the chapters where we describe the key considerations for each phase of the program lifecycle, we will indicate which of the hard-stuff parameters matter the most. Now we can get an understanding of elements of the hard-stuff radar.

6.3.1   Validation Radar

The validation radar in Figure 6.7 focuses on the relationship between the progress in time and the validation by the organization. The meter on the right-hand side indicates whether you are ahead or behind with the production of deliverables in comparison with the forecast delivery date.

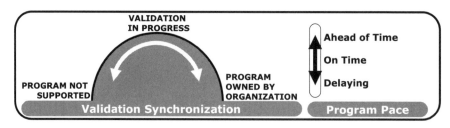

Figure 6.7 The Validation Radar

In addition, you need to follow up on how many of the deliverables have been validated by the organization. Validation of the deliverables is critical, as it influences user acceptance, perception, and eventually trust. The moral of this radar: Making progress within preset deadlines is important, but without acceptance by the organization it is of no use.

6.3.2 Supply and Demand Radar

The next hard-stuff dimension is headcount. As illustrated in Figure 6.8, there is a relationship between the workload of the implementation and the dedication of organization resources for the program.

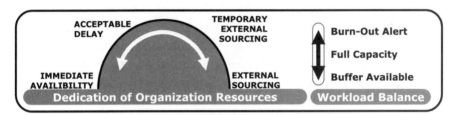

Figure 6.8 The Supply-and-Demand Radar

An SAP implementation is not accomplished over a few months' time. The resource allocation is continuously fluctuating over the course of several years depending on the workload required in each phase of the program life-cycle. That is why you need to monitor the supply and demand of resources on the program. The right-hand side of the supply-and-demand radar indicates whether your workload is balanced. This meter will fluctuate, but you should not allow it to stay too long on the highest or on the lowest level.

The left-hand side of the supply-and-demand radar monitors the capacity of the organization to dedicate resources to the program. In the end, the organization needs to take ownership, and the best way to make that happen is by gradually involving people at the operational level. In some stages, the pressure to do so will be higher than in other stages. This meter also monitors organizational life with financial closing periods, holiday periods, seasonal activities, and so on.

6.3.3 Budget Radar

Realistic budgeting is an essential preliminary step you should take care of way in advance. Budgeting for the full program—not only the software implementation—will save you a lot of negative press during the implementation. Once the program is up and running, budget follow-up should be part of your focus. Figure 6.9 illustrates two meters for monitoring budget follow-up.

Figure 6.9 The Budget Radar

The right-hand side of the budget radar is a traditional view: It shows how much of the budget is used in function of the progress and the phase of the program. But next to that, you also need to look at how much buffer you still have. The meter on the left-hand side displays your flexibility in terms of budget reallocation. Every project stream will have budget reallocation requests as you go. This is where you will start to balance savings potential and quality.

6.4 Going Forward From Here: How to Use Chapters 7–14

The six radars presented in this chapter will be used throughout Chapters 7 to 14, in Part II of this book, to indicate what the program looks like in a certain phase and to warn you about potential danger zones. Like physical radar systems, they are early warning systems of approaching dangers.

In the context of what these radars tell us, the remaining chapters are dedicated to a chronological overview of the four project streams of organizational change: Learning, Communication, Organization, and Performance. The discussion of each phase ends with a list of deliverables and moments of truth (i.e., opportunities for increasing your impact).

6.5   A User-Centric Implementation

As discussed in Chapter 1, integrated process thinking brings along a shift in power over information. Hamburger flippers need to become food-processing managers, and cashiers need to become customer-service experts. Software implementations in the era of the functional castles reinforced the fragmented thinking by putting the technology in the middle. SAP implementations in those cases will never deliver the promise of integrated processes.

This brings us to the only mathematical truth about SAP implementations. It is summarized in following equation: $OO + NT = EOO$. In this equation:

- *OO* stands for the Old Organization
- *NT* stands for New Technology
- *EOO* stands for Expensive Old Organization

As Figure 6.10 illustrates, a technology-centric implementation designs processes based on the features of the system and the availability of the data. The organization—and finally the user—will need to adapt to that structure. A question you might ask yourself in this case is: How well does that serve your customers?

The right-hand part of Figure 6.10 indicates the shift towards a user centric organization. This is adapted from what marketers call a customer-centric organization that they compare to a product-centric organization (Peppers & Rogers, 2004). Integrated processes link the customers of an organization directly to its profits.

Increasingly, these customers are being served by information-empowered front-line workers. Therefore, the new implementation philosophy should take the user—who is the most fragile interface with the customer—as a starting point. Processes in that case are designed according to how users are organized to best serve the customers. As a last step, the information that is required to optimize the processes is captured in the systems that are built and configured to support organization's performance.

There is no need to mention that this user-centric philosophy will heavily influence our traditional way of approaching implementations; hence the importance of building a learning relationship between the implementation team and the organization.

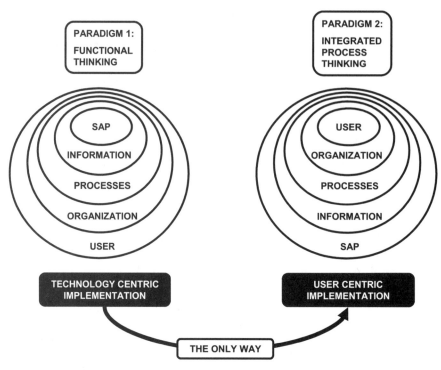

Figure 6.10 Shift Toward a User-Centric Implementation

6.6 Conclusion

It is essential that you monitor a number of parameters that directly or indirectly affect success in changing the organization while running your SAP implementation program. Each of these parameters has to be interpreted in light of the phase of the program lifecycle where you are engaged.

That is why you need to build a radar that shows you the status of these parameters, covering both the soft and hard side of change. In this chapter, we have provided you with the radars that we believe are most critical in making change happen. Throughout the next chapters, we will indicate how you need to interpret the radars in each phase. As a starting point, Chapter 7 goes into the key considerations of the program initiation phase.

PART II
Unfreezing

The program initiation phase is probably the most underestimated and, simultaneously, the most important phase in the lifecycle of an implementation. People tend to be very impatient once the decision has been taken to implement SAP. However, without proper preparation the risk for failure is significant.

7 Program Initiation

7.1 Phase-Specific Characteristics and Needs

In the subsections that follow, we explain how you should use and read the soft-stuff and hard-stuff radars, taking into account the specific characteristics and needs of the program initiation phase.

7.1.1 Soft-Stuff Radar

Figure 7.1 illustrates the status of the Soft Stuff Radar at the moment of program initiation. Let's get a better understanding of the following phases:

▶ **Learning Relationship Radar**
In this phase, you will have to be direct, provocative, and receptive at the same time; i.e., constantly testing and adjusting.

Nobody at this time is aware of the change, let alone interested in your ideas about it. As a result, the permission level meter indicates that your communication is at the level of "spam." You have no relationship with the receivers of your messages, and you are barely making sense to them because your messages do not match their frame of reference.

▶ **Agent Radar**
Program initiation is the phase where you parachute behind the "enemy lines," making provocative proposals. Initially, you will act as commandos, breaking the foundations of current context and beliefs. However, you are still alone at this point in time. This is why the team- stage meter displays as "inactive."

▶ **Target Radar**

There is no "learning heat" at the level of the organization. The organization is "sleeping in unconsciousness," and you are about to make the first wake-up calls. The first ones to wake up and follow your initiatives are the enthusiasts. In this very early stage, the visionaries are not yet at work.

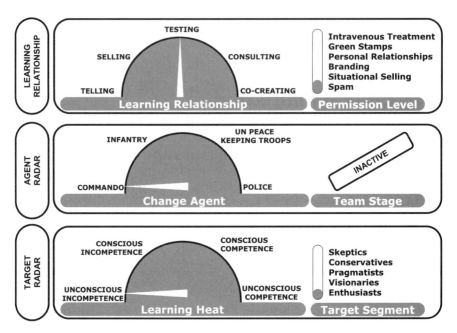

Figure 7.1 Soft-Stuff Radar at Program Initiation

7.1.2   Hard-Stuff Radar

In this phase, the hard-stuff radar is inactive because time, money, and headcount requirements still need to be defined.

7.2   What Happens at the Level of the Program

Many activities that happen at the program level relate to the unfreezing of the organization. These include assigning the program manager, developing the business case and the feasibility study, and kicking off the program.

7.2.1 Diagnostic Interventions

Schein (2002) introduced the concept of Diagnostic Interventions as the best way to involve members of the organization in the change program. By asking them relevant questions about the present state, you not only learn about possible resistance to change, but you also begin to influence their thinking and get them involved in the planning. You need to recognize that no matter how neutral and innocent the questions may be, they will influence the thinking of the people in the organization and will, therefore, be an intervention with an unfreezing consequence.

7.2.2 Supplier Management

If you don't have enough project- and program-management experience in-house to make your SAP implementation happen, you must find it in an outside supplier. What you must be aware of in that case is that the responsibility of your supplier increases significantly. At that time, you outsource part of the responsibility for delivery to an external party. This changes the whole relationship, and it means that you will have to pay much more attention on managing your supplier and following up on its deliveries.

We have seen SAP implementations fail or run into significant delays because external resources were pulled away to other customers during the implementation. It is normal that during a large-scale SAP implementation running over a number of years, people come and go. But you must ensure that at all times knowledge is kept and continuity is guaranteed. You must manage your suppliers accordingly.

Proactive resource management allows you to better manage the inflow of external resources. With regard to external resources critical for the success and the continuity of the program, you must discuss with the supplier the need to block these resources' availability to other customers.

The same is true for purchasing your SAP software. You have to take into account the lead time to negotiate the contracts, get them signed, have all other administrative formalities in place, and have the software delivered to you.

7.2.3 Other Ongoing Initiatives

As mentioned in Chapter 4, no other major activities should be started or ongoing during the implementation. Ideally this is true, but—given the lifetime of a SAP implementation—it is wishful thinking.

Given the speed with which things change these days, your company will face challenges during your SAP implementation that will demand action. You cannot just ignore them, so you should adapt your expectations at the start and accept that there will be other high-priority initiatives in parallel with the implementation of SAP.

The art is not to delay them or ignore these other initiatives, but to carefully select the ones that are really critical and to integrate all ongoing activities with each other. Clearly, this needs to be centrally managed. This requires a high level of capability maturity from the organization and an extensive sponsor involvement, especially when your organization has a decentralized decision-making structure. Shifts in decision-making structures are critical changes for an organization.

7.3 The Organization Stream in this Phase

As you are probably aware, an SAP implementation requires your organization to change both from a strategic perspective and from an operational one. A change of this magnitude should start at the top, and the activities in the program-initiation phase should be aimed at authorizing and reinforcing the change.

7.3.1 Assigning a Program Manager

The assignment of a program manager is the first visible step of unfreezing the organization for change.

The fact that a high-profile employee is taken away from his or her current position for the program is an important symbol, communicating that the program is of strategic importance.

7.3.2 Developing the Business Case

When deciding to implement SAP, the business case is present, but mostly in an immature state. The decision has been taken based on the outcome of executive meetings, no matter how the need for SAP has come to the surface.

It is important that the business case be explicitly described in detail. A written business case triggers discussions that are required to make sure that all minds are heading the same direction. The business case ensures that everybody is aligned on the reasons why the company has decided to implement SAP.

You should be aware of the difference between a business case and a feasibility study because they serve different purposes, as explained here:

▶ The business case supports the decision to change the way you are doing business today. It justifies the transition to something else.

▶ The feasibility study contains the arguments and concrete steps for moving forward with the SAP implementation; it confirms that the program is feasible. The decision to go ahead with the implementation should be based on the outcome of a feasibility study, not on the business case.

Let's have a closer look at the process of making a business case.

Planning for the Business Case

The first task of the program manager is to develop a plan for the business case. This plan must include:

▶ Identification of the major stakeholders and other sources of information.

▶ Timeline by which the business case must be finished (draft, final version, official presentation).

▶ Budget (use of external resources, purchase of research information or benchmarks, etc.).

▶ The complete reporting of the business case.

Developing a SMART Business Case

Once the plan is complete, you can start gathering information. You can do so by having interviews with stakeholders or by examining other key sources that can provide valuable information. Where necessary, some additional research can be done internally. External research information and benchmarks might be purchased from third-party providers.

You can use the approach represented by the acronym SMART to check the elements that must at least be covered in the business case:

▶ **Specific Goals**

These are the reasons for implementing SAP: desired outcome and benefits to be realized. There are two ways you can be explicit and specific about the goals:

▷ **Pulling Factors**

The benefits must be concretely quantified in financial or non-financial terms.

▷ **Pushing Factors**

Organizational change demands a sense of urgency. Randall et al. (2003) state that one of the better ways to create proper sense of urgency is to point at clear dangers for the organization if the SAP implementation does not happen.

▶ **Measurements**

Remember: If you can't measure it, you can't manage it. The realization of the benefits is the return on investment (ROI) for the organization. It is by measuring the realization of the benefits that you can evaluate the ROI of the program.

▶ **Attainability of Program Goals**

This is mostly clarified through a description of the program-related risks.

▶ **Relevance of Goals**

When putting together the business case, ask yourself: "Is the presence of economic value sufficient as a business case to justify the implementation of SAP?" A high-level and preliminary estimate of the costs is necessary.

▶ **Traceability**

A business case is not complete without an itinerary of interim goals and a first mapping of the efforts over time.

Presenting the Business Case

It is not enough to put the business case together and distribute it to executive management for confirmation. The business case must be presented, feedback must be obtained, and you may need some rework from time to time. Section 7.4 on the communication stream explains how the presentation of the business case should be approached.

Approval of the Business Case

We also recommend that you do not ask for validation (confirmation) of the business case immediately after the presentation. You need to allow at least a week or two of reflection. Don't forget: When considering implementing SAP, we are talking about huge investments both in time and effort.

Another objective of the business case must be to get an approval to do a feasibility study. In the business-case presentation, you must point out the importance of the feasibility study and demand the approval for making it. This means you have to be prepared to know what the scope of the feasibility study is, who will be involved, how much time it will take, what the objective is, and how much it will cost.

7.3.3 Feasibility Study Justifies the Business Case

The feasibility study must not be confused with the business case. The feasibility study has a specific purpose that is different from that of the business case. In this subsection, we highlight the difference between these two deliverables.

Objective of the Feasibility Study

As mentioned earlier, the business case must provide the justification for deciding to implement SAP and the underlying benefits for the organization. Just because the business case turns out to be affirmative, does not mean that the SAP implementation is feasible for the organization. There are many other factors that determine whether the SAP implementation is doomed to fail or can be expected to be succeed.

That is what the feasibility study must confirm. True, this will take some time and it will cost some money. But consider the cost as an insurance fee: If the feasibility study shows that you shouldn't do the implementation, it will only cost you the time, effort, and money spent so far. If it turns out to be positive, then at least you can decide to move forward with full confidence. That is also why the result of the feasibility study is a moment of truth.

Contents of the Feasibility Study

The feasibility study must cover all aspects that might influence the success or failure of an SAP implementation. These are as follows:

- ► **Business Scope**
  The business scope of the program must be described in detail. This includes not only a list and description those things within the scope of the program, but also—and this may be even more important—of things that are outside its scope.

- ► **Functional Scope**
  The feasibility study must highlight the processes that will be affected by the SAP implementation, as well as the functional departments that will be involved.

- ► **Technical Scope**
  All systems and existing interfaces that are involved or affected must be listed. The feasibility study must describe whether they will be replaced, improved, or linked to the future SAP environment. You must highlight which processes each system is supporting and who the (key) users will be. Rate each system for business criticality.

- ► **Benefits Analysis**
  The study must question whether the anticipated benefits that the organization wants to realize with the implementation of SAP can be achieved. At this time it is important to involve senior and middle management. If senior and middle management are convinced that the anticipated benefits defined by executive management cannot be realized, it will be very difficult to get their buy-in. And without buy-in from senior or middle management, an SAP implementation will not succeed.

- ► **Functional and Technical Requirements Analysis**
  All functional and technical requirements must be listed for analysis.

- ► **Gap Analysis**
  The functional and technical requirements must be mapped against the functional and technical characteristics of the SAP environment. A gap analysis must show the feasibility of the use of SAP for the company.

- ► **Timelines**
  Is the timeline in which SAP must be implemented feasible and realistic?

- ► **Required Resource Availability**
  The required resources must be identified and listed. The study must specify at what time they are required and how much they need to be involved. Their availability must be analyzed. The company should not only look at internal resources, but also at external resources (SAP, other third-party service providers).

▶ **Effort Estimation**
The effort required to achieve the SAP implementations must be estimated. This is one of the most difficult activities. You need to have a very
good understanding of what it means to implement SAP, the iterations it
takes, and underlying benefits in order to make a qualitative estimate. We
recommend including buffers in the estimation.

▶ **Budget Estimation**
The same is true when estimating the budget. This can to a certain extent
be derived from the effort estimation. Other items, such as cost of hardware, software, and maintenance, must be added. The required budget
must be estimated to a comfortable level of detail. Here again we recommend including buffers: It is better to have budget left over than to have
to go and ask for more money when the program is ongoing.

▶ **Risk Management**
All potential risks must be analyzed. For each risk, the impact (low,
medium, high) and its probability of occurrence (low, medium, high) must
be specified.

▶ **Organizational Readiness**
The feasibility study requires evaluation of the organization's readiness to
deal with such an implementation. This evaluation should look at the
company's track record in doing such implementations, and in managing
or dealing with projects. The culture of the organization and the capability
maturity will have an impact on the readiness.

▶ **Relationship to Other Programs and Projects**
Any possible interference with other ongoing projects must be described.
It is not enough to only identify them, but you must also specify where
and how they relate to each other. Interdependencies (timelines,
resources) must be specified and described.

▶ **SAP Feasibility**
Ideally the decision to implement SAP should be taken after all functional
and technical requirements have been identified, listed, and described in
detail. SAP should then be selected based upon a gap analysis; i.e., comparing the functionality and technical characteristics of SAP with the
requirements that were listed.

Although SAP may be an obvious choice because of its market leadership,
you need to confirm that SAP matches the organization's requirements suffi-
ciently. As we mentioned in Chapter 4, SAP is an off-the-shelf product; it can
be configured but it should not be changed too much. This is comparable to

buying a car: You can buy one, tune it a little, or paint it your favorite color, but you are not going to take out the engine and build your own.

Why it is Worth the Time

The conclusion of the feasibility study will include a recommendation to go ahead or not go ahead with the SAP implementation. The outcome of the feasibility will rarely be a clear go ahead or a clear stop. Senior management must thoroughly review the outcome of the study to make a decision.

Also, you have to realize that the contents of the feasibility study are a basis for the program charter. The program charter, as explained in Chapter 8 (Program Setup), is a kind of internal contract of service-level agreement on what the SAP implementation must achieve, who does what and when, who has which responsibilities, and so on.

The effort and duration required to make a feasibility study depends on the size of the organization, the scope, and the complexity of the SAP implementation. As a rule of thumb, we believe that a proper feasibility study can take six weeks to three months.

7.3.4 The Commando Team

Putting together the team, pulling its members out of their day-to-day business and assembling them in one physical location is a crucial step in bringing the focus and the energy together. From a soft-change perspective, it implicitly communicates that the whole of the organization will be involved from the start.

It is important to think carefully about who will be part of that team. The team represents the entire organization from both the functional (including IS) and the geographical perspective. Participants should know the organization's history thoroughly and have extended networks of relations in the organization so they can access knowledge and multiple points of view.

It is also important to include experienced SAP experts in the team, so that the system implications can be analyzed at any time. Experts should come from outside of the organization, even if you already have people in your organization who are acquainted with SAP. External experts will provide objective information, and they will not have been conditioned by the culture and the current ways of working of your organization. These people must have the maturity to challenge the status quo and question your current ways of working.

7.4 The Communication Stream in this Phase

In the program-initiation phase, the main target groups you need to focus on are executives and other key stakeholders. Here we will highlight how you should approach these stakeholders at this specific time.

7.4.1 Knowledgeable Facts About Executives

From our experience, we know that chief executives sponsoring your program are not always the easiest persons to deal with. At the same time, you will need them as an authorizing and reinforcing driver behind the program during the complete lifecycle. Moreover, during the phase of program initiation, executives are your one and only point of reference in the organization. Therefore, it may be good to know what sets executives apart from other people in the organization. Here are some of the differences:

▶ Sometimes executives are said to have attention spans comparable to that of a seven year old; i.e., between 30 seconds and five minutes. This is because they operate in a world of continuous context-switching. Unfortunately for you, this enhances their ability to detect when you are beating about the bush. As a result, your communication with them should be brief. According to Jensen (2003), you should apply the following law when communicating to executives: "Anything that has a staple through it will not get read."

▶ Executives want to have a stake in the solution. They want to build up arguments, make decisions, take actions, and move on. That is what they are good at; otherwise they would not be in that position. In terms of your communication, this means that you should prepare for a conversation instead of a monologue. An executive who cares about the topic will interrupt with a question after approximately one minute of your monologue. As a result, you should be presenting facts and asking for opinions, or presenting alternatives and asking for pros and cons.

▶ Executives are said to hate surprises. Sponsors of the program hate to be surprised about the program in front of their colleagues. Therefore, you should have preliminary meetings with all the sponsoring board members before you present at an executive meeting. Ask for their input and viewpoints upfront, and they will back you up and guide you during the meet-ing and the decision-making. True, this takes time and may add several iterations.

▸ Numbers will only set you free to the extent that they support your argu-ments. You should only use statistics and numbers to the extent that they significantly support the arguments you are making. Keep all the statistics as a backup for the conversation, and stick to the numbers they really need to know about.

Your awareness of these characteristics will determine how you approach the validation of the business case, the feasibility study, and the involvement of the program sponsors. The purpose of these guidelines is to save you from coming out of an executive meeting with more questions than you had when you entered.

7.4.2 Stakeholder Mapping

A stakeholder is "any party that affects or is affected by an organization and its policies" (Mitroff, 1987). In other words, every interested party is some-one with a relationship to the program.

Stakeholder mapping is quite straightforward. If the exercise is carried out well, a discussion will follow in which the different perceptions are tested against one another. A consensus is then reached regarding the list of inter-ested parties, and this is how you arrive—sometimes to your own surprise—at a more complete picture than if you had done this exercise on your own. The result can take the form of a stakeholder map that can look like the example in Figure 7.2.

In practice, you must remember the following three things:

▸ An organization is not necessarily a *thing* but a series of relationships between a wide series of parties. The mapping of the stakeholders is a first step in bringing relationships to the surface.

▸ The point is not to have a beautiful map, but to have a thorough discussion on the impact of the program on the organization. If the exercise is carried out well, then most of the presuppositions, misunderstandings, and pre-conceptions will come to the surface. These are the point of discussion, until the team has a common view of its stakeholders. Mapping or identi-fying does not mean that we are searching for "the truth" or "objectivity," but rather that we are looking for a common perception. Starting from this point, SAP implementations will end up being what they think and say, as their ideas and visions realize themselves (Morgan, 1998).

▶ A stakeholder map (shown in Figure 7.2), is the landscape through which you have to navigate the change. It can look fairly rough in the beginning and it can change over time.

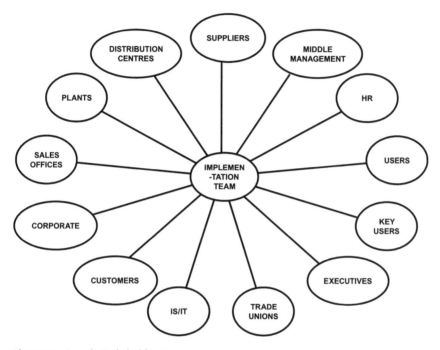

Figure 7.2 Sample Stakeholder Map

7.4.3   Stakeholder Analysis

If stakeholder mapping brings you fruitful discussions about the impact of the program on all the affected parties and vice versa, your next step is to determine their level of involvement. You cannot involve all stakeholders to the same extent all the time.

On the chart in Figure 7.3, you should be able to map every single stakeholder you listed during the previous step. You will need to do so according to the following two dimensions:

▶ **Impact of Stakeholder in Organization**
What is the stakeholder's organizational power or influence to reinforce initiatives in your organization? This dimension also takes into account informal opinion leaders.

▶ **Impact of Stakeholder on the Implementation**

How important is the commitment of this stakeholder to the success of the implementation?

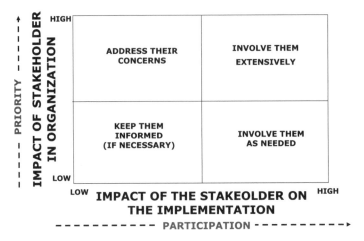

Figure 7.3 Stakeholder Analysis

Sometimes the result of this analysis may be surprising. You may end up mapping in the top right-hand quadrant of this chart those stakeholders who tend to escape your attention because they work in another location. Conversely, you may start to attribute less time and devotion than you would normally to the needs of a department next door, because they appear in the bottom left-hand quadrant of the chart. In short, this analysis will help you to set priorities in the relationships with all stakeholders.

Roughly speaking, most sponsors are situated in the top left-hand quadrant, agents in the top right-hand quadrant, and targets in the bottom right-hand quadrant.

7.4.4 Anticipate Sponsor Readiness

As the previous stakeholder analysis will allow you to set priorities on relationships with stakeholders, it is useful during this phase of program initiation to predict their level of resistance. As the sponsors are the first targets you should focus on, each individual sponsor can be mapped on the chart in Figure 7.4.

The phase of program initiation is not completed until the majority of the sponsors take ownership over the program. Two dimensions are important here, as seen here:

▶ **Trust**

Can you rely on the sponsor's support or are they avoiding ownership of the program?

▶ **Agreement**

Are you in agreement about the content of the program?

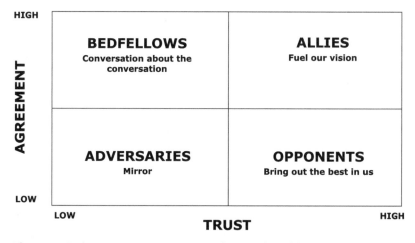

Figure 7.4 Radar to Anticipate Sponsor Readiness (Adapted from Block, 1987)

The point of the diagram in Figure 7.4 is that we need to get all sponsors on the right-hand side into a relationship of trust. We need a healthy mix of:

▶ **Allies**

They fuel our vision.

▶ **Opponents**

They bring out the best in us.

For those sponsors situated low in trust, there are two types you are likely to encounter:

▶ **Bedfellows**

These are the most difficult to get a hold on because they seemingly agree on the surface during face-to-face discussions and meetings. However, as you follow up on their commitments and actions, you will discover discrepancies. The advice here is to start an individual conversation about what is going on with their level of commitment (a conversation about the conversation) to bring to the surface whatever is blocking them. It takes courage to start these conversations, but it is best to have them in this stage of the program.

▶ **Adversaries**
Just like Bedfellows, they are low in trust, but at least they are straightforward about it. It is not likely that you will run into sponsors of this type, openly declaring that they are against this program. However, if you do, you should approach them in the same way as Bedfellows: with a conversation about their commitment.

Remember, the essence of sponsor readiness is trust, not agreement.

7.5 The Learning Stream in this Phase

In this phase of program initiation it may seem strange to start talking about the learning stream. There are, nevertheless, some aspects that need to be taken into account early on to set the learning strategy.

7.5.1 Analyze the Learning Needs

It is good to understand that the basic ingredients of change are reflected 1:1 in terms of learning needs. As Figure 7.5 illustrates, learning is a social skill comprising the following:

▶ Know-How (learning by doing, with others)

▶ Know-What (cognitive skills as well as facts)

▶ Know-Why (relevance and motivation)

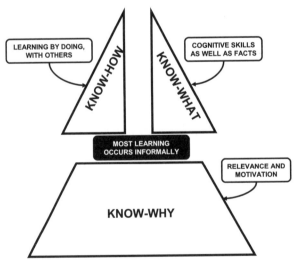

Figure 7.5 The Three Basic Ingredients of a Learning Perspective

Know-How

Traditionally we tend to think of Know-How in terms of specific instructions that can be tested by oral examination. Effective training programs take real-life practice as a benchmark. For most users, successful real-life practice implies awareness of what happens before and after their functional cubicles are involved. As most of our brains have a limited storage capacity for this kind of stuff, we need to make sure that we only provide what is necessary at the exact moment that it is necessary.

Know-What

The Know-What is generally thought of in terms of formal learning recognized through testing and certification. It consists of facts, figures, and specific ways of doing things. However, integrated-process thinking requires that the "what" of learning changes to another cognitive skill that includes decision-making, problem solving, situational awareness, and teamwork.

Know-Why

In a world of integrated processes and information-empowered front line workers, it is Know-Why that emerges as the most critical skill for adults to have. Know-Why is the motivation, the carrot that leads the learner to seek peak performance, personal and professional. It is the deeper knowledge about the cause-and-effect relationships underlying a discipline or practice.

7.5.2   Leadership Requirements

As the program-initiation phase has the sponsors of the program as a main target for communication, we should point out some things about expectations of management with regard to their learning phases. It can take five or six months for a corporate officer to get from unconscious incompetence through conscious incompetence to conscious competence about the Know-Why of the program. In fact, we can say the duration of this phase is determined by the speed of all the corporate officers to go through the learning phases. The purpose is to get them all consciously competent about the need to change and about their ownership of the change.

Unfortunately, when the rest of the organization is going through the learning phases, the corporate officers themselves are in a phase of unconscious competence, leading to impatient reactions and, sometimes, unreasonable expectations. To them, the insight has become trivial and they are apt to forget how long it took for them to absorb and own the insights of the change.

7.5.3 Vision and Strategy Formulation

The business case and the feasibility study requires you to formulate a vision and a strategy prior to deriving the three performance ingredients (i.e., goals, structure and management actions). This is an intensive and time-consuming activity with many iterations during the validation by the organization.

According to Christensen (1995), strategy formulation starts with a definition of the driving forces. Figure 7.6 shows some of the steps involved in formulating the strategy of an organization. What is not visible in the figure is that these steps should be professionally facilitated, that they are spread out over time, and that they involve many iterations.

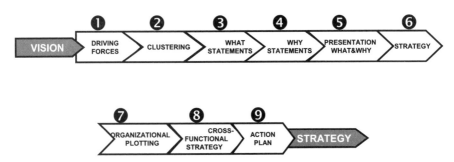

Figure 7.6 Sample Steps for Strategy Formulation

1. In a first step, all the driving forces are mapped that shape the organization as it is today. Basically, this comes down to a SWOT analysis, as follows:

   ▶ **Strengths**
   What are the strong points of your organization?

   ▶ **Weaknesses**
   Which points must be improved?

   ▶ **Opportunities**
   Which internal and external factors are present to improve or leverage the current situation?

   ▶ **Threats**
   Which internal and external factors present a threat to the functioning of your organization?

2. Second, during the clustering phase, all the input is evaluated and clustered into meaningful segments or clusters.

3. The third step is to formulate a uniform and clear description of the clusters. This statement should describe the current situation by answering the question: "What is going on?"

4. Fourth, to achieve a clear strategy, the starting point must not be based on symptoms, but rather on underlying causes and mechanisms that generated the current situation. Therefore, the next step is to look for driving forces, shaping mechanisms, and underlying causes. These are summarized into statements answering the question: "Why is this happening?"

5. As a fifth step, it is important to have an open discussion on the executive level to gain a shared understanding of the current situation.

6. It is only at the sixth step that you will be ready to formulate how your organization can protect itself against some driving forces and take advantage of other driving forces. Finally, "strategy" is nothing more than summarizing these actions into one clear and compelling statement.

7. The seventh step is to roll out the strategy over the current organizational levels. This eventually translates into a set of benefits that need to be realized at organizational, process, and performer level.

8. In an eighth step, you need to make it more concrete by defining how each person in the current structure can contribute to making the future strategy succeed. The logical outcome for SAP implementations is the setup of a cross-functional implementation program. However, thanks to the previous steps, you now have a sharp and compelling definition of the Know-Why, Know-What, and Know-How.

9. Finally, when it comes to deciding how money and manpower should be spent, the strategies can be used to identify and prioritize projects, which is what the business case and the feasibility study is all about.

These nine steps of strategy formulation will eventually result in strategy mapping, described further in the next subsection.

7.6   The Performance Management Stream in this Phase

You must start paying attention to performance management even at the very beginning of your SAP implementation program. It is at this early stage that you set the basics, determining to a certain extent how you will move forward in the next phases of the program. We will explain how to approach the startup of the performance management stream.

7.6.1 Identify Performance Ingredients

As Figure 7.7 illustrates, the vision of an organization is crucial. The vision should be reflected in the three basic elements, which we have identified earlier in Chapter 3:

- **Goals (Motivation/Why)**
  These are the benefits that you aim to realize by implementing SAP. That is why setting the benefits and verifying their feasibility is so important. The benefits chosen will determine what the future organization and its processes will have to look like if we want to realize the strategy.

- **Structure (Knowledge/What)**
  A description of how the organization needs to be structured to support the realization of those benefits.

- **Management (Skills/How)**
  How will you bring the benefits into practice? Which skills are needed to achieve the goals and to operate in the supporting structure?

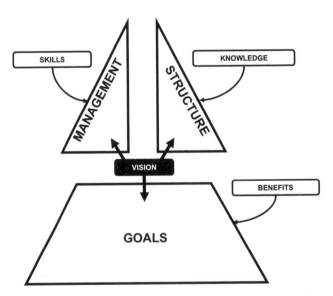

Figure 7.7 The Basic Performance Ingredients (based on Rummler & Brache, 1995)

We want to remind you about the importance of achieving clarity on the level of the program benefits:

- They link the business case to the vision of the organization.

- They are examined and refined during the feasibility study.

- They set certain conditions for the supporting structures and management actions.

- They are the basis for following-up the future performance of the organization in function of its strategy.

7.6.2 The Performance Management Cycle

Performance management is not something static; it is a dynamic and iterative process. It starts with clarifying the strategy in the following steps:

1. **Clarify Strategy**
   This includes making sure that all relevant parties within the organization are involved for alignment.

2. **Translate into Operations**
   The second step in the cycle ensures that the strategy is translated into day-to-day operations. This includes the definition of clear goals that need to be realized to realize the vision.

3. **Manage and Follow-up**
   In the third step, performance must be followed up and managed. By *managed*, we mean that appropriate action must be taken ensure that the organization is performing.

4. **Learn**
   In the learning phase of the cycle, the results of the performance measurement over time allows you to interpret the information and to derive conclusions.

5. **Continuously Improve**
   In the fifth step, you can identify areas of improvement from your learning. These improvements reinforce your strategy or make the realization of the strategy more efficient.

7.6.3 Identifying Performance Levels

The three performance ingredients that we identified in the previous paragraph need one further refinement before we can actually make them tangible. Figure 7.8 illustrates how the three performance ingredients operate on the following three different organizational levels (Rummler & Brache, 1995):

- ▸ Organization
- ▸ Process
- ▸ Role/Performer

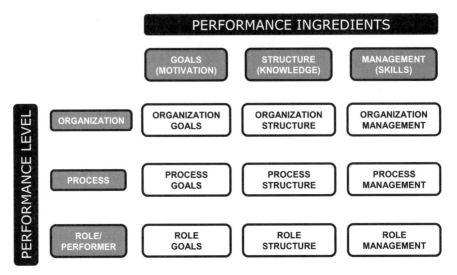

Figure 7.8 Nine Areas of Performance (adapted from Rummler & Brache, 1995)

The basic message of Figure 7.8 is that if a company wants to realize its vision and strategy, clear goals have to be identified at organizational, process, and (individual) role levels. Every design of organization, process or role must be in function of the concrete benefits. As a result you will find that there are nine distinct areas of performance (Rummler & Brache, 1995). The identification of these nine areas is essential when you want to measure and improve the performance of the SAP implementation.

As an example, imagine that your company's strategic goal is to be perceived as being very responsive to the customer demands. Suppose that, in your market, quotations are usually delivered to the customer within 48 hours, and one of the ways to be perceived as responsive is to reduce this lead time by 50% to 24 hours. This is a benefit that you might want to realize by implementing SAP.

The organizational benefit is to be perceived as being more responsive in comparison to your competitor; the process benefit is to reduce the lead time to 24 hours of your current request-for-proposal-to-proposal-out process. If however, the design of the process includes five approval steps before the proposal can be sent to the customer, there is a significant probability that your proposal won't reach the customer within 24 hours. At the role level, this might mean that the person putting together the proposal should possess middle-management rather than operational-level skills.

7.7 Moments of Truth of This Phase

We find moments of truth in the program initiation phase. These are discussed in the subsections that follow.

7.7.1 Identify the Program Manager from the Very Beginning

Normally the program manager has not been part of the team of executives that has taken the decision to implement SAP. But he or she should be involved from the very beginning for the following reasons:

▶ The program manager must be unconditionally convinced about the validity of the business case. He or she is the one who will be responsible for realizing the benefits that SAP must bring. A program manager who does not fully support the business case will lack the drive and motivation to make the change happen.

▶ The program manager has to convince others about the validity of the business case. In the program initiation phase, the people to be challenged and convinced are the executives. To guarantee success, the program manager must "live" the business case, and that can only be the case if he or she is the originator.

▶ While putting together the business case, the mind of the program manager will already be "prepared" for the further steps. An SAP implementation and the realization of its underlying benefits represent a very complex undertaking. It takes time to make sure that you understand all the dimensions. Writing the business case facilitates better and faster understanding.

The selection of the program manager should happen in close alignment with HR because dedicating a program manager for a long period of time impacts the continuity. What's more, the assignment of a person in the role of program manager requires a serious assessment of that person's career perspectives, skills, knowledge, and motivation.

7.7.2 Confirmation of the Business Case

At this moment, the decision of the executive committee to implement SAP is officially confirmed. It shows a strong intention of the organization to implement SAP, provided there is a positive conclusion to the feasibility study. Confirming the business case is a formal milestone.

7.7.3 Bringing the Feasibility Team Together

Focus is one of the most important requirements when putting together the feasibility study. Besides, most of the contents of the feasibility study are gathered during workshops. That's why it is important to bring the feasibility team together in one and the same location, preferable neutrally at headquarters level. The organization's representatives must be pulled out of their day-to-day operations and work environments.

7.7.4 Outcome of the Feasibility Study

The feasibility study concludes whether the SAP implementation is feasible for the organization or not. If the feasibility study turns out to be positive, the program really kicks off. At that moment, the whole organization gets prepared to make the change happen.

7.7.5 Deliverables of this Phase

The deliverables of the program initiation phase are as follows:

▶ Business Case

▶ Feasibility Study

▶ Strategy Formulation

Figure 7.9 illustrates how the deliverables of this phase relate to each other. Spend some time looking over these deliverables in your own SAP-related setting to understand how you can go about achieving them.

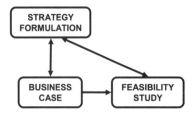

Figure 7.9 Organizational Change Deliverables of Program Initiation

7.8   Conclusion

The importance of the program initiation phase is often underestimated, sometimes unconsciously. So is the amount of work that needs to be done in this phase. Nonetheless, this is where the basis for the success of your SAP implementation program is established. It is the first step in unfreezing the company and preparing it for the change. It is also the phase in which the company must strengthen its self-confidence in that the SAP implementation is the right way to go.

In Chapter 8, we will explore the details of the program preparation phase. This will be the first tangible and visible step of the program; mobilizing resources and getting work done.

Once the program has been initiated and approval has been given to move forward, the program must be established. In this phase, the organization is preparing to start of the real work. People, other resources, and infrastructure are put in place. The program is kicked off officially.

8   Program Setup

8.1   Phase Specific Characteristics and Needs

In this section of the chapter, we'll explain how you should use and read the soft-stuff and hard-stuff radars, taking into account the specific characteristics and needs of the program setup phase.

8.1.1   Soft-Stuff Radar

The soft-stuff radar in Figure 8.1 only shows some minor differences during program initiation compared to the previous phase.

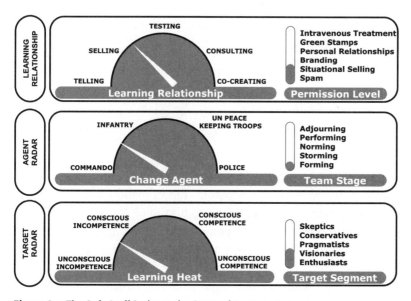

Figure 8.1 The Soft-Stuff Radar at the Stage of Program Setup

▶ **Learning Relationship Radar**

As the vision and the strategy have been defined and validated during the previous phase, they will help you sell the program to all stakeholders; you are now in selling mode. As a result, the permission level meter indicates that your communication is at the level of "situational selling." That is, you still have no relationship with the receiver of your messages, but your message is validated by the organization, even when it conflicts with the receiver's frame of reference.

▶ **Agent Radar**

Your focus is slowly moving from sponsor readiness to agent readiness in this phase. Step-by-step, you will be expanding the team of commandos and preparing the field for the infantry to take over. You are at the earliest stage of forming your team, but because of its small size you have few problems managing it. Moreover, the members of the "commando" team at this stage are experienced business people and experienced SAP experts. They should have the maturity and the experience to work as a team from the very start.

▶ **Target Radar**

By now, the validation rounds and strategy formulation has stimulated the visionaries (the majority of them at the sponsor level) to join the enthusiasts and to link the benefits of the SAP implementation to the organization's vision and strategy. At a very premature stage, this causes some members of senior and middle management to feel uncomfortable about the upcoming changes. You should look for signs of this "conscious incompetence" and help these people envision what the change looks like for their specific environment.

8.1.2 Hard-Stuff Radar

Figure 8.2 illustrates the start-up of the hard-stuff radar at the phase of program setup.

▶ **Validation Radar**

At the end of this phase of the program, the validation synchronization must indicate "program owned by the organization." The deliverables due at the end of the program setup phase must be completely signed off before you can move on. It is important that the program pace remains indicating "on time." From a change-management perspective, it isn't good if the program is already running into delays. However, validation is the point at this moment, not pace.

▶ **Supply and Demand**

At this time, you are recruiting key people from the organization into the program. Many of these people are at the level of middle management. The supply and demand must be managed so the balance between program needs and operational needs is guaranteed.

▶ **Budget Radar**

Little attention should be paid at this time to the budget radar. In this phase, a lot of the attention goes to setting up the budget, not yet on follow-up.

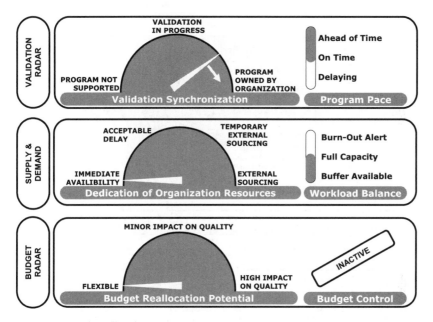

Figure 8.2 Hard-Stuff Radar at Program Setup

8.2   What Happens at the Level of the Program

In the program setup phase, it's expected that a lot of attention goes to the program itself. There are many critically important things to do, such as putting together the program's organizational structure.

To kick off the program, a number of activities must be performed. They are described in the following subsections.

8.2.1 Setup Program Organizational Structure

Setup of the program's organizational structure is a critical factor for the success of the SAP implementation. It defines who contributes at which level. The larger the scale of your SAP implementation—both from a geographical and a functional perspective—the more complicated your program structure.

> **Note**
>
> It is beyond the scope of this book to discuss in detail the way the program should be structured. In Figure 8.3, we show you a sample of a generic structure that has proven to be successful in a multitude of multinational environments.

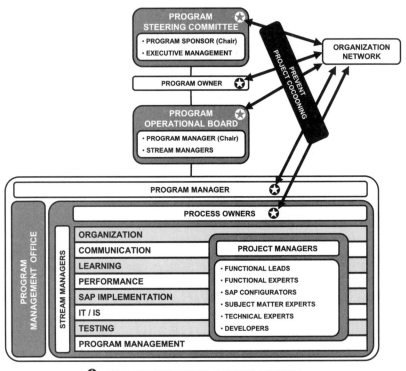

✪ = NEED TO BE RECRUITED FROM THE BUSINESS

Figure 8.3 Best-Practice SAP Program Organizational Structure

It is very important to understand that the program's organizational structure must correspond to the way your operational organization runs and how it deals with change. It is also possible that the structure will change during the lifecycle of the program to meet the needs within each phase. This is fine, as long as you make sure that the knowledge gathered within the program remains captured or gets transferred.

As illustrated in Figure 8.3, the following element roles are essential for a sound program organizational structure:

▶ **Program Steering Committee: Making Executive Decisions**
The steering committee is responsible for taking decisions that affect the whole of the program, such as program scope changes, critical risk mitigation issues, changes in benefits to be realized, or replacement of the program manager.

▶ **Program Sponsor: Maintain Executive Sponsorship**
It is important that executive sponsorship and commitment is maintained throughout the program lifecycle. A full-blown SAP implementation will affect the whole organization. That is why it is important to involve executive managers. The sponsor should be of executive level and should chair the steering committee.

▶ **Program Owner: Take Ownership**
The program must be owned by an executive who bears the responsibility to make change happen throughout the organization. Ideally this person is the CEO. An SAP implementation will affect the organization on all levels, and this includes a transformation of operations.

▶ **Program Manager: Keep the Program Together**
The program manager is the link between the program and the business. He holds the final responsibility for delivering the program, and for delivering its benefits.

▶ **Operational Board: Take Operational Decisions**
The operational board is responsible for making program operational decisions such as the setting of priorities, replacement of key resources, system scope changes, and issue handling.

▶ **Stream Manager: Safeguard Delivery**
The stream managers could alternatively be called *delivery managers*. They follow up with the project managers to make sure projects are delivered in time within their stream. Each delivery of a project is a step in the realization of the change required. Stream managers have expert knowledge with regard to the stream that they are managing.

▶ **Process Owner: (Re-)Engineer Processes**
As explained in Chapter 1, the organization must shift from thinking in functions to thinking in processes. That is why process owners have an important role within the program. They are responsible to make sure that the new ways of working are designed and implemented in function

of the identified goals (benefits). This responsibility goes across the delivery streams.

▶ **Project Manager: Delivery**
Project managers are responsible for delivering the projects that they are managing according the rules.

▶ **Program Office: Support the Program**
The program office is responsible for the administration of the program. It includes budget maintenance, program reporting, organization of meetings, booking travel, administration of time and expenses, and so on.

8.2.2 Program's Project Portfolio and Critical Path to Timely Delivery

As illustrated in Figure 8.4, the focus should be on defining the critical path to timely delivery of the SAP program during the program setup. This means that you define in detail the interdependencies and possibilities for parallel delivery of activities and deliverables. The next step is to define the buffers of time and budget to protect the critical path that you just defined.

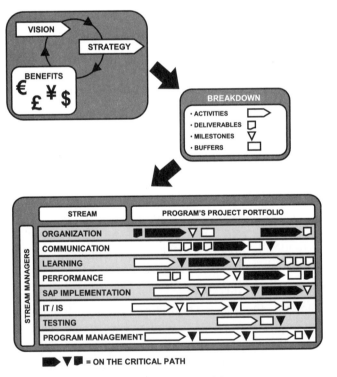

Figure 8.4 Vision to Program's Project Portfolio

The concept of a program implies that you will not change the organization with a so-called "big bang" approach. You will change the organization step-by-step with a series of intermediate milestones ("a succession of small victories") and the final delivery of each project in the portfolio. Therefore, during the program setup, each project of the portfolio needs to translate program benefits into its own scope in terms of deliverables, budget, time plan, resource planning, and so on.

8.2.3 Setup Program Administrative Office

In this phase of program setup, you may still find it difficult to believe that program administration requires almost one full-time staff person during the complete program lifecycle. This person should be extremely computer-literate, service-oriented, and lazy by nature. That third characteristic will drive him or her to automate as much as possible and make the administrative life of program members easy. The typical tasks of a program administrator include the following:

► Time administration from A to Z.

► Program plan reporting.

► Program budget reporting.

► Safeguarding documenting standards.

► Assisting each project team with their administration and program reporting.

► Setup and maintenance of the knowledge portal (see also Chapter 9).

Although this person is not expert in any aspect of SAP, the drive to automate and improve the reporting of "how we are we doing" will, in the end, turn out to be a success factor.

8.2.4 Organizational Change is in the Details of Delivery

Organizational change is not a separate action or a secret magical plan. Neither is it about outdoor activities or feel-good New-Age therapy. Organizational change is about the way you plan, do, check, and adjust all of your activities, even the most technical ones. It is the motivation that makes you take care of the details, because you know they make a difference.

Now let's explore the activities that take place during the organization stream.

8.3   The Organization Stream in this Phase

All activities that must happen within the organization stream in this phase still have the purpose of unfreezing the organization so it is ready for change. In comparison to the program-initiation phase where one can say that most of the activities aim to unfreeze the organization's mindset, the activities in the program setup phase unfreeze the organization physically.

8.3.1   Implementation Team Setup

Once the feasibility study is finished and the executive committee gives you the go-ahead, you need to launch the program as soon as possible. From our experience, we know it is difficult to find the appropriate resources inside the organization. It is even more difficult to free them up for the program. Even if you are working with internal staff resources and executive management supports their participation to the program, their positions need to be backfilled to ensure continuity of operations. This is where you need to involve HR.

A frequent mistake is to recruit agents from a population of "non-performers" or "social misfits." They are being sent to the SAP-program to try their luck over there. One regional director of a multinational company once put it this way:

> *"It's really no wonder that some SAP roll-outs in other countries fail to deliver their promises. When I look at how they are staffed, it looks more like a garbage bin than the driving force they are supposed to be. The next thing you know is that they are labeled as a pure IT-project with zero impact on processes."*

Later, he added:

> *"I am convinced that the success of our SAP roll-outs is that I have personally assured that our best people were on the team. Taking the best performers away from their current job and dedicating them—that is for the full FTE—to the project was the hardest part. But the results are there: We fulfilled every single strategic goal of the program."*

In addition to internal resources, you will need external resources, mainly SAP experts in the functional modules (FI/CO, SD, MM, PP, etc.) that are part of the scope. You will also need some SAP Basis experts for setting up the environment and to install the software. You will be assigning these people to important but temporary positions.

As mentioned earlier, you must select your suppliers well in advance and maintain good relationships with them. The same is true for purchasing the system. You have to take into account the lead time needed to negotiate contracts, signatures, administration, and so on, before it can even be installed. As obvious as these recommendations may seem, remember that you ignore them at the risk of not having the appropriate resources and system in place at the time that you require them. That would mean a false start of the program and a negative first impression.

8.3.2 Program Charter: Transition Service Level Agreement

Once executive management has decided to proceed with the implementation of SAP, based on the feasibility study, the program charter must be drawn up. The program charter sets a clear mission for the team by describing broad performance objectives (Clark & Wheelwright, 1992). Thus, joining the team includes accepting the charter.

Service Elements

Ideally, the service level agreement (SLA) is a translation of a major part of the feasibility study. Further, it describes the program organization—not only the structure, but the role of each individual—and the program management processes. The most important elements that need to be described are as follows:

- Benefits of the program
- Planning and purposes
  - Timing of phases
  - Resource planning
  - Budget planning
- Deliverables per phase
- Risk management and mitigation
- Performance measurement and incentives

More Than a Piece of Paper

To be effective, an SLA must incorporate two sets of elements: the service elements that we just mentioned above and management elements to make sure that the "transition SLA" works properly. The management elements (Karten, 2002) include the following:

▶ How deliverables and milestones will be validated.

▶ How information about the program status will be reported and addressed

▶ How disagreements will be resolved.

▶ How and under which circumstances the steering committee and the program management will review and revise the program charter.

Both service and management elements are necessary if a program charter is to be effective; yet, in many of the program charters, the management elements are lacking.

In this respect it is important to see the program charter as the most concrete outcome of the many-month process of information-gathering, analyzing, documenting, presenting, educating, negotiating, and consensus-building that has taken place for the business case and the feasibility study.

The program charter is to be considered as the transition SLA between senior management and the implementation team. It must be physically signed as an indication of commitment from both sides.

8.3.3 Continuity and Stability During Transition

As mentioned in Chapter 1, HR and IS/IT are not agents of change. We stated that they have another very specific responsibility during organizational change programs: continuity and stability. This is a difficult balancing act that lasts as long as the transition period. This means: the period after the first "go-live" through to the last site implementation. It is important to note the following:

▶ The challenge of HR is not only to mobilize the team and to backfill the open positions on the short term. During this phase of program setup, HR needs to build a strategy that ensures that the organization can bridge the transition period on the level of all HR processes (selection, performance, development, appraisal, and rewarding).

▶ The challenge of IS/IT in the phase of program setup is to plan processes, temporary interfaces, architectural moves, and data requirements to bridge the new SAP world and the old legacy world. From a maintenance point of view, they should also define a long-term skills transition plan.

No need to mention that the pace of execution of the HR and IS plans is completely determined by the SAP implementation.

8.3.4 Identification of Process Owners

In the program's organizational structure, you have identified process owners. This is a basic requirement because from now on your organization will have to start shifting from functional thinking to process-oriented thinking.

Process owners should be middle managers with high career potential. Again, their appointment should take place in close cooperation with HR because you want to make sure they stay on the job long-term.

This is the first major step in unfreezing the organization at the very top. At this moment, you have accepted the challenge to move from an organization that thinks functionally towards a process-oriented organization. Now it is time to define the communication stream for this phase.

8.4 The Communication Stream in this Phase

We'll now explain the communication ingredients and how to analyze the communication needs to develop a communication strategy, and also deal with agent and sponsor resistance.

8.4.1 Communication Links Vision to Perception

The communication cycle in Figure 8.5 depicts the steps it takes to communicate on the level of an organization.

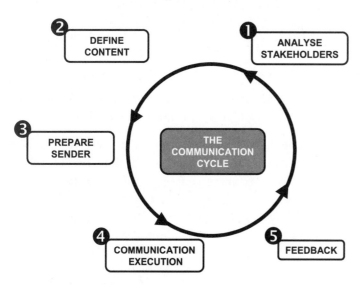

Figure 8.5 The Communication Cycle

Organizational communication, regardless of whether it is formal or informal, starts with identifying the receiver. This is done by means of a stakeholder analysis. The next step is to prepare the content of the communication; here you occasionally will differentiate the content by audience. Next comes the choice of communication channel and determination of who will be the sender. The actual execution of the communication is then followed up by gathering feedback, which in turn, feeds the communication cycle.

Throughout the communication stream, the phases of this cycle are used as containers for organizing the numerous subtasks. In Appendix B.1, you will find an example of a high-level communication plan, making use of these containers.

8.4.2 Communication Ingredients

As stated in Chapter 3, there are three basic ingredients of organizational change. In the context of communication, they translate to the following communication needs (Jensen, 2003):

▶ **Know**
Relating to the Know-What. People need to know the rationale behind the changes, and they need to come to their own conclusions.

▶ **Feel**
Relating to the Know-Why. People need to actively participate in the process of making decisions and need to create their own buy-in.

▶ **Do**
Relating to the Know-How. People need the right tools to implement the change.

Figure 8.6 shows what the three ingredients look like from a communication point of view. The "know-feel-do" model can be used in any communication from email to a telephone conversation or in front of an audience.

Bill Jensen (2003) says know-feel-do forces you to see the receiver of your communication as decision makers and to organize your thoughts according to how they listen. The receiver of a message mostly waiting for the answer to three questions: "What is the one thing you want me to know?," "Why is it important?," and "What do you want me to do as a result of your communication?"

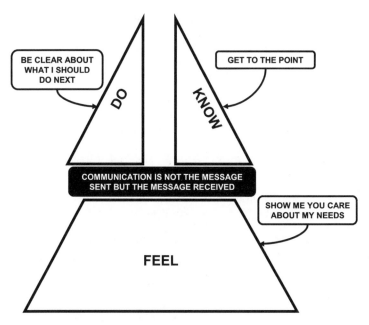

Figure 8.6 Three Basic Ingredients from a Communication Perspective (adapted from Jensen, 2003)

8.4.3 Analyze Communication Needs

The three ingredients of change can also be spread over the lifecycle of an implementation. In general, Unfreezing is the phase where you need to motivate people (Know-Why) and as the program progresses over time, there will be more and more need for concrete facts (Know-What and instructions (Know-How). Table 8.1 provides a sample of communication needs during the lifecycle of a program.

The basic thing to remember from Table 8.1 is that communication needs increase over time and that people have very short memories. As a consequence, you need to reuse and recycle the communication that you sent in the previous phases and add more and more concrete information.

How exactly you need to put this to practice is part of the communication strategy and of the communication plan.

Phase	UNFREEZING	CHANGING	REFREEZING
Communication Needs	▶ Know-Why	▶ Know-Why ▶ Know-What	▶ Know-Why ▶ Know-What ▶ Know-How
Examples	▶ Explain the status quo and why it is not working anymore ▶ Explain the business Rationale	▶ Explain the status quo and why it is not working anymore ▶ Explain the business Rationale	▶ Explain the status quo and why it is not working anymore ▶ Explain the business Rationale
	▶ Explain the Organization Implications ▶ Explain the Process implications ▶ Explain the System implications	▶ Explain the Organization Implications ▶ Explain the Process implications ▶ Explain the System implications ▶ Informing employees about progress ▶ Responding on feedback ▶ Clarifying Roles and Responsibilities	▶ Explain the Organization Implications ▶ Explain the Process implications ▶ Explain the System implications ▶ Informing employees about progress ▶ Responding on feedback ▶ Clarifying Roles and Responsibilities ▶ Declaring small victories ▶ Fast and Honest communication about corrections ▶ One single point of communication ▶ Detailed instructions and procedures

Table 8.1 Communication Needs per Phase

8.4.4 Define Communication Strategy

The purpose of the communication stream is to facilitate the shift from the old frame of reference (functional thinking) to a new one (integrated process thinking).

In Chapter 3, we explained in detail the anatomy of our perception by means of the seven steps of sense making. This is how we create a frame of reference for ourselves to cope with the world that surrounds us. Roughly speaking, those seven steps can be summarized as follows. Keep in mind, when something happens that interrupts our frame of reference, by nature we will always do the following:

1. Explain the present situation with evidence from the past (**The Past**).

2. Infect others with this point of view and have others enrich this point of view (**My Relations**).

3. Label the situation and put it into one or other known category (**My Labels**).

4. Talk our view of the situation into existence: "the glass is half full / half empty" (**A Declaration**).

5. Attach more importance to simple stories with cause and effect than to scientific evidence (**The Story**).

6. Be unaware that the exact point in time that this situation occurred determines our perception (**The Slot**).

7. Filter for hints and cues that confirm our point of view (**The Triggers**).

As stated in Chapter 3, when your purpose is to modify the beliefs, behaviors and assumptions of the existing cultures, then these seven steps will form the anatomy of your communication approach. In Figure 8.7, we show the parallel that exists between the steps in creating a new culture and the anatomy of our perception.

A successful communication strategy during organizational change takes into account the anatomy of our perception and caters to a similar mechanism to create a new culture. Here are the seven essential steps of the high-level communication strategy:

1. Investigate the historical background of the organization and the people you are targeting (**The Past**).

2. Make a stakeholder analysis so you clearly know who will be involved and whether they are sponsor, agent, or target (**My Relations**).

3. Build a clear identity for the program through branding, thereby providing psychological safety (**My Labels**).

4. Build a compelling vision and a clear strategy in understandable simple steps to get there (**A Declaration**).

5. Build a cause and effect relationship between the vision and what is in there for the people (**The Story**).

6. Respect the matter of timing: not to far in advance and not too late for the momentum you want to create (**The Slot**).

7. Be aware of the symbols, the unwritten rules, and the actions that speak louder than words (**The Triggers**).

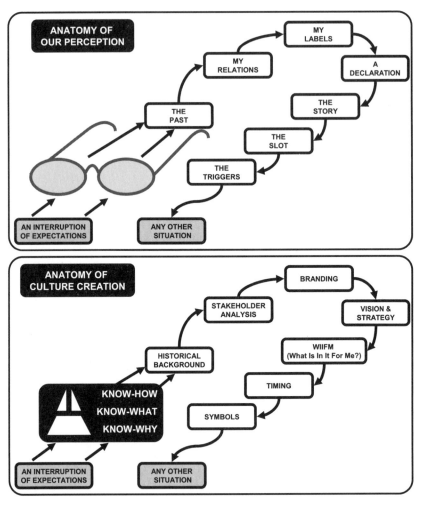

Figure 8.7 Anatomy of Perception as a Starting Point for Creating a Culture

All of these elements (not necessarily in that order) constitute the key points of your communication strategy. This is what you need to monitor during the complete lifecycle of the program. Eventually, when scanning through the communication plan (see next chapter), these steps should be reflected either in communication principles or in concrete actions.

8.4.5 Managing Agent and Sponsor Resistance

In his book *Flawless Consulting*, Peter Block (1981) lists some common types of resistance that are abundant during the lifecycle of an SAP implementation. Remember that we defined resistance as the emotion that results from interrupting our expectations about the "the way things are." We also said that resistance comes to the surface in a game of persecutors, victims, and rescuers. Block's list demonstrates just how subtle that game can get. Let's take a closer look:

▶ **Need More Detail**
Some resistance can appear in the form of requests for additional detail related to the topic or statements made. When requests for more information appear to block discussion or a decision, this could be resistance rather than a need for more detail.

▶ **Give a Lot of Detail**
Rather than requesting details, some offer too much. This can also block discussion and decisions when members are derailed by detailed stories or explanations of events rather than focusing on the topic at hand.

▶ **Not Enough Time**
Stakeholders may resist participating in a consensus process because time is of the essence. While time limitations are often the reality, a preoccupation with the limitation can be resistance to the process for some other reason.

▶ **Impracticality**
Stakeholders may feel consensus is not a "real-world" answer or approach to problem-solving or decision-making. Those who say "people can't reach consensus in the real world; it doesn't work that way" may have deeper reasons for not wanting to move forward with the process.

▶ **Confusion**
Similarly to needing too much detail, a persistent inability to understand an opinion or proposal before the group sometimes can be a way to block the process.

▶ **Silence**
Perhaps the most difficult resistance to identify or address, silence among Stakeholders can mean the process is not working. Consensus is total participation by every member, and silence can be a refusal to participate and can block the process altogether.

▶ **Moralizing**

When discussing the opinions of others, especially controversial topics, stakeholders may feel the need to explain or describe to one another a "better" way to think or what they "should be thinking" or "need to understand." This form of resistance can offend and stifle others. Often it indicates the moralizers are uncomfortable because others disagree with them.

▶ **Push for Solutions**

When proposals are before the group, some resistance can emerge in the form of impatience for possibilities and a need for solutions rather than ideas. If stakeholders disrupt decision-making with a discussion about the impossibility of an idea, this resistance may be more about what they are unwilling to do than about what cannot be done.

According to Block, dealing with these behaviors primarily requires allowing, supporting, and acknowledging the complete expression of the resistance. Often this alone can diminish the resistance. In other cases, when resistance is blocking the process or the decision of the group, there are effective ways to address it, such as the following:

▶ Identify the form the resistance has taken.

▶ Ask a question using neutral language.

▶ Be quiet and listen to the response.

Table 8.2 lists some examples and possible responses.

Resistance	Cues	Say
Need more detail	▶ Repeated questions ▶ Unwavering confusion	"What level of detail is needed to make a decision?"
Giving a lot of detail	▶ Leaning forward ▶ Interrupting others	"What is most important for you to express?"
Not enough time	▶ Focus on time over content	"Which part of the discussion should we give more time to?"
Impracticality	▶ Covertly undermining consensus	"Is there something you feel might be overlooked?"
Confusion	▶ Furrowed brows ▶ Shaking heads	"Is your confusion about the topic or the process?"

Table 8.2 Forms of Resistance and Possible Ways to Deal with It (Block, 1981)

Resistance	Cues	Say
Silence	▶ Folded arms ▶ Leaning backward	"We need your opinion. Can you share what you are thinking?"
Moralizing	▶ Pointing fingers ▶ Shaking heads	"We feel we understand your opinion. Do you feel you understand others?"
Press for solutions	▶ Impatience ▶ Exasperation	"Can we discuss the ideas first?"

Table 8.2 Forms of Resistance and Possible Ways to Deal with It (Block, 1981) (cont.)

8.5 The Learning Stream in this Phase

In the program-setup phase, the learning stream focuses on defining the learning objects and the learning strategy, but also on scanning the learning needs of the implementation team and the training of that team.

8.5.1 Learning Links Strategy to Performance

The purpose of the learning stream is that it links the benefits of the program to the performance of the people. There is only a slim chance for that link to occur when learning is restricted to the usual one-size-fits-all training.

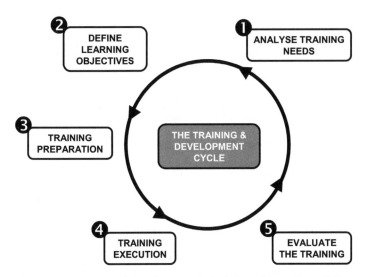

Figure 8.8 Training and Development Cycle (adapted from Sisson & Storey, 1995)

As illustrated in Figure 8.8, training and development are usually represented by a series of consecutive steps called the training and development cycle (Sisson & Storey, 1995). Mostly, the identification of the training needs is the starting point. In the following step, the learning objectives are defined to bridge the gap between the current level of competence and what will be required in the new situation. Then it is time to design and choose activities and programs during the preparation phase. The execution of the training is mostly followed by an evaluation phase to measure how well the objectives have been met.

Throughout the learning stream, we will use the phases of this training and development cycle as containers for organizing the numerous sub-tasks. In Appendix B.2, you will find an example of a high-level learning plan that uses these containers.

8.5.2 Define Learning Strategy

Process thinking puts the front-line employees in charge of the information, making them a hub of skills and knowledge. Front-line employees are action oriented, and they will suddenly need to be competent in a broader sense. Therefore, user-centric learning focuses on relevance, personalization, and timeliness.

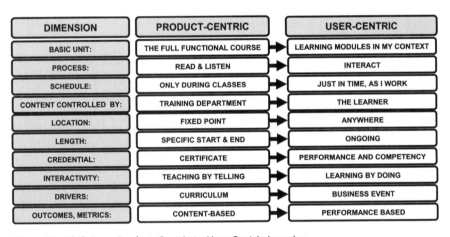

DIMENSION	PRODUCT-CENTRIC	USER-CENTRIC
BASIC UNIT:	THE FULL FUNCTIONAL COURSE	LEARNING MODULES IN MY CONTEXT
PROCESS:	READ & LISTEN	INTERACT
SCHEDULE:	ONLY DURING CLASSES	JUST IN TIME, AS I WORK
CONTENT CONTROLLED BY:	TRAINING DEPARTMENT	THE LEARNER
LOCATION:	FIXED POINT	ANYWHERE
LENGTH:	SPECIFIC START & END	ONGOING
CREDENTIAL:	CERTIFICATE	PERFORMANCE AND COMPETENCY
INTERACTIVITY:	TEACHING BY TELLING	LEARNING BY DOING
DRIVERS:	CURRICULUM	BUSINESS EVENT
OUTCOMES, METRICS:	CONTENT-BASED	PERFORMANCE BASED

Figure 8.9 Shift From Product-Centric to User-Centric Learning

Performance is the measure and the means of learning. Performance is facilitated through technology (such as simulations) that lets us participate fully in an experience without risk. Performance-based learning, or user-centric learning is the result of a transition from functional thinking to integrated process thinking. As Figure 8.9 suggests, this shift will need to be assisted by technological and human coaches providing the low-level and high-level support.

8.5.3 Functional or Cross-Functional Training?

The concept of user-centric learning immediately leads to consideration of the pros and cons of functional and cross-functional training. Within a functional approach, we focus on in-depth knowledge of a subject. A functional approach is aimed at describing every possible option into detail. Most of the time, interdependencies with other elements are not taken into account. In short, functional courses are dense in content are not related to a specific context. An example of functional courses is a course for the implementation team members, as they need to be aware of all the possibilities of the system.

On the other hand, the cross-functional approach is aimed at describing activities that need to be mastered. The starting point here is the specific context in which the activities need to take place. The disadvantage of this approach is that multiple functional elements overlap and thus need to be re-examined repeatedly. In an environment of integrated processes, the context of use prevails over the in-depth content of a course. Cross-functionality of learning objects is therefore a basic principle throughout the entire learning stream.

8.5.4 Learning Objects

To make the cross-functional approach manageable in practice, you will need to work with modular building blocks referred to in Chapter 5. We call them *learning objects*. They will return in multiple cross-functional courses. Learning objects are stored in a catalog. To that purpose you may consider using SAP Solution Manager as a storage catalogue. The catalogue then serves as a container of buildings blocks from which different courses are assembled.

Figure 8.10 shows that in practice this comes down to maintaining learning objects as separate documents that are recycled into multiple courses.

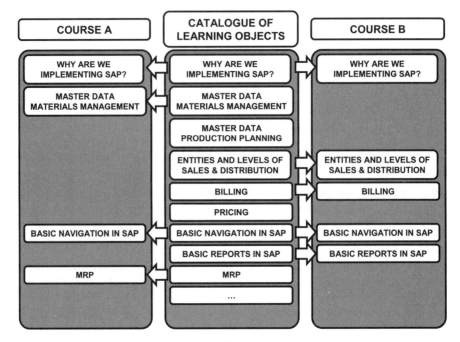

Figure 8.10 Learning Objects Recycled Into Different Courses

8.5.5 Scan Competence of Implementation Team

Earlier, we stated that the targets of the change during program initiation are the sponsors. The next target in line is the implementation team itself.

In Chapter 4, we noted that according to the principle of requisite variety, the complexity of a team should reflect the complexity of the organization it has to operate in, just like a chameleon with the surrounding terrain. As a result you will end up with quite a colorful bunch of people who—at first sight—have nothing in common with each other.

The first reflex of each responsible program manager is to send his team right off to functional (i.e., in depth) SAP courses, each for his or her part of the business they represent. That is an excellent reflex, but it is not sufficient.

Taking into account that these people will be the ambassadors of change for the organization and that their success largely depends on their ability to work as a team, a preliminary competence assessment will do no harm.

Teamwork will imply that members take up one or more additional informal roles. Therefore it pays to know where the strengths and weaknesses of each team member lie.

8.5.6 Train Implementation Team

The skills assessment will give you an indication of which points of development need to be monitored during the program lifecycle. As a result, not only will SAP courses for the business people of the team be necessary, but other initiatives will be as well. These might include corporate courses for the non-business people of the team, as well as the external resources of the team.

In a later stage, when the team is in a first "storming" phase, team building activities—if they are well prepared—can leverage a storming group into a norming team.

8.6 The Performance Management Stream in this Phase

In the program setup phase, performance management focuses on putting together a strategy map.

As defined by Kaplan and Norton (2000), a strategy map is a visual representation of the strategy. It answers the questions, "What are a business's strategic objectives?" and "How do they integrate and combine to create future value for shareholders, customers and employees?". Just as income statements and balance sheets provide a standardized way to communicate a financial plan, so strategy maps are convenient conventions for communicating strategic plans. In simple terms, the strategy map depicts business objectives across all the perspectives associated with measurements of an organization's performance: financial, customer, internal performance, and learning (as we mentioned higher on: learning links strategy to performance).

As illustrated in Figure 8.11, the financial and customer perspectives state the outcomes of the strategy: achieving the appropriate balance between benefits for the organization, on the one hand, and meeting targeted customer value propositions on the other. These outcomes, in turn, are driven by internal performance and all the elements that sustain organizational learning and growth. Once the strategic objectives are validated by the organization, we can define *the key performance indicators* (KPIs) required to measure execution. In this way, strategy mapping becomes the way to map the path to the future.

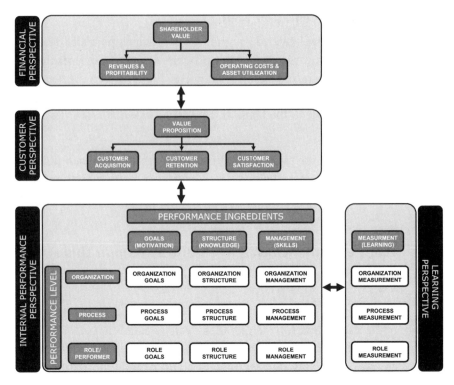

Figure 8.11 Generic Strategy Map
(based on Rummler & Brache, 1995 and Kaplan & Norton, 2000)

Strategy mapping is an activity that may require quite some professional facilitation. In return, it drives strategy execution and measurement because of the following reasons:

▸ Objectives on the map define the highest level of outcomes and drivers that management needs to monitor and review.

▸ Objectives on the map point directly at the processes, sub-processes, and activities that are the priorities for achieving effective change in performance.

▸ Ongoing dialog is generated around the cause-and-effect relationships among objectives, which in makes sure that strategy evolves and matures with the organization.

8.7   Moments of Truth

We find the following moments of truth in the program-setup phase. Let's review these together in the subsections that follow.

8.7.1   Negotiate the Program Charter as a Service Level Agreement

As mentioned earlier, the program charter needs to be considered as the SLA of the transition phase. According to Karten (2002), an SLA is a negotiated agreement designed to create a common understanding about services, priorities, and responsibilities. It is not a quick fix for a troubled relationship. Instead, you should consider it as the following:

▸ **A Communications Tool**
The value of an agreement is in the process of establishing it.

▸ **A Conflict-Prevention Tool**
An agreement helps to avoid disputes by providing a shared understanding of needs and priorities.

▸ **A Living Document**
On a predetermined frequency, the parties to the SLA review the agreement to assess service adequacy and negotiate adjustments.

▸ **A Shared Basis for Evaluating Service Effectiveness**
An SLA ensures that both parties use the same criteria to evaluate service quality.

8.7.2   Signing the Program Charter

The signing of the program charter by the members of the steering committee (including the program owner and the program manager) conveys official confirmation that the organization will implement SAP and the underlying benefits.

The program charter triggers the commitment of the organization to make the change happen. That is why it is important to not lose momentum by taking too much time to finish writing the program charter. Completing the program charter is a high-priority activity.

8.7.3 Installation of the Program

Until the program is installed, the real work can't start. All aspects must be in place in the appropriate way. This creates the environment for achieving the change desired. This specific moment of truth will have delayed effects over time. As mentioned earlier, the company might have difficulties in accepting the program management environment, depending on its maturity.

8.7.4 Having Process Owners in Place

This is a real milestone if your organization is not used to process-oriented thinking. Not having process owners in place reduces the probability for a successful SAP implementation and definitely for the full realization of the benefits that the organization wants to achieve.

8.7.5 Include a Glossary

By all means you should include a glossary in the business case, the feasibility study, and the program charter. One of the biggest sources of misunderstanding between implementation teams and stakeholders is that they define key terminology differently, which leads to conflicts at the moment of delivery. Even members of the same team often interpret terms differently.

Because of the high potential for misinterpretation, the process of developing a glossary is an immensely valuable effort (Karten, 2002). In working together to create it, you reveal and resolve differences in expectations. The result is a shared vocabulary that reduces the odds of future misunderstandings.

The glossary also includes the very terminology: "Business Case," "Feasibility Study," and "Program Charter" to ensure that there is a basic level of agreement about the agreement. Until you do, you will have trouble keeping the validation radar under control.

8.8 Deliverables

The deliverables of the program setup phase are as follows:

► Program charter
► Strategy map
► A program fully prepared to start the implementation of SAP:

- Resources available
- Budget available
- Infrastructure in place
- Ways of working and procedures installed
- Project portfolio

Figure 8.12 illustrates how the deliverables of this phase relate to each other and how they relate to the deliverables of the previous phase.

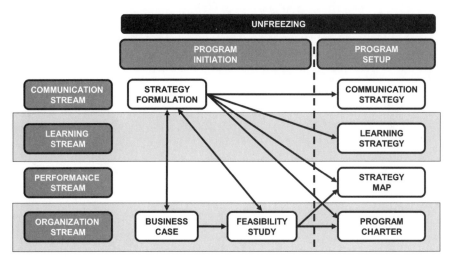

Figure 8.12 Deliverables of Program Initiation and Program Setup

8.9 Conclusion

The activities that happen in the program-setup phase are mainly those that visually unfreeze the organization to prepare it for the change to come. In this phase, the whole organization will feel that something is happening and that things will change.

Many of the activities in this phase are of a strategic importance to the program, as they set the basis for the further execution of the SAP implementation.

In Chapter 9, we cover the design phase of the SAP implementation program. From an organizational change point of view, this means entering into the changing state as you start to model the future for your organization.

PART III
Changing

The design phase is one of the most critical phases in the whole change process. This is where the future organization is designed, including the processes and the way that SAP must support these processes. The way you approach the design phase can greatly influence the SAP implementation's success. The user acceptance at the time of going live is almost one-to-one related to the choices you make in this phase.

9   Design

9.1   Phase-Specific Characteristics and Needs

This section explains how you should use and read the soft-stuff and hard-stuff radars, taking into account the specific characteristics and needs of the design phase.

9.1.1   Soft-Stuff Radar

Note how the soft-stuff radar shows only some minor differences compared to the previous phase. Let's take a more detailed look at these now.

▶ **Learning Relationship Radar**
This radar shows no changes compared to the program setup phase. You are still in a selling mode, trying to convince the stakeholders to take ownership. For the same reason, the permission-level meter indicates that—even though you have no relationship with the stakeholders—your message and the existence of your team are validated by the organization.

▶ **Agent Radar**
The design phase is the phase where a lot of infantry troops enter the field to take over from the commandos. Most often, these are external service providers who are there for a limited period "to get things done" according to the commandos' plan. As the implementation team grows rapidly, with people joining from different backgrounds, there is still no common language, and this problem quickly surfaces at the moment that the first deliverables need to be produced. Misinterpretations lead to conflicts, and

through these conflicts—big and small—people start to redefine their roles and identities within the team. This is the storming phase.

▶ **Target Radar**

You still will have trouble waking up the majority of the pragmatists and the conservatives. In their opinion, you have nothing concrete to offer them, and until you do they see no need for questioning the status quo. Hence, the only ambassadors of change you can count on to mobilize the organization are the sponsors. As time passes, your challenge is to keep them interested and pulling the cart forward.

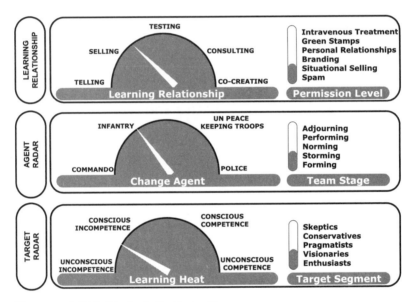

Figure 9.1 Soft-Stuff Radar in the Design Phase

9.1.2 Hard-Stuff Radar

The hard-stuff radar (see Figure 9.2) should not show any peaks or reach alarming levels during the design phase:

▶ **Validation Radar**

In the design phase, many people struggle with the fact that everything still seems abstract without an actual system in place. On the other hand, the design must be concrete enough that the system can be built. As a result, discussions on the design tend to take more time than planned. Certain aspects are often repeatedly discussed even though they were supposed to be finished. In some cases, you have to allow this as you really need people to be engaged. Aiming for your validated deliverables in time but with the appropriate quality requires special attention in this phase. In short, the indications on this radar should not be different from those on the previous phase.

▶ **Supply and Demand Radar**
The design phase will require the middle management and future key-users to relate to an imaginary future. During the design workshops, they should be thinking 100 % about the future, but when the workshops are over they must return to the day-to-day reality and catch up with "lost time." For that reason, you should carefully plan workshops well in advance and keep close contact with line managers to make sure that involvement of their lieutenants in the design phase is guaranteed. You should aim for immediate availability of the business participants and have the courtesy to invite them way in advance. With regards to the workload balance, you will be running on full capacity.

▶ **Budget Radar**
Make sure that your real costs incurred are within budget. If at this stage you are using any buffer, a warning flag should go up immediately. This does not mean that there are no budget discussions taking place. At the end of the design phase, the budget for the rest of the program must be reconfirmed.

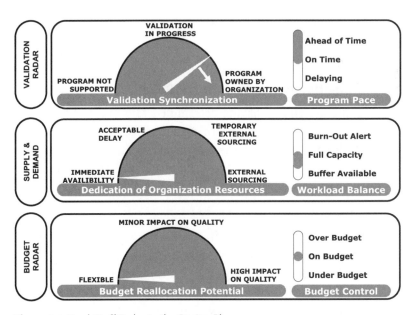

Figure 9.2 Hard-Stuff Radar in the Design Phase

9.2   What Happens at the Level of the Program?

In the design phase, it is important that time frame, budget, and achievability of the benefits are reconfirmed before you start to do anything else.

9.2.1   Reconfirmation of Budget

By the end of this phase, knowing the design in detail, you will be able to better understand the budget requirements for the remaining of the program. You might find out that the budget that was initially defined is far from sufficient. That fact might prompt the organization to question the continuation of the program.

The program manager must explicitly reconfirm the initial budget to the steering committee or present the recalculated one.

9.2.2   Reconfirmation of Time Frame

The same goes for the time frame. You might find out that the time frame for building the prototype was underestimated, based on the design that has already has been approved.

It is important that such issues not be kept hidden but discussed outright to avoid running into delays during the remaining of the program. That would trigger frustration, and would damage the program quality.

9.2.3   Reconfirmation of Achievability of Benefits

Having finished the design and having determined KPIs and future thresholds, the organization must also reconfirm its belief in the achievability of the benefits. If everyone doesn't share that belief, you need to discuss the business case again. As soon as you start to monitor realization of the program benefits, you will gain clarity about the achievability of the benefits.

9.2.4   The Role of Stream Manager

As mentioned in Chapter 8, a stream manager could also be called the *delivery manager*. This is the person making sure that the design deliverables are produced in time and with the right quality. With the help of the program manager, the stream manager identifies which projects are required to produce the total design of the future organization, including its ways of working, roles, and responsibilities.

We can now discuss the organization stream during this particular phase.

9.3   The Organization Stream in this Phase

We'll now share pragmatic, proven ideas on how to approach the organizational stream in order to make your SAP implementation work. These range from design principles to team characteristics.

9.3.1   First Reorganize, Then Implement

As discussed in Chapter 1, implementing SAP requires you to work differently, and most often requires you to reorganize. Many organizations execute the reorganization at the same time as going live with SAP. We discourage this for the following reasons:

▸ People can only accept so much change in a given time. Some people can take big leaps, and others need to be spoon-fed. Remember that a chain is only as strong as its weakest link.

▸ If people need to move to another function in order for SAP to work, you should make those moves as far in advance as you possibly can. Only when people are stabilized in their new positions and departments are running in their new configurations for some time will they be able to accommodate the next wave of change: a new system.

▸ You need real feedback from committed people during user-acceptance testing. Think about the commitment of people who need to test a functionality for which they will not be responsible tomorrow, or for which they currently lack the practical experience. To obtain realistic feedback during user-acceptance testing, people need to be able to focus on what is important from their new point of view.

▸ People absorb more change when they have a need to learn. As long as they are working in their old functions, they will not really experience a learning need. In their new roles, people will come to the training with specific needs on the know-how level, and as a result they will better absorb what is taught.

9.3.2   Mass Participation or Sample Representation?

There are basically two ways of getting the design of a new organization together:

▶ **Mass Participation**

In this approach, you mobilize a huge number of people within the organization to create the design together.

▶ **Sample Representation**

In this approach, you carefully select a sample of people to do the dirty work, after which the deliverables are validated by a larger group of people.

Reasons to apply the mass participation approach are as follows:

▶ To gather as much information as possible on the current ways of working and on future requirements.

▶ To get buy-in from as many people as possible from the start.

In our experience, there also are significant disadvantages to this approach, including the following:

▶ Mobilizing a large number of people burdens the organization from an operational point of view.

▶ It is difficult to come to an overall accepted outcome when the groups are too big.

▶ Many people are not eager to speak up in large groups, even with the proper facilitation techniques.

The sample representation method works as follows:

▶ You select a number of people who represent the organization, and they put together the design.

▶ The outcome is validated within the organization by presenting it to larger groups.

▶ Comments from the validation workshop are consolidated and are used to further improve the first draft of the design.

▶ The final design is developed by the initial group.

We believe that the sample representation method is much more effective, because of the following reasons:

▶ A shorter timeframe is required.

▶ By having the results validated by a larger group of people, buy-in is obtained much more efficiently.

9.3.3 Restrict Pilot VIP Treatment

There should be no privileges for the pilot project. We often see that the area chosen as the pilot for an SAP implementation is more thoroughly represented in the design than is the rest of the organization. There's no good reason for this when you are implementing a global SAP with standardized, globally applied ways of working.

Finding a pilot is not easy, and you may encounter resistance. For example, an entity may agree to serve as the pilot in exchange for extended participation. The underlying objective here is to ensure that specific requirements are included in the global design. Be wary of people eager to convince you that their requirements are global requirements.

That is why we recommend that the pilot be chosen as one of the first activities of the build phase. We will return to this topic later. As explained in Chapter 4, this is one of those activities you will spend 5 to 10 percent of your time on, although they actually belong to the next phase.

9.3.4 Workable Pieces

Putting together the design of the future organization, its future ways of working, and the future roles and responsibilities represents a huge amount of work. So you will have no other choice than to split up the work.

Be aware that the design of the processes does not occur only at a high level. You will need to go to the operational level of describing the process. If you make an inventory of all the processes and sub-processes, you might be surprised to find out how many there are. There will be hundreds. Let's look at some examples:

▶ The sales-to-order process breaks down into the following:
  ▷ Contacting prospect or customer
  ▷ Gathering customer-relevant information
  ▷ Finding out the needs
  ▷ Making a proposal
▶ The asset-management process includes the following:
  ▷ Make-or-buy decision
  ▷ Purchasing of asset
  ▷ Revaluation

▸ Depreciation

▸ Write-off

The question arises of how to split up the work. As mentioned earlier, one of the biggest challenges in changing your organization when implementing SAP is that you have to shift from functional thinking to process thinking. This is absolutely true. On the other hand, SAP works according to modules that are split up functionally: Financials (FI), Controlling (CO), Production Planning (PP), Sales and Distribution (SD), Human Resources (HR), Materials Management (MM), etc.

In our opinion, the best way to split up the work is to assign it to functional domains. In this way, you split up the design of the organization, the processes, the roles, and the responsibilities into functional areas such as finance, sales, HR, and production. The most coherent approach is to start at the top and drill down through the details of each process. During the whole design process, the integration manager has an important role in making sure that processes are fluidly running across all functional domains in the organization.

9.3.5 Process Design Principles

When designing the processes, you need to apply the principles covered in the subsections that follow.

Focus on the Future State First

The classic way to start the design of processes is by mapping the current state (as is) before designing the future state. If you do this, two negative things happen:

▸ **Hanging on to Status Quo**
By mapping the current state, we fill up our minds with all the stuff that is important now. Since there is no reference point to map the current state against, this leads to a document describing why it makes no sense to change.

▸ **Wrong Anchor Points**
At the point of the gap analysis, you will find that some things you highlighted as important in the current process are obsolete, and that other issues that are important for closing the gap have been overlooked. You need to have a clear view of the future state to know what you need to

assess in the current state. Figure 9.3 illustrates the differences between the traditional and the future-focused approaches.

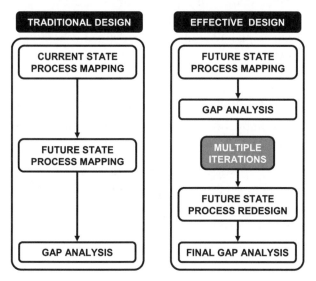

Figure 9.3 Traditional Design Vs. Effective Design

Starting off with the design of the future processes, you can assess the current state more accurately because you know exactly what to look for and which aspects to pay attention to. True, you may find yourself redesigning the future state after the first gap analysis, and you may need multiple iterations to arrive at the final gap analysis, but anything is better than a current state mapping without a point of reference.

Design Vis a Vis SAP

The benefits should be the main drivers indicating how you need to work or what you need to change. After all, SAP is a configurable system that is to a certain level adaptable to your needs. Whenever you come to a point at which SAP would not support the design that you are putting together, you have to think over the design. Changing SAP is the most common mistake that is made.

Many organizations vow that they are not going to change SAP, but end up doing so anyway. It is all about discipline. Therefore, changing standard SAP should be one of those decisions that is made only by the steering committee.

197

As a consequence, when putting together the design, you have to involve SAP experts who have enough seniority, maturity, and experience to immediately evaluate whether standard SAP can support your design. They need the ability and the knowledge to help you identify alternative ways of working that will be both efficient enough to realize the predefined benefits and that will be supported by SAP.

Process Improvement Vs. Process Redesign

Process improvement is about improving the processes as they are today to make them more efficient. Process redesign is about putting together your future processes from scratch.

An SAP implementation involves process redesign, and that is something you have to be very aware of. Upgrades are an exception to that rule, as they are more likely to accompany process improvement.

9.3.6 Drawing up the Processes

Often people start by listing all the processes and sub-processes that they need to design. However, when you evaluate the end result of such an exercise, you soon find out that the list is both incomplete and based on the processes currently in place in the organization. When designing the processes, you need to make sure that:

▶ All affected stakeholders are represented.

▶ Relationships between different processes and sub-processes are clear.

▶ The level of detail is accurate enough to make everybody understand what the process aims to accomplish.

Swim Lanes

It is up to the process owners to draw up the high-level process maps. These maps can be used as a basis to drill down the processes into the sub-processes. Here are some other tips:

▶ To draw the processes, use swim-lane templates, specifying in which functional department the process step is taken. This way you visualize connection points between departments. Figure 9.4 provides you with an example.

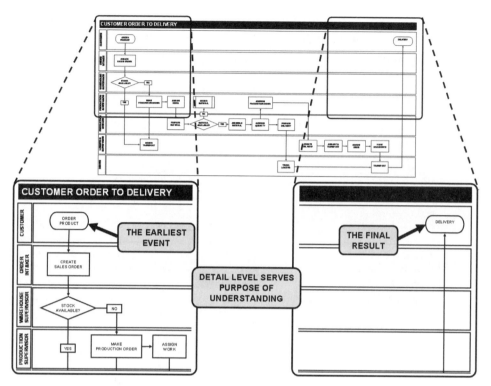

Figure 9.4 Swim-Lane Process Mapping Example

▶ Describe input and output per (sub) process so the added value of the process becomes clear. Highlight other processes from which input is received and processes to which output is delivered. Keep the following in mind:

▶ If you can't measure a process, you can't manage it. Therefore you should define KPIs for all processes.

▶ Ask yourself how the process that you are drawing up contributes to the realization of the corporate goals. If the answer is "no idea," the process is most probably redundant. If it is redundant, eliminate it.

▶ Make a distinction between primary processes (processes that connect the organization with the external world) and secondary processes (internal processes).

▶ Use facilitated workshop methods, making sure you have an experienced facilitator.

▸ Make sure that the functional leads and the integration manager are actively involved in this exercise.

▸ When the process design in each functional domain is finished, the functional leads, the process owner, and the integration manager consolidate the outcome in an overall picture.

There are some pitfalls you should be aware of as well. These are seen in Figure 9.5.

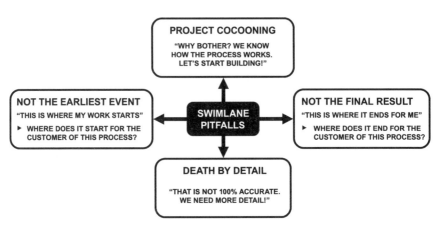

Figure 9.5 Swim Lane Pitfalls

Event-Driven Process Chains

In SAP Solution Manager, the ARIS framework is offered to help you with the design of the processes. The ARIS framework refers to what is called *event-driven process chains*.

The main elements of event-driven process chains are functions and events. Functions are triggered by events and functions produce events. Event-driven process chains can be hierarchically structured, which enables the following:

▸ Better understanding of the total setup and functioning of the processes.

▸ Better use in defining the information systems.

▸ Levels of detail and the complexity that can be applied in accordance to the program purpose.

▸ Inclusion of probabilities and resource capabilities that will enable simulation of the processes.

▸ Facilitated workflow design because people and roles can be assigned.

9.3.7   Write Procedures

For each process step, a procedure must be written. The procedure includes the following:

▶ Detailed description of the actions that happen in that process step.

▶ Responsible person.

▶ Input required.

▶ Output to be delivered.

Optionally, the SAP transaction codes or the menu path to access the respective transaction in SAP. It can also specify which fields are mandatory.

You must take time at this point to identify the differences between the current ways of working, roles, and responsibilities and the future ones. This will allow you to link functional role descriptions (owned by HR) and security profiles (owned by the implementation team).

9.3.8   Design Reports

Special attention must be paid to the design of reports. A common mistake is to request the currently available reports for future use, many times even in the same format containing exactly the same information, even if some of the contents are never looked at.

You should jump in immediately when you see this happening. At all costs, you should prevent the status quo from determining the future reports. In this respect we make following recommendations:

▶ Start from scratch.

▶ Design in the functions of the benefits.

▶ Design in the functions of the future ways of working.

▶ Involve middle management in the design workshops.

9.3.9   Authorization Design

We mention the design of the security profiles (access to the system and its functionality) because this is much more important than people often think. Security profiles must be set up in accordance with the newly designed functions, roles, and responsibilities. If the authorization design does not match those factors, you will find that people can't perform the jobs they are expected to do.

It is not only important to think about the setup of the authorization, but also about the process of identifying and approving and assigning them. In addition, regulatory imperatives such as Sarbanes-Oxley, BASEL II, and FDA Part 11 may require you to redesign your security setup.

9.3.10 Validate the Design

The validation of the designed processes is a precise ritual. Applying the sample representation design method that we mentioned earlier, there are five steps to take into account:

1. **Validation of the Design by the Operational Board**
   First, you must present the design to the operational board. Its sign-off confirms that the design is in sync with the benefits that your organization wants to achieve. If certain elements trigger questions about the fit with the strategy or the vision, these must be presented to the steering committee, which means troublesome scheduling and risk of delays because of unavailability of executive management. Therefore, it is best to tentatively schedule a session with the steering committee and the operational board in advance.

2. **Validation of the Design by User Groups**
   Present your design to a number of representative user groups, key users, middle management, and senior management. Make sure it is not only a presentation, but a workshop format that enables open discussion and voting on important elements. Be open for the feedback that you get, and make sure the atmosphere is constructive. Resist the temptation to make any promises about requested changes. Use the fact that the operational board has signed off on the design to reinforce the idea that the change requests that are raised must be relevant.

3. **Fine-Tuning of the Design**
   Document all changes in detail (description, workload, impact, etc.) and present them to the operational board. The board has to validate each individual change request and prioritize them. Then, you should rework the design in function of the approved change requests. However, if one of the change requests triggers a scope change, you need to get confirmation from the steering committee. Communicate properly to the organization which change requests have been accepted and rejected, also explaining the reasons why.

4. **Confirmation of the Design by User Groups**
Once the design has been fine-tuned with the change requests, you have to distribute it again. At this point it is not necessary to gather the user groups physically as in the second step. However, the representative of each user group must formally confirm the design.

5. **Confirmation of the Design by the Steering Committee**
Once the organization has confirmed the design, it must be presented to the steering committee. The committee has to formally sign off on the design and evaluate how it fits with the vision and strategy of the program.

9.3.11 Career Perspectives

While recruiting people from your organization, you will need to put this recruitment in a career perspective; otherwise you may be putting employees' long-term commitment at risk. With the help of HR, there are two elements you should focus on:

▶ **Motivation**
We have seen a lot of people on SAP programs who have been sent to the SAP program as if it were a dead-end street. These people show a low level of motivation and commitment. Nevertheless, you are putting the future of your organization into their hands. People should be motivated to join the SAP program by showing them how it accelerates their careers. Of course, this all depends on how well people take responsibility for the roles they are assigned, but proactive people with good career potential always benefit from taking part in an SAP program.

▶ **Retention**
You need to ensure that the resources of your organization stay with the program until the end. Therefore, it is important to offer people some career goal they will be able to pursue as a result of successfully participating to the program.

9.4 The Communication Stream in this Phase

If you want to communicate effectively, you need to know who you want to reach, how to reach them, at which time, and with which contents. This section goes into the details of these issues.

9.4.1 Communication Channel Inventory

One of the first things you need to do as you get to know the organization is to make an inventory of its communication habits. The subsections that follow give you a better and more detailed idea of what is involved.

Listing the Channels

When you list all the communication channels, you can start with common media (mail, phone, etc.). Next, you should also look at contact moments of each stakeholder (team meetings, management meetings, training, etc.). Finally, you should look beyond "push" channels to include "pull" channels (i.e., channels where people come to pull out what is useful to them). These include knowledge portals on the intranet and help files.

Here are some useful questions that can help to investigate the effectiveness of the existing communication channels:

▶ Questions regarding formal communication channels are listed here:

  ▷ How quickly and how frequently are official decisions communicated?

  ▷ Which stakeholders are reached by each channel?

  ▷ How able and effective is the existing communications staff; e. g., is there a dedicated person or a department for internal and external communication?

  ▷ How does the organization gather feedback on its communications?

  ▷ How familiar is the organization with advanced communications technology and what is the current level of interaction on those media?

▶ Questions regarding informal communication channels are as follows:

  ▷ Who are the authority figures?

  ▷ Who are the opinion leaders?

  ▷ What are the attitudes about sharing information?

Remember that this step is not just about listing the channels, but is also about the communication habits.

The Stakeholder Channel Matrix

The second step is to group all of the previously mentioned channels and habits into three clusters:

▶ Formal communication channels.

▶ Program-specific communication channels.

▶ Informal communication channels.

In the stakeholder channel matrix, you list all the stakeholders in rows and all the channels in columns. As illustrated with the sample in Figure 9.6, you need to indicate which channel is a primary channel, which ones are additional, and which ones are not applicable to reaching that specific stakeholder.

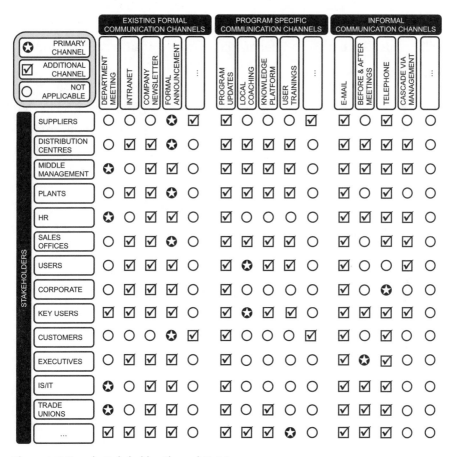

Figure 9.6 Sample Stakeholder Channel Matrix

Then it is time for a first assessment. Horizontally, you will see the level of repetition (i.e., reaching the stakeholder over multiple channels). Each stakeholder should be reached at least once via a formal channel, at least once via a program specific channel, and at least once informally.

You should compare the level of repetition to the way you positioned the stakeholder during the stakeholder analysis (see Figure 7.3 in Chapter 7). If a stakeholder belongs to the upper right-hand quadrant ("involve them extensively"), the level of repetition should be as high as it can get.

Vertically, you can see how important a certain communication channel is and whether it is worth an extra investment of time and money. If a certain channel happens to be the primary channel for many stakeholders, you should consider it as a strategic asset of your program.

9.4.2 Plan and Prepare Content

Follow this advice when developing the substance of any communication:

▶ **Consider the Receiver**
You should be sensitive to the characteristics and attitudes of your audience. Each stakeholder is different, although their differences may be subtle. As each stakeholder has his or her own set of "what's-in-it-for-me's" (WIIFM), a single message intended for multiple audiences may require rewriting for each. According to Jensen (2003) this implies that the content for each stakeholder complies with the acronym CLEAR:

  ▷ **Connected:** How is this relevant to what I do?

  ▷ **List next steps:** What, specifically, should I do?

  ▷ **Expectations:** What does success look like? (What does failure look like?)

  ▷ **Ability:** How I will get things done: Tools and support?

  ▷ **Return:** My WIIFM.

We recommend using the CLEAR model as a checklist each time you develop the content of a communication.

▶ **Historical Background**
The best starting point is the frame of reference of the stakeholder you are addressing. Familiarize yourself with past events and previous communications to each stakeholder. The receiver's frame of reference should determine what your message contains and how you construct it.

▶ **Simple Separated Messages**
You should try to divide complex messages into separate parts and consider sending them as separate messages. If you deliver the parts together, be sure to clearly explain the relationship between the parts.

▶ **Local Vocabulary**

Use terminology that the local audience understands, such as formally defined and recognized words with unambiguous meanings. This will require you to get out of the project cocoon and discover how much specific jargon you have been producing during the program. Avoid using this jargon. Instead, try to translate vision and branding into the local language. You can dramatically improve your chances for success by involving local key persons.

▶ **Make it Appealing for Every Receiver**

This may be the very last thing on your mind, but you should be aware that nicely formatted messages have a better chance of being read than plain text. You are addressing a big audience, which means different kinds of people. Most of them are visual people, others are auditory, kinesthetic, or a combination of these three. Table 9.1 illustrates the difference between these three types.

Visual People	Auditory People	Kinesthetic People
▶ React most strongly to visual stimuli.	▶ Experience the world through their ears and dialogue.	▶ Experience things physically and emotionally.
▶ React best when they can see or visualize their information.	▶ Taking their cues from sounds.	▶ Appreciate using touch, movement, and space.
▶ Relate most effectively to written information, symbols, notes, diagrams, and pictures.	▶ Information becomes more meaningful for them when it is spoken out loud.	▶ Learning most often occurs through imitation and practice.
▶ Typically they will be unhappy with a presentation where they are unable to take detailed notes. To some extent, information does not exist for a visual learner unless it has been written down.	▶ They will tend to listen to a lecture, and then take notes afterwards, or rely on printed notes.	▶ Impacted effectively through touch, and movement, and space, and learn skills by imitation and practice.
	▶ Often information written down will have little meaning until it has been heard. It may help auditory learners to read written information out loud.	▶ Predominantly kinesthetic learners can appear slow, in that information is normally not presented in a style that suits their learning methods.

Table 9.1 Three Types of Audiences

9.4.3 Prepare Communication Plan

A solid communication plan is one that is based on clear principles, which are translated into concrete procedures and actions.

Define Communication Principles

You should start by defining communication principles and have the majority of your team subscribe to them. It will make life so much easier when the going gets tough. Examples of generally accepted communication principles include the following:

▸ Repetition of important messages increases the chance that everyone will at least receive the message once. This is often challenging for executives, as they easily get bored.

▸ Redundancy in communication channels is more challenging than repetition. Redundancy is communicating the same message in different ways.

▸ Face-to-face communication is preferable.

▸ Involve line managers as communication agents.

▸ Build and re-use the know-why, since awareness of the know-why is the starting point to build the frame of reference for every communication. The point here is to make a conscious use of branding, an idea we return to later in this chapter.

▸ Plan on frequently discussing the future.

▸ Listen proactively (which means: ask explicitly for input, feedback, and second opinions).

Guidelines and Procedures

The next step of communication planning is to determine guidelines and procedures for the execution of each communication based on the communication principles.

▸ Examples of guidelines at a more detailed level are as follows:

  ▸ Who composes the messages

  ▸ How you obtain the feedback

  ▸ How message senders prepare for distribution.

  ▸ The frequency of communications "to all"

  ▸ A military-style and centralized approach for communication and issues-handling, both one month before and one month after the go-live.

▸ Consider taking extra precautions when sending critical messages. For instance, communicating to external stakeholders is often necessary when the business change is expected to build market share, improve customer service, or enhance company image. Asking for a formal review by the steering committee may be necessary in such cases where inaccurate or misleading messages can damage the business.

▶ If possible, test each communication by locating one or more test receivers who are close to the demographic target audience. Possible questions to be answered include the following:

  ▷ Is the communication stated in terms the stakeholder understands?

  ▷ Is there more content than needed?

  ▷ Is the intent of the message adequately communicated?

  ▷ Is the chosen vehicle appropriate?

  ▷ Are there any technical errors?

▶ Consider each individual team member (including external consultants and key users) as an ambassador of the program and provide them basic guidelines for their daily communication. The checklist in Figure 9.7 can give team members some guidance for their communication.

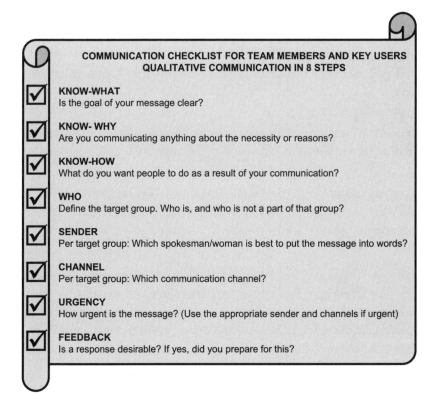

COMMUNICATION CHECKLIST FOR TEAM MEMBERS AND KEY USERS
QUALITATIVE COMMUNICATION IN 8 STEPS

☑ **KNOW-WHAT**
Is the goal of your message clear?

☑ **KNOW- WHY**
Are you communicating anything about the necessity or reasons?

☑ **KNOW-HOW**
What do you want people to do as a result of your communication?

☑ **WHO**
Define the target group. Who is, and who is not a part of that group?

☑ **SENDER**
Per target group: Which spokesman/woman is best to put the message into words?

☑ **CHANNEL**
Per target group: Which communication channel?

☑ **URGENCY**
How urgent is the message? (Use the appropriate sender and channels if urgent)

☑ **FEEDBACK**
Is a response desirable? If yes, did you prepare for this?

Figure 9.7 Communication Checklist for Team Members and Key Users

9.4.4 Branding

When we addressed culture and the anatomy of culture in earlier chapters, we introduced the concept of *branding*. Now we explain how it can help you with organizational change during an SAP implementation.

What is Branding?

A brand is the image of the program you want to create in the mind of the stakeholders. It is your promise to deliver the outcomes and benefits to the stakeholders. The best brands imply a warranty of quality. A brand can deliver up to four levels of meaning (Kotler et al., 2005):

▶ **Attributes**
A brand first brings to mind certain product attributes. For example, your program's name may suggest such attributes as standardized processes, common data, better customer service, and so on. The program may use one or more of these attributes in its name and catchphrase.

▶ **Individual Benefits**
Stakeholders are not interested in individual attributes. They want benefits. Therefore attributes must be translated into functional and emotional benefits. The attribute "standardized" could represent the functional benefit: "It will reduce the complexity, and lead times will consequently be reduced."

▶ **Values**
A brand also says something about the stakeholders' values. This is the translation into the WIIFM.

▶ **Personality**
A brand should project a personality. Motivation researchers sometime ask: "If this brand were a person, what kind of person would it be?" A brand attracts people whose actual or desired self-images match the brand's image.

The challenge of branding is to develop a deep set of meanings for the brand. The most lasting meanings of a brand are its values and personality. They define the brand's essence. The brand name, logo design, and brand identity are all a big part of branding because the image, colors, slogan, and so on, must reflect the vision of the program. The brand should also have emotional content that people can aspire to and identify with.

How Branding Works

All of the above factors are necessary, but not sufficient. In the context of SAP implementations, your purpose is to create a new culture, and this requires trust and community building. Let's take a look at this next:

▸ **Trust**
Through branding, the implementation team opens an "emotional bank account" (Covey, 1990) for each stakeholder. The account status displays the value of the relationship between the team and the stakeholder. Trust is the currency of this bank account. As with a financial bank account, deposits and withdrawals are made that affect the value of the relationship. If you stick to your promises, people will make deposits of trust, and the value of your brand will grow. When you make mistakes, the "emotional reserves" will compensate for it, but the value of the brand will decrease.

▸ **Community Building**
If the value of the brand is high, more people will want to open an emotional bank account, because depositing trust on your brand gives high returns. That is how you create community: First you provide an image, and then you walk your talk for each individual stakeholder. Pushing an advertising campaign on stakeholders who have a negative balance in their emotional bank accounts will only create cynicism.

Why Branding is Important

There are two reasons why it is important to create an attractive brand that reflects the vision of the program:

▸ **Psychological Safety**
If a brand's trustworthiness reduces anxiety and doubt, branding creates the emotional link that is necessary for people to experience psychological safety. As mentioned in Chapter 2, people need a sense of psychological safety that it is OK to try something new and to give up something old and familiar. However, this building of trust takes time.

▸ **Reaching the Tipping Point**
Stakeholders base their ultimate trust about a brand (to support or not to support) on its clarity of purpose. To truly commit, stakeholders try to assess the authenticity with which the implementation team acts across its entire relationship network. Because that network is largely invisible to them, stakeholders use close relationships (friends, colleagues, opinion

leaders, etc.) and symbols (logo, language used, leadership declarations, physical presence, etc.) to assess the program (Ind, 2003).

9.4.5 Communication Styles of the Sender

How you deliver a message is almost as important as the message itself. The effectiveness of your communication style is related to the amount of information you transmit. You can choose from the following communication styles; some are more effective than others:

▶ **Withhold and Uphold**
Knowledge is power. Implementation teams who adopt this style will only release information when they are forced to do so. Giving little information results in reduced effectiveness (confusion, disorientation, cynicism, etc.).

▶ **Identify and Reply**
This is what happens in the absence of an overall communication strategy. Team members provide information at a personal level; addressing each staff member within his/her personal frame of reference. This is more effective than the previous style, but not always optimal. The biggest shortcoming of this style is that you have not created a general frame of reference, which leaves the door open for many deviations and exceptions. What's more, it is time-consuming and not very effective.

▶ **Underscore and Explore**
This style is optimal, because here it permits two-directional traffic within a general frame of reference. You first create the frame of reference through vision and strategy formulation and branding; and only then do you resume communication. Because you have started by staking out the playing field, it immediately becomes clear what will be given a chance and what will not. The communication that takes place thereafter is limited to this marked out playing field. This saves time and orients everyone in the same direction.

▶ **Tell and Sell**
Implementation teams with this mindset think that you can never over-communicate. Unfortunately, you can. Teams that are adopting this style have a well-cared-for presentation and layout, but no guts for interaction. They talk at people instead of having a conversation. Sending out more information than people can absorb, at a frequency that people cannot follow will turn your communication into background noise. No adjustments are made because feedback is lacking. Tell-and-sell teams have the

biggest communication budget of all, the best logo, the most appealing brand, the best catchphrases, but no interaction or participation.

► **Spray and Pray**
This style is symptomatic for teams with a lack of vision and clarity. Such teams strive to be paragons of openness, whose credo is: "We share all information with the organization, like an open book." This results in very low communication effectiveness, because too much information has the same effect as too little: confusion and disorientation.

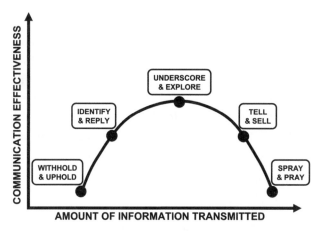

Figure 9.8 Communication Styles (based on Clampitt, et al., 2000)

The message here is that more information is not always better. Figure 9.8 illustrates that good communication is truly an exercise of balance and interaction. This can only be learned by making mistakes and continuously adjusting in a learning relationship with the stakeholders.

9.4.6 Build and Use a Stakeholder Database

This database functions just like the customer relationship management database of a marketing department. Several kinds of data are maintained in there and tagged to each individual. These include:

► Employee name and most important contact information: email address and phone number.

► Organizational entity they belong to, which:

    ► Allows you to target communication per organizational unit.

    ► Allows you to phase certain communications by grouping and excluding certain organizational units.

- Functional role, which:
    - Is the basis for the role analysis and security profiles.
    - Allows you to communicate per functional role.
- Organizational change role, which allows communication to agents, sponsors, and targets separately.
- Which groups received which communications? This allows you to track history and to occasionally report back to non-believers that you effectively communicated a certain message at a certain date, that they signed the presence list, etc.

The purpose of maintaining this information over time is to get a detailed view of an individual's track record during the organizational change. Most of all, this database will ensure that you did not forget anyone. People will not come and tell you that you forgot them in your communication. Rather, they will discover that you forgot them, be offended (as most of us would be), and be less willing to cooperate.

Once again, change is in the details. People are very sensitive with regards to being included in a communication program.

9.5   The Learning Stream in this Phase

In this phase, the learning stream focuses on designing the whole training effort, from means that are used to contents for each of the target groups. It also covers the planning of the training.

9.5.1   Differentiate Target

Identifying skill gaps and addressing these deficits in a learning plan is fairly straightforward. In terms of learning needs, you will need to tag each participant with one or more of the following labels, allowing you to better serve their training needs.

- **Transaction Users**
  These are the users in the strict sense of the word. The frontline workers, those who will do the bulk of the work in SAP. We will always refer to this group as "users."
- **Key Users**
  These members of the user community perform multiple roles at the same time and assume responsibility for the learning of their teams.

▶ **Info Users**

These are users that need to make use of SAP for reporting and management-information purposes only.

▶ **Specific Single Users**

These users that will use the system for specific narrow and well-defined tasks. Typically they will only need to be skilled in using one or two SAP transactions.

▶ **Supervising Non-Users**

You may wonder why we would bother to include this group as a participant in the training. In the aftermath of unsuccessful implementations, this group is often referred to as "the black hole of middle management," indicating that this group has not been trained to make informed decisions in a world of integrated processes.

9.5.2 Define the Blend

The magic of learning is in the right mix of human and technological learning assistance. Providing an array of learning vehicles will enable the learner to select media optimal for his or her learning style, and a mix of different learning activities is more effective than reliance on just one approach.

The optimal blend differs from one organization to another. According to Brennan (2003), the choice of learning content development and delivery methodologies is based on the following dimensions:

▶ Training Conditions:

  ▷ Is it urgent to complete the training?

  ▷ Will results be reported externally?

▶ Resource Availability:

  ▷ Do we have the subject matter experts?

  ▷ Do we have the development expertise?

  ▷ What is our budget?

  ▷ Is outsourcing the most cost-effective option?

▶ Content Characteristics:

  ▷ How valuable is the subject matter to the organization?

  ▷ Is the content informational, procedural, behavioral, or conceptual?

  ▷ How should it be reinforced? Is group interaction necessary?

▸ Will the content need to be updated frequently?

▸ How long will it take to teach this material?

▸ Target Audience:

  ▸ Do they have access to physical classrooms and/or labs?

  ▸ Do they speak the same language?

  ▸ Do they have Web access?

  ▸ Are they connected to the LAN?

  ▸ Are they refreshing existing knowledge or learning something completely new?

  ▸ How will they use what they learn?

  ▸ What is their preferred style of learning?

  ▸ How much time can we afford to train them?

  ▸ How do we motivate them?

  ▸ Are they in the same time zone?

  ▸ How closely does their learning need to be tracked and reported?

After considering these questions, you will be choosing a combination or blend of one of the types of learning shown in Table 9.2.

Delivery Method	Primary Strengths	Primary Weakness
Classroom-based instruction	Familiar, engaging, social, and formal	Expensive, passive (lectures), difficult to scale, impractical, tough to schedule, time consuming, and difficult to localize
Web-based courseware (with or without simulations)	Interactive, convenient, easy to distribute, practical for technical training, customizable, just-in-time and easy to assess performance	Can be boring, risk of learner distraction, needs localization, needs basic PC skills, and simulations are complex and expensive to develop
CD-ROM-based courseware (with or without simulations)	Interactive, convenient, portable, practical for technical training, and easy to assess performance	Costly to develop/update and distribute, boring, with risk of learner distraction

Table 9.2 Different Learning Forms (Adapted from Brennan, 2003)

Delivery Method	Primary Strengths	Primary Weakness
Live virtual classes/ Webinars	Convenient, scalable, easy to develop and deliver, interactive for small groups	Lack of interaction, too passive, risk of learner distraction, lack of infrastructure for delivery, and plug-ins
Conference calls	Convenient, scalable, and easy to develop and deliver	Background noise, too passive, lack of interaction, risk of learner distraction, and difficult to schedule
Job aids (e. g., manuals and checklists)	Portable, convenient	Difficult to update and distribute, lack of interaction and feedback, and risk of learner distraction
Electronic performance support systems (EPSSs)	Practical, timely, and engaging	Expensive to develop and impractical for certain topics
Online portals with supplemental materials	Convenient and inexpensive to maintain	Difficult to maintain neatly, lack of interaction, and not top of mind for most
Communities of practice: chat rooms and online message boards	Interactive, social, and convenient	Difficult to maintain and impractical for certain topics
Mentors (e. g., in person, over the phone, or over the Web)	Convenient and interactive	Expensive and impractical for certain topics

Table 9.2 Different Learning Forms (Adapted from Brennan, 2003) (cont.)

9.5.3 Design the Training Track

Most probably, you will lack the time to ponder what the individual training track should look like. Yet it pays to check on the individual level whether learners are addressed at more than one level of learning. These levels are illustrated in the learning pyramid shown in Figure 9.9.

The learning pyramid illustrates how much of each level of learning we remember later on. For example, we remember 10% of what we hear, 30% of what we see, and 80% of what we do. The pyramid illustrates the saying: 'What I hear I forget, what I see I remember, what I do I understand."

When you translate this principle to the SAP training environment, the total learning package for an individual should contain a balanced blend. Here are some examples:

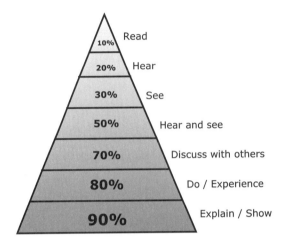

Figure 9.9 The Learning Pyramid

- ▶ Sample Blend 1:
  - ▷ Detailed process and new procedures training in large groups.
  - ▷ A series of transactions via exercises in small groups.
  - ▷ E-learning modules for the basic transactions.
  - ▷ Role-play workshops.
  - ▷ Daily centralized key user meetings after go-live.
- ▶ Sample Blend 2:
  - ▷ Base course via e-learning.
  - ▷ Theory and practice in classes of 12 persons.
  - ▷ Web-based testing to test the learning.
  - ▷ Full-time coaching on the job after go-live.
- ▶ Sample Blend 3:
  - ▷ On-the-job coaching regarding processes.
  - ▷ Minimal training in classroom.
  - ▷ Exercises via e-learning.
  - ▷ One-day-a-week coaching on the job after go-live.

9.5.4 Define Roles

The starting point for the planning any training activity is to determine your target public. Although it may seem early to be doing this, assigning users to their future roles is essential. This is certainly one of the elements that causes major resistance within the implementation team. It corresponds directly to the definition of future roles as described in the organization stream. The tendency of most implementation teams is to not even think about roles and security profiles until one or two months before go-live.

If they are set up with the appropriate level of detail, all future organizational roles match with a security profiles in SAP. In terms of SAP, a role can always be delimited by a set transaction codes. In practice, these transaction codes are organized into smaller groups. Some common examples of functional roles are listed here:

▶ Manufacturing operator
▶ Manufacturing supervisor
▶ Material handler
▶ Inventory clerk
▶ Manufacturing manager
▶ Manufacturing engineer
▶ Supply chain planner
▶ Production planner
▶ Production planner power user
▶ Fixed-asset accountant
▶ Plant accountant
▶ Plant manager
▶ Credit analyst
▶ Financial master data specialist
▶ Distribution manager
▶ Distribution supervisor
▶ Goods receiving clerk
▶ Wave planner
▶ Material planner

9.5.5   Match Role, Person, Learning Object

Successful planning of the learning stream will require you to start well ahead of time and to keep an overview of things.

Assign Persons to the Roles

It is now time to attach persons to each of the roles. This is predominantly a task for the entire organization. In fact, this assignment is a first big opportunity to interact with the organization at large. Whether conducted in focus groups, interactively over the intranet, or by e-mail, the organization should take ownership of this exercise through a formal validation.

Define Courses

As explained earlier, a course is a combination of learning objects. There are no strict rules in defining or delimiting a course, but as a rule of thumb a course equals a process and a learning object equals a sub-process. Some examples of courses are given here:

▶ Outbound transport

▶ Inbound transport

▶ Invoice verification

▶ Billing

▶ Profit analysis

▶ Procurement of raw materials

▶ Inventory

▶ Materials resource planning

▶ Warehouse management

▶ Sales planning

▶ Pricing

▶ Production planning

▶ Sales order management

▶ Maintenance order management

▶ Goods issue and billing

Assign Courses to Roles

The most common mistake made in the planning of the learning stream is to link users directly with courses; that is the fastest way to lose an overview of the ability of the users. Using the roles as an intermediate step for the course planning not only pushes the organization to think very concretely about the future, it also allows you to design the learning objects according to the roles. Moreover, this approach allows you to follow up on learning needs for people who are new to a certain role or those who change roles.

At the end of this step, you have built up a structure that connects users to courses via their roles. As Figure 9.10 illustrates, a user can have more than one role, and one needs to master one or more courses to perform a role.

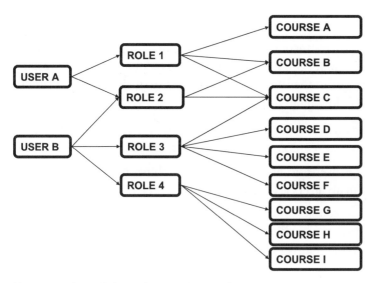

Figure 9.10 Using Roles to Connect Users to Courses

Before you inform the organization about the course package for each user, make sure you add information about the course duration. This is usually the next step.

Determine the Course Duration

Another crucial element in the planning of courses is the estimated duration of the course. For class-based courses, the duration is best communicated in terms of full days (eight hours) or half days (four hours).

▶ The course duration will be multiplied by a certain ratio to determine the time it takes to write the course. Depending on the quality of the course the ratio of course days to writing (preparation) days will vary from 1:8 to 1:13. There are numerous tools for automating screen capture and document editing. However, experience shows that these companions hardly get us under the ratio of 1:8.

▸ The course duration indicates the time that a user will be away from his or her regular job, and more often than not this triggers a lively discussion with middle management. In some cases, you may have to come back for a second round of validations. Our advice is to accept this give-and-take as a necessary ritual for the organization in coming to terms with the change. As stated in the previous chapter, think of it as a diagnostic intervention.

Define Sessions

With all the information concerning the previous steps, you are now ready to create sessions. A session in this context is a day for a full room of participants (in other words: the combination of course, participants, and a certain date). Keep the following in mind:

▸ Each user now has one or more courses to follow, and as a result you are able to communicate the course time per user, but also a time per session.

▸ Thanks to the user-role and role-course combination, you now know exactly how many users are attending which course.

▸ For class-based courses, you will have rooms with an optimal capacity of 10 to 12 participants, so divide the total users per course by this number. This results in the number of sessions that you need for a certain course.

Plan Sessions

You finally ended up with many sessions, which need to be rolled out over time. For class-based courses, you will be able to reduce the overall training period by using more than one room at the same time.

A useful term in the discussions at this stage is "time-to-task." This is a way of stressing that the time between acquiring knowledge and using it should be as short as possible.

Finally, we highly recommend that you mandate follow-up of the sessions, users, invitations, the confirmations, the waiting lists, etc., in a separate training administration system by one or more dedicated members of the local training-and-development department. All of these steps are summarized in Figure 9.11.

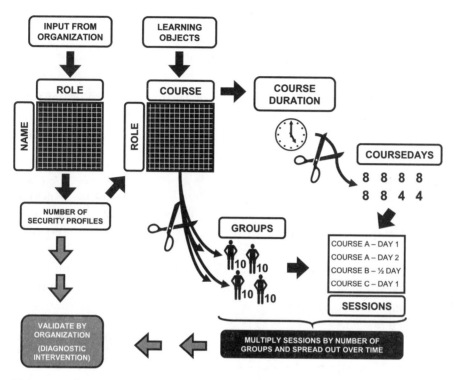

Figure 9.11 Planning of Classical Courses

9.5.6 E-learning

As it is the case for class-based courses, the course duration for e-learning splits up into two parts: course days and writing days. The planning of e-learning courses follows a similar track, with some notable differences, as Figure 9.12 illustrates. Let's take a look at the differences next:

▶ The first big difference lies in the duration of the preparation. As a rule of thumb you should double the ratio of course days to writing days when it comes to e-learning. This is mainly because you need very detailed scenarios and major didactic talents in order to have a successful product.

▶ Next to that, you need to allow yourself some time to get to know SAP Tutor or other simulation software.

▶ Executives are always eager to find out how much time they can save by using e-learning as a substitute for a class-based course. However, just like classical courses, e-learning courses will require users to be away from their jobs, but this time in a different manner. This time is hidden in the organization, and if you don't follow up the progress, people may end up with no training at all. Therefore we highly recommend that you follow up in detail. Here are some ways to do that:

▶ **Pre-announced Tests**

Users need to prove that they have taken the e-learning modules attentively. A simple test that is announced in the beginning of the course will make sure that users pay more attention while taking the course and will give you a simple indication of progress.

▶ **Teamwork**

As the learning responsibility is completely moved to the organization, middle managers and supervisors need to take care of the course organization. Contrary to what most would expect, the success of e-learning in the workplace is determined by teamwork. Teamwork in this context means making sure that the team takes over a colleague's task while he or she is e-learning. Without management reinforcement, this won't happen.

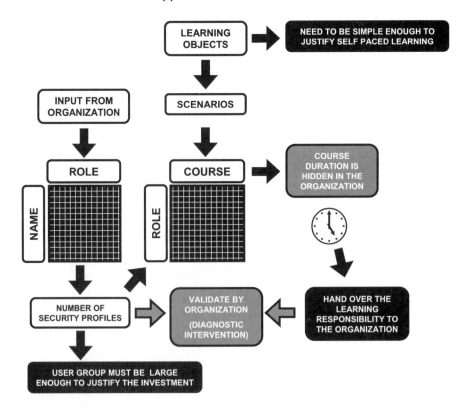

Figure 9.12 Planning of E-Learning Courses

No e-learning should be initiated without a clear intent. You should target business issues that you believe promise a sizable payback. This translates to the following three simple rules:

▶ The course you target for e-learning should be simple enough to justify self-paced learning beyond the control of a trainer.

▶ The number of participants to this course should be large enough to justify the investment.

▶ The individual learner needs to be motivated. Budget time to follow up on this essential element.

9.5.7 E-learning with SAP Tutor

The SAP Solution Manager license agreement includes five licenses for SAP Tutor, which comprises the recording software, SAP Tutor Recorder, and SAP Tutor Editor as an authoring environment for the development of e-learning material.

You can create SAP Tutor simulations for your program, but commercial use is excluded. The playing software SAP Tutor Player is included within the framework of the SAP Solution Manager license agreement and is free for all SAP users in the organization.

SAP Tutor Recorder and Editor

To record learning material, use the SAP Tutor Recorder. When working in the application, the software will record all the screens and input in the background and create, on the basis of that information, a simulation for interactive use. After recording the content, you can edit the learning material with the SAP Tutor Editor. For example, you can change the order of the screens, insert texts, highlight certain parts, and define interactive fields. Users can now work in a simulated system that highly resembles their working system.

Learning Maps

Once you have created the learning objects, you can generate a Learning Map. A Learning Map is an orderly index of learning objects, providing information in HTML format on learning units and links to the learning material. Learning Maps are the equivalent of a course and can be made available at the user's workstation at any time, using the SAP Solution Manager as document server.

Integrated Advantages

The fact that SAP Tutor is integrated into SAP Solution Manager offers some additional advantages:

▶ Learning Maps are linked to Service Desk, which means that part of an incident notification is filled out automatically and the user can add a text for feedback or to address problems with the Learning Map. This allows technical problems to be transferred directly to the support organization.

▶ SAP Solution Manager allows mailings to specific user groups to inform them about a Learning Map. Users can assess Learning Maps by means of a feedback option. The assessments of all users about a Learning Map are saved anonymously. SAP Solution manager offers several ways to follow up the progress on the level of the learning map as well as on the level of the roles and the individuals.

9.5.8 Plan and Prepare Logistics

An important question for the planning and the preparation of the logistics is whether you will host the training yourself, outsource it to a third-party, or a use combination of both. The logistics work includes taking care of the timely and qualitative delivery of participant materials.

9.5.9 Plan Systems and Support

The planning of systems and support is almost a project by itself, involving questions regarding the training system for class-based training and questions regarding an e-learning platform. Here are some basic elements to take into account for each of the previously mentioned options:

▶ Training system for classical training:

  ▶ How will we manage security profiles in the training environment?

  ▶ How will we manage user IDs and passwords?

  ▶ How will we manage interfaces with external systems or legacy systems?

  ▶ How will we manage printers and documents?

  ▶ How will we manage multiple training clients?

  ▶ How will we manage the master data?

  ▶ How will we include the training system in the chain of system transports?

▶ How will we manage the series of numbers (e.g., material numbers that include a piece of the user code or the reservation of a range of numbers per training room) because all the participants cannot modify the same data at the same time.

▶ How will we load the training system with all the master data?

▶ How will we manage and refresh transactional data?

▶ How will we guarantee the availability of the training system?

▶ How will we test the training system?

▶ For an e-learning platform:

▶ How will we make it available to the users?

▶ How will we manage user IDs and passwords?

▶ How will we track individual progress?

▶ How will we guarantee the availability of the training system?

▶ How will we test the training system?

▶ How will we manage updates to the system?

▶ How will we integrate it into a knowledge portal?

▶ How will we handle reporting of learner progress?

9.5.10 Reduce, Re-use, Recycle

In Chapter 6, we introduced the notion of learning objects. To really benefit from the use of learning objects, there are some principles that all the team members need to be aware of, as summarized in the three Rs:

▶ **Reduce**
As a result of the SAP implementation, users will need to master a lot of completely new information on three levels: know-how, know-what, and know-why. Unfortunately, there are limits to what users can absorb. A basic principle is to reduce the learning objects to the strict minimum of what is needed.

▶ **Re-use**
This principle involves all the players on the team, even those who have nothing to do with the learning stream. To save time during the very short period of course preparation, it is the responsibility of all project members to contribute to the re-usability of their deliverables. The most common deliverables that can directly be re-used for learning purposes are

process descriptions and test scenarios. However, the re-use principle is not restricted to prior deliverables; most of the times it involves knowledge that is in the heads of the team members. These people need to budget extra time to work with technical writers.

▶ **Recycle**
This principle derives from the need to design learning objects so they can be used in multiple courses.

The adherence of all the team members to these three Rs determines whether you will be able to save time as an implementation team.

9.5.11 Recruit Technical Writers

From the moment the courses are defined and materials and deliverables of the project exist to be re-used, you can start recruiting the first group of technical writers. Their main responsibilities are to:

▶ Create a style guide and the necessary templates to implement the style guide for each type of output that is required.

▶ Research, learn, and document company policies and procedures, and report any problems or discrepancies to technical and business teams.

▶ Develop end-user documentation and training material, including presentations, data for demonstrations and exercises, instructor guidelines, training aids, online help, simulations, and procedures based on company and industry standards.

▶ Communicate individual status of projects.

▶ Develop and maintain training data.

▶ Coordinate with training and documentation management to ensure training issues are identified and resolved.

▶ Prepare lessons before class to ensure smooth, accurate delivery.

9.6   The Performance-Management Stream in this Phase

Within the design phase, the strategic part of performance management is translated into an operational approach.

9.6.1 Translate Benefits into KPIs

We have argued that if you want to achieve the benefits your organization has identified, you will need to change your way of working and the design of your organization in accordance with those benefits. In the program-initiation phase, the benefits that the organization wants to achieve by implementing SAP were identified, described in detail, and qualified.

In a 1990 book *Improving Performance*, Rummler and Brache described a method of process designing that has largely influenced best practices ever since. It has inspired us as well in our pragmatic and down-to-earth approach to ensure that the benefits that you have identified can be achieved.

The first step is to translate the benefits into organizational and process KPIs. The following are examples of KPIs:

- On the organizational level:
  - Yearly increase of turnover
  - Integrated information flows
  - Integration of processes
  - Headcount
  - Yearly increase of cash flow
  - Cash-conversion cycle expressed in days
  - Market share
- On the process level:
  - Lead time sales-to-order
  - Lead time order-to-delivery
  - Lead time delivery-to-cash in
  - Purchase-to-order just in time (JIT)
  - Lead time closing process
  - Closing process effort, expressed in full-time equivalents (FTEs)

9.6.2 Set Future KPI Thresholds

Based on the current KPI values obtained by internal and external benchmarking, the future performance thresholds for these indicators can be set on the basis of the benefits that your organization wants to achieve. Table 9.3 shows an example of KPI thresholds settings.

KPI	Current Value	Desired Benefit	Future Threshold	Realization Date
Headcount	30,000	Reduce head-count by 10 % in the next three years after go-live	27,000	29,000 on Go-live date + 1 year; 28,000 on Go-live date + 2 years; etc.
Lead time Order-to-delivery	two days for parts sales	Reduced lead time of 50 % within one year after go-live	24 hours	Go-live date + one year
Percentage of orders entered within four hours of receipt (sub process of Order-to-delivery)	70 %	Reduced lead time order-to-delivery of 50 % within one year after go-live	90 %	Go-live date + one year
Percentage of orders entered within 24 hours of receipt (sub process of Order-to-delivery)	80 %	Reduced lead time order-to-delivery of 50 % within one year after go-live	100 %	Go-live date + one year
Percentage of credit checks done within timeframe (sub process of Order-to-delivery)	90 % within 24 hours	Reduced lead time order-to-delivery of 50 % within one year after go-live	90 % real time; 10 % within two hours after order receipt	Go-live date + one year

Table 9.3 KPI Threshold Setting

The threshold setting in Table 9.3 is necessary for each KPI. It shows how sub-processes can help to realize a benefit at higher level.

It is important to recognize the interdependency of the KPIs. For instance, the benefit aiming towards reducing the lead time with 50 % of order-to-delivery in the parts sales may be one of your desired benefits. However, if the lead time between order and delivery for parts sales can be no more than 24 hours, it can never be realized if the credit check takes 24 hours. These interdependencies may require you to review the design of the process once again.

9.6.3 Define KPIs at Job/Role Level

Once the KPIs are defined at process level, they must be converted into KPIs at the role level. This means that each function description must include KPIs for that role. Realization of these role KPIs is part of the individual performance appraisal. Examples of such KPIs are as follows.

▸ For an order-desk person: Enter x number of orders per day.

▸ For a credit manager:

  ▹ Maximum bad debts: x% of total amount of portfolio managed.

  ▹ Review all credit limits minimally once a year.

▸ For a collection agent:

  ▹ Maximum amount of overdue receivables: x% of total amount of portfolio manager.

  ▹ Decrease average days outstanding of portfolio with 10%.

It is very important to have the KPIs and their thresholds presented to and validated by the steering committee.

9.7 Moments of Truth

We find the following moments of truth in the design phase. You can get an idea of these in the following subsections.

9.7.1 Take a Customer Relationship Management Approach

This customer relationship management (CRM) approach means that you can connect the stakeholder database to the learning administration system. If you want to do a detailed follow-up of the stakeholders, you should not only track their communication histories but also do a follow-up of the stakeholder's history with the program. The more you know about the stakeholders, the better you can guide them through the transition.

9.7.2 Validation of the Learning Plan

On the level of the learning stream, there are some important issues to address on the organization level.

One of these is mapping of the learning stream onto the overall program plan and finding synergies with other project streams. This includes discussions with the leaders of those streams, as you will be asking them to deliver their work in chunks that are re-usable as learning objects. The most popular requests include the delivery of testing scenarios, testing data, blueprints, and communication deliverables.

Executives love numbers, so you will need statistical acumen. The training budget of an SAP implementation is a big deal. In this stage, this requires you to quickly build and simulate loads of scenarios. The most important variables that you will need to be able to swap back and forth are class-based training hours, e-learning training hours, time-to task and preparation-to-participation ratios.

9.7.3 Steering Committees are Program Charter Review Meetings

A program charter that is not managed dies upon implementation. Management responsibilities include providing a point of contact for problems related to the agreement. Important problems, issues, and concerns will surface even when you are delivering according to the targets of the program charter. Therefore, holding reviews regularly, for example by making it a fixed agenda point on every steering committee meeting, is essential to keeping the program charter alive and the sponsors involved.

In fact, the intention to conduct these reviews should be documented in the managerial aspects of the program charter. Interim review meetings can be held when significant concerns arise regarding the validity of the program charter.

On the other hand, changes to the program charter should not be made randomly. It is best to limit changes to significant circumstances such as those arising from scope change and other unanticipated events. Each circumstance that is qualified for making adjustments to the program charter should be listed in the management elements (Karten, 2002).

9.7.4 Validation of the Design is a Process

Signing off on the design means that the organization agrees to the future ways of working that were presented. It means that the organization believes that these new ways of working help the company to realize its strategy. The signed-off design is the basis for the next phase: building the prototype.

9.7.5 The Sign-Off of the KPIs and Their Threshold Values

Signing off the KPIs means that the organization agrees that the KPIs that were defined are the ones that need to be measured to follow-up on the performance of the organization, i.e., the realization of the defined benefits.

The sign-off of the threshold values might even be more important, as the organization confirms at that moment that it is convinced that these objectives must be met to ensure realization of the corporate strategy.

9.7.6 Swim Lanes: Accept No Substitutes

From the moment that the design is validated, the process maps or swim-lane diagrams are by far the most vital communication tools of the program. In the program charter, this is validated even before the design phase has started. This is because they will serve as an essential input for multiple other steps and deliverables, such as:

▶ Security profiles.
▶ Local coaching (swim-lane diagrams provide know-what, that connects the know-why of the business case to the know-how of a training manual).
▶ Training manuals.
▶ User acceptance testing.
▶ Job descriptions.
▶ Standard operating procedures.

Therefore, we advise taking a disciplined approach to creating and updating swim lanes.

9.7.7 Involve Impacted Non-users

You should make sure that all affected parties of a business process are involved from the beginning. For instance, in the design of the sales and distribution processes, you should involve sales representatives because they will be the main contact persons when the sales back office has specific information requirements. "They are not impacted by the system, so they should not be involved as closely" is a wrong approach on your part and a bad excuse on their part.

9.8   Deliverables

The deliverables of this phase are the following:

- ▶ Process maps:
  - ▶ Event driven process maps
  - ▶ Swim lane diagrams
- ▶ Security profiles
- ▶ Reports
- ▶ Validated KPIs
- ▶ Roles
- ▶ Stakeholder database
- ▶ Learning plan (for an example, see Appendix B.3)
- ▶ Branding
- ▶ Communication plan (for an example see Appendix B.2)

Figure 9.13 illustrates how the deliverables of this phase relate to each other. For the map of all the organizational change deliverables over the complete program lifecycle, see Appendix C.

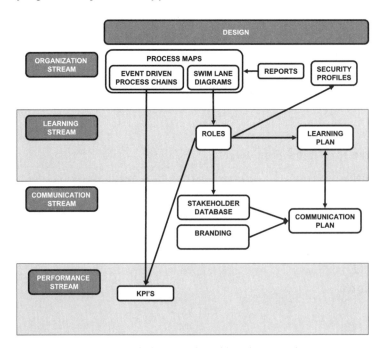

Figure 9.13 Organizational Change Deliverables of Design Phase

9.9   Conclusion

The design phase sets the basis for the future ways of working, and it defines what your future SAP environment will look like. All four streams (organization, communication, learning, and performance management) need a high degree of attention, as the fragile translation of strategy into operations takes place here.

In Chapter 10, we will cover the build phase of the SAP implementation program, although some building already will have taken place during the design phase.

During the build phase, most of your attention will go to the development and the configuration of SAP as the system that will support your new organization and its future ways of working. The change becomes more and more concrete, so—although you will be tempted to stay in your laboratory until the prototype is finished—you will need to prepare your organization at the same time.

10 Build Phase

10.1 Phase-Specific Characteristics and Needs

This section explains how you should use and read the soft-stuff and hard-stuff radars, taking into account the specific characteristics and needs of the build phase.

10.1.1 Soft-Stuff Radar

During the build phase, your team will be programming and configuring different components of the system without really caring about integrating the components. On the soft-stuff radar, you will notice that the changes happen gradually as the program finds its way through the organization:

▶ **Learning Relationship Radar**
It is during the build phase that the black holes of the design come to the surface: Some things that were obvious on paper all of a sudden give rise to new questions that can only be answered by asking the right people in the organization. That is why we highly recommend adopting a consulting style when interacting.

You will only get the appropriate level of attention and time from people in the organization when they perceive you as important. For that reason, you will need to make use of the branding efforts.

▶ **Agent Radar**
This radar shows no changes compared to the previous phase. The infantry troops continue their work methodologically and step-by-step, according to the project management method you are following.

However, brilliant methodologies and intelligent project management tools will not prevent the implementation team from running into a conflict from time to time. Conflicts at this stage are not limited to the implementation team itself. Design and build issues stimulate lively discussions between team members and pragmatists of the organization. Remember, conflicts are not a bad thing; it is how you solve them that matters most. Smart program managers have the ability to learn from the conflicts and to bring the team into a norming phase.

Having no conflicts, clashes, or discussions at this stage is actually a warning flag of low involvement of the team and the organization.

▶ **Target Radar**

The pragmatists' and the conservatives' opinions will not have changed much at this point. The questions you ask them and the insights you bring them will not persuade them to blindly trust you.

Given the relatively long time between this stage and the actual go-live, they see no need to panic about it or to feel uncomfortable. As for you, you will still feel as though you are pushing a big boulder uphill in trying to convince them that their positive participation is vital. Don't blame pragmatists for it; they are 100 % dedicated to their jobs, and most of the time your "diagnostic interventions" are intrusions into their frames of reference. Approach their resistance with respect.

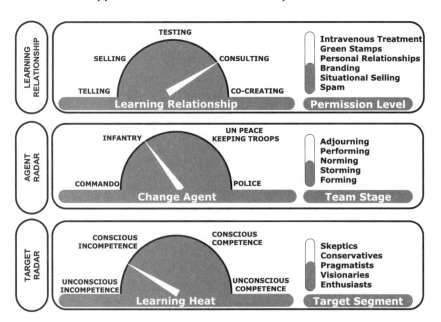

Figure 10.1 Soft-Stuff Radar in the Build Phase

10.1.2   Hard-Stuff Radar

The hard-stuff radar in the build phase shows a gradual change, as illustrated in Figure 10.2.

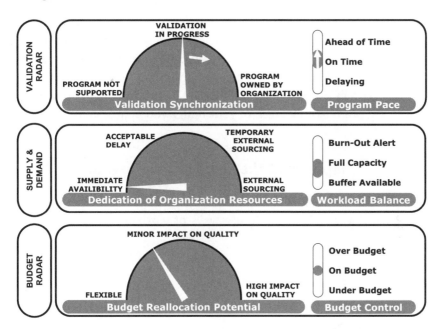

Figure 10.2 Hard-Stuff Radar in the Build Phase

You can get a more detailed idea about the phases in the upcoming bulleted list:

▶ **Validation Radar**
You should start this phase with no delay. What's more, during this phase you will need to plan for the next phase and try to build in extra buffers. From a validation point of view, the build phase is less congenial than others, as the team tends to develop and configure the system on its own. Therefore, validation may lag slightly compared to the development progress.

▶ **Supply- and -Demand Radar**
The supply-and-demand radar is very important for the pilot organization. This group is are heavily involved in the build phase, and activities and workload must be managed carefully if you don't want to lose its commitment. As a result, the supply and demand radar should show no significant difference with the previous phase.

▶ **Budget Radar**
Here you need to track spending carefully. The budget required for building the system is easily underestimated. Development of interfaces is often much more expensive than forecast, mainly because of false assumptions about the availability of specific functionality in the legacy systems. Lacking of certain functionality means decreased integration, and because that is often unacceptable, additional development in the legacy systems may be required. As a result, you may be confronted for the first time during the program lifecycle with a budget reallocation request to stay on budget. Be aware of how much of your buffer you may be consuming.

10.2 What Happens at the Level of the Program?

During the build phase, it is important to make sure that the system is built in a pragmatic way so that the future ways of working are properly supported.

10.2.1 Avoid a Disconnect

At this moment, the program is in running mode. Build projects start up, and the projects relating to the test phase are being prepared. The operational organization must be involved when building the system to avoid disconnection between the following:

▶ Design and realization

▶ Program and operational organization

In this phase, the project-cocooning pitfall is a common risk. More often than not, the SAP experts and the implementation team return to their cocoons to build the system far away from the organization.

10.2.2 Iteration Processes

During the build phase, there must be continuous verification and validation loops between the program team and the organization.

From experience, we know that during the build phase many questions arise on how the processes and the system are supposed to run. This is because, during the design phase, it is almost impossible to touch the level of detail that is required when setting up the system. This is where the build phase and the design phase overlap.

Where issues arise that may trigger scope changes at strategic, functional, or system level, approval must be obtained from the operational board or the steering committee.

10.2.3 Prepare the Organization for Testing

In Chapter 4, we indicated that you will always be spending a small percentage of your time finishing the previous phase and preparing for the next. In the build phase, the organization must be prepared for testing. This means that users who will be involved in the testing must be properly trained.

10.3 The Organization Stream in This Phase

During the build phase, the organization stream focuses on preparing the deployment. A number of activities will still relate to the design, as there is a natural iteration between build phase and design phase.

10.3.1 Selection of the Pilot

As advised in the previous phase, you should postpone assigning a pilot to keep the design from being too much influenced by local desires. However, once the design is validated, you should not waste another second before choosing a pilot. When selecting the pilot, you must keep the following issues in mind:

▶ The pilot should be an entity within the organization that is representative for the whole of the organization.

▶ It should be located in a part of the world where the organization is highly represented or where its major business is realized.

▶ Complexity is estimated to be average.

▶ High commitment from local management is required.

▶ The pilot organization must agree to play an important role after the go-live and during the complete roll-out lifetime

Building the system means the building of a prototype that can be fully tested and presented to the organization. The prototype is built fully in accordance with the pilot, with regard to the following:

- Organizational set-up
- Functional elements
- Interfaces

The pilot organization will be more heavily involved than any other entity in data cleansing and data migration during the build phase.

10.3.2 Defining the Workflows

Workflow increases the level of integration and saves a lot of time in the execution of a process. Workflows ensure that people who are required to take action are informed, and that information and electronic documents flow correctly across the organization.

Documents or transactions can be accessed directly from the message that is received and support the user in organizing his or her work. Workflow can also be used to automate approval processes; e. g., in the case of incoming invoices or outgoing payments. Effective workflow design must specify the following:

- The process steps or processes that are connected.
- A description of the trigger of the workflow:
  - A person
  - An event
- The functions subject to the workflow and the sequence in the flow.
- The documents that are subject to the workflow.
- The related SAP transactions that have to be accessed.

The implementation of workflow might be subject to second-wave activities. We will come back to this in Chapter 13.

10.3.3 Documenting the SAP Organizational Structure

An important step is documenting how the organizational structure in SAP will be used to support the needs of your organization. The organizational structure in SAP must reflect the operational structure of the organization. Each of the following organizational entities must be identified, named, and described:

- Legal entities
- Groups of companies (legal entities) that belong to each other

- Credit control areas
- Sales organizations
- Sales divisions
- Sales channels
- Purchasing entities
- Plants
- Warehouses

10.3.4 The Functional Design

Even though the functional design theoretically belongs to the design phase, in practice it happens early in the build phase. When implementing SAP, it is not sufficient to design your organization and its future ways of working. There are other elements to be designed that, from an operational perspective, are at least as important as the processes.

They are what we would call functional elements, and their design highly depends on your organization's strategically-defined ways of working. We are talking about the following:

- Charts of accounts
- Price lists
- Profit-center structure
- Profitability analysis
- Cost-center structure
- Document types (transaction types)
- Document-number intervals
- Reporting requirements
- Business-partner numbering

You should not underestimate the time it takes to design these functional elements into full detail. For instance, the description of one single account drills down to the level of detail that includes items such as: a long and a short description for the account, balance sheet or profit-and-loss account, allowable currencies, and sort keys. This activity will trigger much discussion as you discover many gaps between global design and local use.

It will be more difficult to make people accept the new functional elements than it will to change the way they work. This is because people don't work with processes; they are part of them. But they do work with the functional elements, many times per day. If these don't fit their needs, people will avoid using them as much as they can. When refining the value proposition you need to link back to this insight.

Once the organizational design and the functional design are finished, the whole of the outcome must be converted into a system design. This design is put together by SAP experts. The system design describes in detail how SAP must be set up to support the future-state organization—in terms of configuration and development—and how connections are made to other systems.

10.3.5 Setting Up the Functional Organization

As we argued in Chapter 1, HR is not an agent of change but an agent of continuity. We also added that this does not exclude HR from the organizational change process but rather gives HR a specific challenge to meet. Every SAP implementation—no matter how small—has an impact on the roles. This is because the system requires certain tasks to be grouped according to one or more SAP transactions. This can be both an opportunity and a threat for the current organization.

Most often, neither HR nor the implementation team is aware of the impact of the systems' redesign on the organization. In Figure 10.3, we outline the challenge for HR. As business processes get translated into SAP terminology, tasks get translated into SAP transactions. However, in practice these tasks need to be performed by people. This means that these tasks need to be translated into functional roles (bundles of tasks and responsibilities). On a local level, these functional roles may even get translated into position descriptions.

The difficulties for HR start at the interconnection between a person and the position, functional role, and tasks he or she needs to perform. At this level, the following aspects of the HR function may be affected to a greater or lesser extent:

▶ Role agreement between employee and manager

▶ Recruitment

▶ Job sizing and evaluation

▶ Compensation and benefits management

- Training and development
- Skills and competency management
- Minimum legal obligations
- Enforcement of contractual obligations
- Workforce allocation and planning
- Project planning
- Performance management and target setting
- Basis of statistical reporting (internal and external)
- Compliance with regulatory obligations

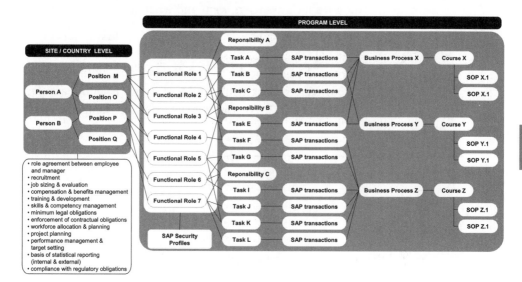

Figure 10.3 The HR Challenge: Connecting People

The point is that you either need to look at the impact on all of these elements in advance or accept that at the end of the implementation the status of all of these elements will not reflect reality.

10.4 The Communication Stream in this Phase

During the build phase, the communication stream focuses on making sure that the organization remains properly informed about the program. Subsequently, the focus is on managing resistance. Then, a knowledge portal must be set up.

10.4.1 Refining Value Proposition

When we described the functional design, we noted that it will be more difficult to make people accept the new functional elements than to make the elements work in other ways. This brings us to the insight of John Gourville (2006), who says we need to pay attention to the psychological costs when new products force consumers to change their behavior. When we apply this marketing logic in the world of SAP implementations, we can refine the value proposition for the users. Users overvalue the existing benefits of legacy systems by a factor of three, and executives and developers overvalue the new benefits of their innovation by a factor of three. The product of this clash of irrational estimates is a mismatch of nine to one between what the SAP implementation team thinks users want and what users really want.

How can you overcome this disconnect? Gourville says the first step is to ask what kind of change we are asking of users. As Figure 10.4 shows, we need to figure out where the changes for the users fall in a matrix with four categories: Easy Sells, Rough Spots, Long Hauls, and Smash Hits. Each has a different ratio of WIIFM (What's In It For Me) versus behavior change required from the user.

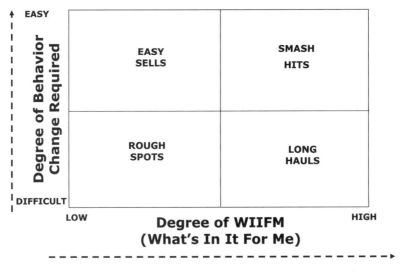

Figure 10.4 WIIFM versus Behavior Change Matrix (adapted from Gourville, 2006)

As a result of the mapping of Figure 10.3, you will be able to estimate the resistance for each change. Accordingly, you will know which topics need more time for conversation or in which order you want to communicate them (we recommend communicating the bad news first).

▶ **Rough Spots**

Limited WIIFM and significant behavior changes. These changes typically refer to transactions that require more clicking and data entry than before with no visible result for the user. An example is the situation of production workers who need to put in production data in a timely fashion. Most often, this is an essential action for the process on the whole, but another burden on top of their workload. If the communication of such a topic is restricted to the know-how and know-what (i.e., the instructions and the procedure), these users (and their supervisors) may quit on data accuracy and timing. If you want users to commit to these rough spots, it is going to require a lot of context (know-why) and a thorough monitoring of the supervisors as agents of change.

▶ **Long Hauls**

Significant WIIFM and significant behavior changes. These are typically the transactions that require a completely different way of thinking, a considerable number of clicks and screens, and many parameters to look after at the same time. For example, the local procurement of materials that had a paper flow of approvals and signatures is replaced by a paperless procurement workflow with automated approvals linking to a corporate and centralized catalogue. In the beginning, this is a tremendous change for the users, and only after a while they will start to see the benefits of this automated and centralized approach. We really want people to persist in this long period of learning how to work in a totally different way. This will only succeed when we communicate regularly the know-hows (refreshers course, quick reference cards, coaching on-the-job, etc.), the know-whats (e.g., feedback about the KPIs to all the procurement users) and the know-whys (the context of why we are doing this).

▶ **Easy Sells**

Limited WIIFM and limited behavior changes. These are the very small changes in very basic actions. Examples include the printing of transport documents and any other transaction that requires no different logic than the one that users had to apply previously. For these changes, sticking to the know-how and the know-what may work out fine, although we recommend that you take every opportunity you get to reinforce and link back to the know-why.

▶ **Smash Hits**

Significant WIIFM and limited behavior changes. These are the time savers and visible process improvements compared to the old situation. Examples may include a better overview of stock levels, or better search functionality. Most of the times, these are kind of features that users themselves are keen on telling their colleagues about, although initiating them yourself can do no harm to your relationship with the users and the trust they put in you.

10.4.2 Dedicating Sender

The person you select as the sender of a message is a symbol of how important the message is. The audience should recognize the sender as having the authority and power to send the message. For instance, if the objective is to confront skepticism that is endangering the program, the message should come from one or more sponsors.

However, authority and power are not the only characteristics that qualify a sender. They are only valid for formal communication. For informal communication, there are other rules that apply. According to Duck (2001), there are three types of people who have the power to make a message travel through a community:

▶ **Cassandras**
Most often, these are the middle managers and line supervisors who are quick to recognize an impending change and to cry out an early warning. They usually know more about the effect of the upcoming change on their people because they spend so much time in the thick of the operational action. According to Duck, a reliable Cassandra can give an early warning and cause you to rethink your action plan before things get out of hand.

▶ **Networkers**
These employees are keenly attuned to what is happening in the organization. They interact regularly with different departments and different levels of employees. They can be helpful in identifying which plans are working and which aren't because they regularly interact with a variety of people across disciplines. According to Duck, they can be thought of as thermometers because they accurately register the emotional temperature of the organization around them.

▶ **Influencers**
They can affect the opinions of others. According to Duck, these opinion leaders are like thermostats because they can literally cool a place down or fire it up. Other people seek their opinions and often base their own attitudes and actions on what the opinion leaders say and do.

The point here is to be aware that you need a combination of all these types of senders in the community of agents and sponsors and should spend extra time with these people.

10.4.3 Designing Knowledge Portal

With the word *portal*, we explicitly aim at the use of your organization's intranet for a double purpose:

▶ Single point of information.

▶ Major interaction platform with the user community.

Most interactions during the lifecycle of your program are "one-to-many" communications with a considerable amount of reference materials. People may want to check back to previous communication and reference materials. Finally, based on the feedback from the receivers, you will need to update or correct any reference material that you shared previously. These specific requirements make the intranet a suitable communication channel.

The best way to take maximum advantage of this channel is by using it to interact with most stakeholders from the earliest phase. We believe there are some key approaches you should adopt in using the intranet to drive your program communication. Some of these are:

▶ Declare the intranet to be the single point of contact, and guide people to it each time you have something to tell and each time you have told something. Examples include the following:

  ▶ Broadcast "scoops" from time to time via this channel.

  ▶ Make it an attribute of your branding by including the web-page address in the footer of all team members' email, at the end of all communications, etc.

  ▶ Make all communication handouts of meetings and announcements available on the intranet, and keep an archive available.

▶ Make it evolve over time according to the communication needs:

  ▶ In the period of Unfreezing, the contents will be rather static. The biggest part at this time is know-why communication such as: historical background, describing the status quo, the vision and strategy, and the benefits of the program.

  ▶ During the phase of changing, know-what facts are added as the program evolves. Now you can really benefit from interaction via the intranet. Some implementation teams, for instance, make successful use of the intranet for opening up their databases of data to be cleansed and add visual indicators of percentage completed and how far one is ahead or behind with respect to the schedule and to other data cleansers. Of course, this requires clear rules of the game, but it is a tremendous advantage compared to sending spreadsheets around.

▸ At the time of go-live, the intranet should have evolved into its final stage: *a knowledge portal*. This should include an intuitive interface for finding any course material, learning map, quick reference cards, frequently asked questions (FAQ), key users' telephone lists, etc. We once even built a "transaction search engine" that returned every learning object, quick reference card, FAQ, and news flash item that was related to a certain transaction. To do that, you should make sure to tag every news item and learning object with the right transaction codes at the moment of creation.

▸ At regular intervals, you can use the intranet for short surveys. If you conduct this is kind of temperature reading regularly, you can identify patterns and correct your course accordingly. The same is true for Web statistics and learning statistics (see also Chapter 139).

▸ You should double-check that all future users, key users, and other stakeholders that you intend to reach via the intranet have easy and all-time access to this channel. For example, some future users may at present not have to work with a PC.

▸ The level of using and leveraging a knowledge portal depends on the intranet infrastructure and the resources available for authoring and developing intranet applications.

From our experience, the current level of using the intranet for other purposes has no influence on the interaction that you can expect for the program. As a consequence, the statement that "people currently don't make use of the intranet" is not a valid argument for not investing in a knowledge portal.

10.4.4 Conducting a Temperature Reading

The goal of a *temperature reading* is to track the evolution of the change cycle country by country, or site by site, depending on the size of your organization and the scope of your implementation. But temperature reading is more than just making a diagnostic. Most of all it is a team-strengthening technique, regardless of the geographical spread of your team.

A temperature reading can help workgroups reduce tensions, strengthen connections, and surface information, ideas, and feelings that might otherwise be suppressed. A temperature reading consists of five segments (Karten, 2002), which are as follows:

- **Appreciations:** What is working well?
- **New Information:** Which information is still missing?
- **Puzzles:** Which problems and puzzles are confusing?
- **Complaints with Recommendations:** What would people recommend, and what are the lessons learned?
- **Hopes and Wishes:** What are the hopes for the future?

Following is an example of a temperature reading that we did concerning the work streams on large multinational SAP implementations. On a bi-monthly basis, each work-stream leader conducts a structured interview with each country or site correspondent. The interview is a five-minute conversation based on the five segments mentioned earlier. The final question is "What is the temperature at this moment?" The respondents are given the following choices:

- You can count on us to take the initiative.
- We are ready to contribute and let go of our old habits.
- We believe in the added value of this program.
- We know what is expected of us.
- We know what will happen and why.
- We have no idea what this is about.

This last item gives you the opportunity to follow the change curve for each country or site on a regular basis (monthly, bi-monthly, etc.). Figure 10.5 illustrates how this can be summarized and presented.

Ideally, a temperature reading is conducted in a face-to-face setting, but most of the time you will either lack the budget or the time to bring the stakeholders together. Yet, at the time of going live, you are going to need the commitment of every single stakeholder. You should aim to conduct a temperature reading regularly and to give your feedback both in words and actions on a regular basis. Be aware that this diagnostic sets an expectation for course correction or justification.

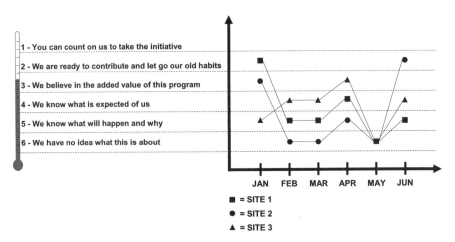

Figure 10.5 Example of a Temperature Reading

10.5   The Learning Stream in this Phase

The learning stream's activities mainly relate to translating the training design into reality. It covers the production of the materials, the recruitment of the trainers, as well as the always-underestimated training enrollment and administration.

10.5.1   Defining the Curriculum

As a result of the extensive planning during the previous steps, you are now able to present a learning curriculum that is known and validated by the organization. This curriculum now serves as a target for the learning team to work on.

Before you know it, you will be chopping this curriculum down into smaller pieces for the technical writers, and you will be scheduling and time-boxing the writing efforts and chasing the implementation team for input.

10.5.2   Setting Evaluation Criteria

At the end of the implementation, we would like to have an idea of the extent to which the learning stream has improved the performance of the organization. You should work with executives and business unit managers to determine the levels of rigor appropriate for measuring the business impact of different types of training and development.

Even before doing so, you should be aware of the different levels of training evaluation (Kirkpatrick, 1998), as we illustrate in Figure 10.6

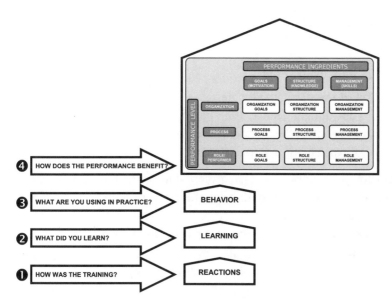

Figure 10.6 The Four Levels of Evaluation (adapted from Rummler & Brache, 1990, and Kirkpatrick, 1998)

Each of these evaluation levels tells you something different. Therefore, they will be measured at different points in time and in different ways. How you put this in practice and whether you will automate this will be the subject of discussions focusing on time and budget.

We highly recommend that you take all of the following seriously, as they will serve as an early warning system:

▶ Reactions (or, satisfaction) will give you an indication of how well the training initiative is perceived. This is more than just smiley sheets about coffee, temperature, and trainer friendliness. The undertone of the wording will give you an impression of the extent to which users will decide to trust the program. Eventually, trust is the currency of change and the evidence of know-why.

▶ Learning evaluation, mostly by means of testing, will indicate the level of know-what that has been acquired by the learner.

▶ Measuring behavior in this context means observing users' know-how in how well they are solving exercises and how they react in role plays and on-the-job coaching.

▸ Finally, the measurement of performance can only be done in practice by means of the performance ingredients (goals, structure, skills) on all levels (organization, process, and role). This is where the learning stream links to the perfomance stream.

10.5.3 Participant Materials

The preparation of the participant materials is the task that will take up the largest part of your budget. Hence, time-boxing, strict planning and follow-up are necessary to control the workload. The following points are important in the practice of participant material preparation:

▸ The input for your work is not lying there and waiting to be picked up. You will need to find your way through the test scripts and scenarios and the process descriptions to know the process responsible. This is when you will experience the re-usability of the program deliverables.

▸ Guidelines, templates, trainer agreements, and strict appointments with the process leads ensures that you can deliver within the budget of the allotted time. We highly recommend chopping the total number of preparation days into smaller pieces; e.g., make introductions, describe process, describe master data, make exercises, validate by functional team member, make corrections, etc.

▸ Flexible timing. There is a slim chance that you will be able to complete every preparation according to plan. You have to take into account that as you go, the implementation team is still building and testing in parallel. In other words: You are not documenting an end state but a process and a system that is unfinished.

▸ The anatomy of a good course contains all three basic elements, which are:

   ▹ The know-why learning objects: the company strategy, the driving forces, and the consequences of integrated process thinking.

   ▹ The know-what learning objects: the process descriptions and overview, the master data, the roles and responsibilities.

   ▹ The know-how learning objects: navigation, exercises, reporting.

▸ The base course is a special course. The specific purpose of a base course is to speed up all the other courses, by tackling the very basic issues. We recommend having all participants (including the supervising non-users) follow this course. Typically, a base course takes half a day and includes the following topics:

- The know-why (about 50 % of the course).
- The basic navigation and screen layouts of SAP.
- Search functions in SAP.
- Basic reporting in SAP.
- The use of support materials (help, documentation, portals, etc.).

10.5.4 Recruiting Trainers

Training is a joint effort of the trainers, assisted by the process experts and reinforced by the key users. Bear in mind that external trainers—no matter how charismatic they are—will only be able to give you the functional training. The context, the business processes, and the procedures that are specific to your organization can only be taught by the functional team members and the key users, because they need to be able to relate to the current context of the learners.

You should be aware of the fact that the most competent experts in the field usually don't qualify as good trainers. Look for didactic skills and emotional intelligence. The responsibilities of a trainer in the learning stream are the following:

- Deliver training to target groups and evaluate the training.
- Communicate individual status of projects.
- Leverage assistance of key users and extended team members to ensure that the curriculum meets the business requirements.
- Coordinate with training and documentation management to ensure training issues are identified and resolved.
- Manage classroom timelines and solve any problems that arise in class.
- Communicate any issues that arise during training, such as database problems and system access.
- Prepare lessons before class to ensure smooth, accurate delivery.
- Coach customers/end users on adult learning and delivery mechanisms.

10.5.5 Administration and Enrollment

This is where the training-and-development department comes in and has a shared responsibility with the implementation team. The mission is to track the learners from enrollment to qualification. The responsibilities for the training administrators during an SAP implementation are the following:

▸ Register students and ensure that they are in the proper classes and have taken the prerequisite sessions.

▸ Track and coordinate training data refresh cycle to coincide with the training schedule (working with the team member taking care of the training system).

▸ Coordinate site-specific training services and facilities, such as lunches, breaks, and accommodations.

▸ Ensure that the training system is available and that all hardware, software, and materials are in training rooms before class begins.

▸ Maintain training records and order all supplies for the training and documentation team.

▸ Report any problems to training and documentation team leader or project manager.

As the example in Figure 10.7 points out, training administration is a shared effort. As a consequence, drawing in advance a small process flow describing exactly who does what can save a lot of time and discussion when the going gets tough.

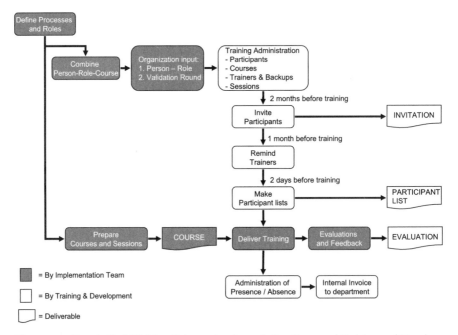

Figure 10.7 Sample Task Division Between Implementation Team and Training and Development Department

10.5.6 Training the Trainers

The training of the trainers themselves does not only apply to implementation team members who will try their luck as first-time trainers.

Seasoned trainers need to be trained on the company policies and procedures and the way that the business processes are handled in your specific organization. In our experience, this is an important activity that needs to be hard-scheduled or else it will fall off everyone's plate.

10.5.7 Staying in Synch With Overall Program

As the learning stream takes up a considerable amount of time and budget of the program, you want to make sure that you track and report. There are some learning stream dependencies that require the program to deliver some things earlier than initially planned or in a different form than they initially thought.

In the other direction, the learning stream will be paced by the overall program, and any movement in the program schedule should be checked against needed course corrections in the learning stream.

10.6 Performance Management

In this phase, it is time to link the know-whys to KPIs.

10.6.1 SMART KPIs

We used the SMART acronym in the previous chapter when discussing the business case. Here, you will need it but for another purpose. During the build phase you should be able to link the benefits of the program to the KPIs; i.e., making sense of the KPIs before throwing them at people's heads. The diagram in Figure 10.8 can serve as a checklist while doing so. From Figure 10.8, you can easily understand that there are actually three kinds of KPIs, as follows:

▶ **Do New Things**
  These KPIs will measure new things that were not in place before the process redesign.

▸ **Do Things Better**
Basically, these KPIs come down to putting new tagets on existing KPIs.

▸ **Stop Doing Things**
These KPIs measure the fading away of bad habits.

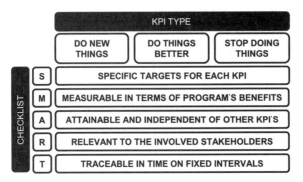

Figure 10.8 KPI Reality Check

10.6.2 Monitoring the Benefits Realization

Based on the business case of each work stream, the benefits realization needs to be followed up. Based on the insights of Kaplan & Norton (2000), this can happen according to the four-step approach.

▸ What are the target benefits from the business plan? These should be divided according to this benefits distribution, described here:

  ▸ **Cost Avoidance**
  Examples include a more efficient way of order intake, which leads to a less than proportionate growth of administrative overhead.

  ▸ **Cost Savings**
  For example, think of a structural cutback of resources for procurement administration thanks to an automated workflow that replaces the paper trail.

  ▸ **Revenue Growth**
  Suppose, for example, there is an increased market share thanks to a more structural market approach and the implementation of the CRM module.

▸ **Data Gathering**
This business case needs to be translated into local improvement initiatives and data-gathering needs to ensure success on a local level

▶ **Measure the Baseline**
The relationship between the benefits distribution and hard currency (euros/dollars) needs to be known before you can start to measure. After that, you can set a target.

▶ **Calculate and Calibrate**
Calculate and calibrate the influence of early wins that have taken place before the baseline setting and scope changes.

Finally, you should be able to indicate which persons are responsible for owning the KPIs that you will be setting up. Some of these KPIs will eventually be taken over long-term to follow up general performance.

10.7 Moments of Truth

We find the following moments of truth in the build phase. Read the subsections that follow to fully understand these.

10.7.1 Involvement of the Pilot Organization

As mentioned earlier involvement of the pilot is essential for the success of the SAP implementation. Once the build phase has started, it is not easy to change the pilot again. That is why it is important to work closely with the pilot organization and to have a good relationship with it as a basis for open, honest, and direct communication.

10.7.2 Delivery of the Prototype

The delivery of the prototype is the basis for moving forward to the deployment phase. The prototype is the first concrete proof of success of the program, and it will be used for acceptance testing by the end users. That is why it is so important that it is delivered in time, with the right quality.

10.7.3 Learning Moments of Truth

▶ The validation of a set of design principles, such as:

  ▶ Develop training material based on templates.

  ▶ Ensure 75 % is re-useable for training end users during roll-outs.

  ▶ One common language/or not.

▶ Informing the users of their future roles and of the corresponding training will focus their minds on a future point of reference.

10.7.4 KPIs Need Positive Targets

For a KPI to work and for people to be motivated, you will need to set goals that are realistic and attainable. What's even more important is to set positive targets instead of negative ones. For instance, you may be targeting fewer than 2 percent of deliveries with mistakes or 98 percent of deliveries successful. They both measure and target exactly the same thing, but which one will motivate people most to perform?

10.8 Deliverables

The deliverables for this phase are the following:

▶ Functional design
▶ Workflows
▶ Organization structures
▶ Refined value propositions
▶ Knowledge portal
▶ Learning curriculum
▶ Participant administration
▶ Individual training plans
▶ SMART KPIs

These deliverables are outlined in Figure 10.9.

For the complete map of all deliverables during the program lifecycle, please refer to Appendix C.

10.9 Conclusion

During the build phase, the main challenge is to avoid a disconnect between program team and organization and to make sure the SAP system is built in a way that it pragmatically supports the new organization and its future ways of working. During this phase, the organization, learning, and communication streams prepare for the deployment of the system.

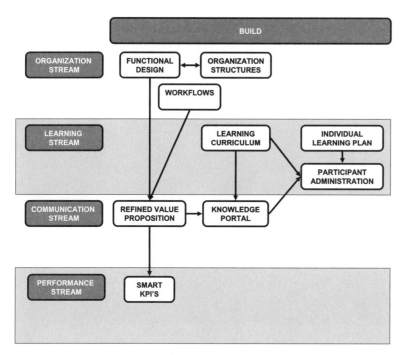

Figure 10.9 Organizational Change Deliverables of the Build Phase

In Chapter 11, we will treat the test phase of the program lifecycle. This is a milestone in your program, which is seldom approached with the required discipline.

The test phase is a hidden opportunity to strengthen the learning relationship between the implementation team and the organization. User acceptance of the system is only a starting point. What matters most is the user acceptance and awareness of the new organization and of the redesigned processes.

11 Test Phase

11.1 Phase-Specific Characteristics and Needs

In this section, we explain how you should use and read the soft and hard-stuff radars, taking into account the specific characteristics and needs of the test phase.

11.1.1 Soft-Stuff Radar

When you reach the testing phase, the soft-stuff radar (see Figure 11.1) should indicate that some interaction has taken place and that a relationship has been established between the implementation team and the organization. Now you are going to use the relationship, and leverage the trust that you have been building up during the previous phases:

▸ **Learning Relationship Radar**
In multiple test rounds, you will be involving key users in user acceptance testing (UAT). During these UAT rounds, you need to take a very structured approach, with predefined scenarios and detailed scripts. As a result, the pattern for your interaction is fixed, and you can adopt a "testing" interaction style.

Testing is also the ideal moment of setting up personal relationships. Therefore it is essential that the UAT rounds are led by team members who later will be assigned coaching roles or who will assume major roles in the organization after the implementation.

▸ **Agent Radar**
At this stage, the members of your implementation team need to begin functioning as a team. This is the "norming" team stage.

As mentioned when discussing the permission level metric, you should make sure that UAT rounds are led by future coaches, in other words: the UN Peacekeeping Troops.

▶ **Target Radar**

Pragmatists and conservatives are fully involved during testing. However, they will have trouble imagining that they are actually looking at their future day-to-day work while performing the UAT rounds. It still doesn't fit their frames of reference. Nevertheless, you will see signs of conscious incompetence as each individual reacts in his or her own way. Again, this is natural resistance, and you should approach it with respect.

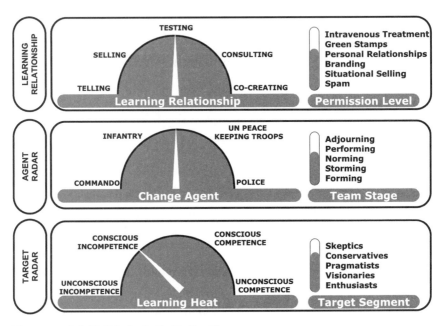

Figure 11.1 Soft-Stuff Radar in the Testing Phase

Another form of resistance, or rather reluctance, will come from middle managers who don't want to release people to spend time on UAT rounds. This will show up on the hard-stuff radar that we're about to discuss.

11.1.2 Hard-Stuff Radar

On the hard-stuff radar in Figure 11.2, you will see that we have indicated some *danger zones*. You should try to stay out of the danger zones, because getting the meter out of a danger zone in this phase will always involve damage repair. Our advice is precaution and prevention.

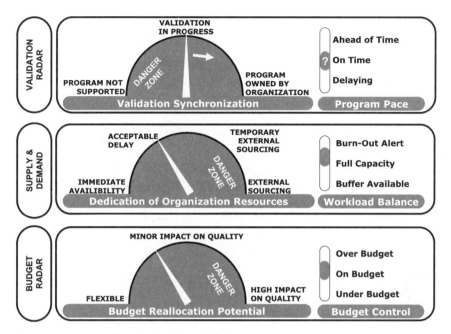

Figure 11.2 Hard-Stuff Radar in the Testing Phase

▸ **Validation Radar**

From an organizational change point of view, testing is a major step toward acceptation and validation. It is in this phase that the prototype is accepted or not. If at the end of the test phase the radar is in the danger zone, a judgment call is made and timing, scope, or both will be affected.

Sign-off of the testing and sign-off of the prototype are crucial before the program can move to the next phase.

▸ **Supply-and-Demand Radar**

In this phase, the whole of the organization is burdened to a large extent. You need many key users to participate in the testing. It is important to follow up on their workload balance because this will not be the last time that you involve them that intensively. The test phase is also a stress test for people. If some people crack now, they will also crack in a later stage, so you should work out a proper solution for them today, not tomorrow.

The danger zone indicated on this radar underscores the point that UAT testing should be done by users and *not* by external resources.

▸ **Budget Radar**

What needs special attention is follow-up on requested changes that may result from the testing. Uncontrolled change requests will backfire on the completion of the prototype and put all consecutive activities on hold. You will wake up in the danger zone with a swollen budget.

Make sure that large change requests are described in detail, including the effort required, so that budget priorities can be set.

11.2 What Happens at the Level of the Program

The test phase is one big moment of truth, as the results of the testing directly impact the buy-in of the new ways of working and its supporting SAP system.

11.2.1 One Big Moment of Truth

During this phase, the organization is watching you very closely. It is the role of the program management to carefully manage expectations and to complete this phase successfully.

This will be the period where the maturity of both the program and the organization will be put under pressure. The whole phase is one big moment of truth. Decisions are made here on moving forward to the next phase, or not.

During this phase, the organization risks fooling itself by too quickly stating that things are fine or that issues will be solved during deployment. Resist the pressure to buy into these stories, because managing a rollout and solving system issues discovered during the testing is "mission: impossible."

11.2.2 Producing Test Plans

The testing is approached the same way as all the other activities: It is captured into projects with clear deliverables. One of the projects is about developing very clear test plans. These test plans describe in the finest detail which key user is supposed to test what and when. By doing so, you ensure that all functionality is properly tested by the people affected, and also that testing is on schedule.

11.2.3 Different Types of Testing

There are different stages within the whole testing phase, which fulfill different testing requirements. These are described in the upcoming subsections:

Unit and System Testing

As explained in Chapter 4, some activities of a certain phase are already started in the previous phase. This is the case for unit and system testing because they happen during the process of building the system. When a certain set-up is finished, the SAP configurator and the developer test their own set-ups. Unit and system testing is a very iterative process. It stops when each part of the set-up functions as expected.

It is important that attention be paid to unit testing and follow-up. The outcome of unit testing must give you an indication of what you can expect during the integration tests.

Integration Testing

Integration testing is an activity that takes place during a specific organized time frame within the testing phase. It is where all key users, SAP experts, and other functional or technical developers test the whole of the system from a process perspective.

User-Acceptance Testing

During the UAT, the organization is involved heavily. This where key users and end-users are involved in testing the system. Successful UATs are the basis for deciding to move forward, toward the deployment phase.

Volume and Performance Testing

This part of the testing focuses on ensuring that the system can handle a huge number of users at the same time and that the system can handle large volume transactions without unduly affecting the performance of the system. Volume and performance testing must be set up so they can happen during the integration and acceptance testing cycles.

Now let's see how the organization stream works in the testing phase.

11.3   The Organization Stream in This Phase

Clearly, the organization is highly involved in the testing. The organization stream's activities directly relate to making sure that the system is supporting the new ways of working.

11.3.1 Develop Test Scenarios to the Smallest Detail

Test scenarios are step-by-step instructions for the testers so that they know exactly what to do. The total list of test scenarios must cover the testing of as many situations that can occur as possible. Test scenarios include the following:

- Header, which includes:
  - Title
  - Description
  - Objective
  - Function within organization that is affected
  - Transactions used
  - Estimated duration
- Body, which includes:
  - A step-by-step activity plan
  - Expected outcome of each test step
  - Comments
  - A column in which the step can be marked as successful or not
- Footer, which includes:
  - Formal sign off conclusion: Yes or No
  - Open space for comments

11.3.2 The Test Cycle

We find that the test cycle is often significantly underestimated. The purpose of testing is not only to make sure that the system works. The testing is also an important activity from a change-management or acceptance point of view.

You will note that the phases are explained in the test cycle in depth. That is because each phase is important to ensuring proper acceptance from the user:

- **Unit Testing**
  Unit testing is the first step in the cycle of testing. Agreed, it happens in parallel to the build activities, but it is a mandatory and important testing step.

> **Note**
>
> Unit testing is only performed by SAP experts, configurators, and developers.

▶ **Integration Testing—Round 1**
The next step in the cycle is the first round of integration tests. This is a crucial cycle, as it is the first time that the prototype gets tested as a whole. The efficiency of the work done during the build phase comes to the surface.

During this period, fixing bugs gets the highest priority. Apart from other problems they pose, bugs threaten to block others from continuing with their testing. The duration of this cycle is typically two to four weeks, depending on the scale and the size of the implementation. At the end of this test cycle, an evaluation milestone must be planned for the feasibility of deployment and go-live of the pilot.

▶ **Integration Testing—Round 2**
After all bugs and issues are resolved, a second round of integration tests is recommended. The number of bugs should have significantly decreased by now.

The duration of Round 2 is typically half the time of the duration of integration test Round 1. At the end of the phase, a second evaluation milestone must be inserted to evaluate whether the acceptance test phase will be kicked off. We stress that it might be better to delay the acceptance tests if you conclude that the quality of the system is insufficient.

> **Note**
>
> Note that the purpose of the integration test round is to increase the quality of the UATs. If there are too many mistakes or bugs found during the UATs, the degree of acceptance of the system by the user may decrease significantly.

▶ **User Acceptance Test Preparation**
During this period, the acceptance tests phase is prepared. The last bugs and issues are solved and the environments are prepared. Users are given access to the test environment.

▶ **User Acceptance Testing—Round 1**
It may sound trivial, but make sure that the first day of this testing period is an introduction day in which you explain the whole of what is supposed to happen in the coming weeks. On that day, you brief everybody about what needs to be done and about what is expected.

When performing the acceptance tests, it is important that you organize the testing at a single location. You need to be able to closely follow up on the progress, and it is important that the test participants interact with each other and with the implementation team. This facilitates better acceptance.

On the level of the supply-and-demand radar, you need to make sure that the testers are available and that you made proper arrangements regarding holidays. The duration of the first round of acceptance tests is typically four to six weeks. During that period, sufficient support must be foreseen for adequate bug-fixing. At the end of this cycle, you have to do the following:

▶ Draw up a final conclusion of the results. (Hint: organize workshops on the last two days of the testing period. Organize a debriefing meeting on the last day of the testing period.)

▶ Make sure all change requests are documented properly.

▶ Make sure that test scenarios are signed-off if appropriate. Make sure there is common approval for signing off test scenarios. Test scenarios that are signed off don't need to be run again in the next round of acceptance testing.

▶ Evaluate the feasibility of the deployment and the go-live of the pilot.

▶ **System Fine-Tuning**
Based on the conclusions and comments of the users and based on the registered change requests, you need a period to improve the system and make changes.

Don't underestimate this phase. There might be more requests than you would have expected. Don't forget that it is only when people are using the system that they recognize issues that did not show up during the design phase. This is normal. In most SAP implementations, this is not taken into account, and the organizations expects this step to concern only testing of the current system setup. Make sure you budget four to eight weeks for this phase.

Correctly handling this step increases the degree of acceptance, because necessary changes are made to the system to ensure a better fit to the ways of working.

▶ **User Acceptance Testing Round 2**
This is the final round of testing. All test scenarios that were not yet signed-off must be retested. It should be approached the same way as UAT Round 1.

Typically, this phase lasts three to four weeks. At the end of this cycle, movement to the deployment phase must be explicitly confirmed, based on the sign-off of the prototype.

You have probably noticed that the duration and effort can take up to 18 weeks in the longest scenarios. This depends on the size of the organization and the scope of the SAP implementation. The estimates given earlier refer to a full-blown SAP implementation of a multinational organization.

For a small implementation in a smaller environment, the testing cycle would take about eight weeks if you want to do it properly from a quality and a change-management perspective.

11.3.3 Test the Processes

No matter how thorough you are about testing the systems, the processes need to be tested separately. You may wonder how on earth it is possible to test a new process in an old organization that is still running on legacy systems.

However, when you investigate each step of the future process in detail, you will notice that there are a surprising amount of process steps that can already be tested on shop-floor level. The testing of the processes on-site is an important step because of the following reasons:

▶ It provides a chance to test the process steps in practice.

▶ It allows people to experience the way the SAP implementation will influence their daily work.

▶ This tests the support of the local hierarchy and its readiness to cooperate with the implementation team.

▶ It sets a benchmark for multiple testing rounds and post-go-live comparison.

▶ It provides the opportunity for local coaches (UN Peacekeeping Troops) and key users (Police) to test their cooperation skills.

▶ It tests whether your instructions have been communicated to the shop-floor level and how well they are understood.

The example in Figure 11.3 illustrates the process steps that have been tested in the logistics area of an SAP implementation for five sites. The first six columns describe the roles involved in the test and to which process steps they contribute. The column in the middle describes the process steps, ranging from critical path to essential but not critical to necessary for long term. The five last columns indicate whether the test of the process steps proved successful or not. The possible test results include:

▸ Passed

▸ Passed with workaround

▸ Defect

▸ Not applicable

▸ Applicable but not tested

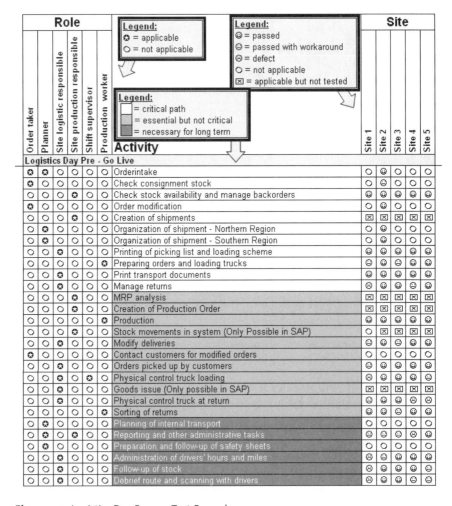

Figure 11.3 Logistics Day Process Test Example

The table in Figure 11.3 allows you to keep an overview of the process readiness and a comparison of one site to another. It is important that these local process-testing initiatives are taken seriously and that they get the full support of middle management and supervisors. Ideally, the tests are done twice with a period of three to four weeks in between. The first time, some learning is needed and people may not perform well because they do not know exactly what is expected of them.

However, things should go much better the second time, and you should be able to apply a zero tolerance on defects on the critical path. If, after two test rounds, there are still defects on the critical path, you should consider a third test round.

Finally, you need to make sure that you do not restrict these kinds of testing to the process steps that involve SAP transactions. The added value of this test is that it integrates the future process into the complete activities of a local logistical day, including daily communication and administration tasks. This is the only way to make the testing representative and the only way to build psychological safety at the most basic level.

11.3.4 Test Reports and Documents

Under the time pressure of the test phase, testing of the reports and the documents is often forgotten about. You will need some determination at this point to claim the importance of correct documents and reports. We strongly advise you to persist for the following reasons:

▶ Most documents (invoices, delivery notes, quality certificates, transport documents, etc.) are intended for external stakeholders such as customers and legal authorities. As a result, the quality of the documents influences their perception on your organization.

▶ Increased attention for the quality of documents pays back in terms of user acceptance, provided that users are involved in helping you to improve the documents.

▶ Correct reports increase the acceptance of middle management, provided that you involved those managers during the design.

11.3.5 Key User and Coach Assignment

The test phase is the ideal time to start detailed assignment and planning of the key users and coaches. This is where you need to dig out the stakeholder map drawn up at the start of the program. You need to make sure that every entity (i.e., a group, a department, a team, a night shift, etc.) that involves users is represented by a key user and a coach.

Key Users

Key users represent what we have earlier called the local police (see Chapter 6). An effective key user network has following characteristics:

▸ Key users are dedicated by their entities and supported by their middle management and peers.

▸ They are known by all users of their entities.

▸ They represent their entities within the implementation team.

▸ They represent the implementation team in their entities.

In your communication, you should pay extra attention to the key users by informing them first about any new communication and occasionally asking them to coach and to assist you in delivering the message to their specific audiences.

Coaches

Like UN Peacekeeping Troops, coaches are responsible for handing over the know-why, know-what, and know-how to the local Police. Assigning coaches is not necessary at the same level of granularity as the assignment of key users. One coach can easily represent more than one entity and have a local presence two to three days a week during the last month before go-live. Examples of typical pre-go-live coaching assignments include the following:

▸ Attaching people to functional roles (via position description), and having the subsequent security profiles and trainings validated.

▸ Communicating the vision and strategy (know-why) and translating these to the level of the entity.

▸ Communicating the future processes (know-what) and highlighting the what's in it for me (WIIFM).

▸ Local testing of processes.

▸ Implementation and follow up of key performance indicators (KPIs).

▸ Following up data collection and data cleansing.

► Supporting local training initiatives and evaluate the learning of the users after they went to training (know-how).

► Assisting with the local technical systems deployment.

An effective coaching network has all the characteristics that we indicated for a key-user network. On top of that, the coaching network has direct access to all implementation team members, and report in on a weekly basis to information and experiences.

How should communication occur during testing? Let's answer this question next.

11.4   The Communication Stream in This Phase

During the test phase, you are involving the organization at all levels. Therefore, it is important to assess how the stakeholders feel about the change.

11.4.1   Ready–Willing–Able Assessments

Duck (2001) suggests using ready, willing, and able (RWA) assessment to understand overall emotional reactions to various elements of the change process.

As illustrated in Figure 11.4, the RWA assessment focuses on three aspects of preparedness that match the ingredients of change mentioned in Chapter 3: readiness to change, willingness to change, and ability to change.

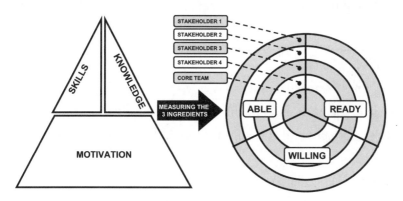

Figure 11.4 RWA Measures the Three Change Ingredients (adapted from Duck, 2001)

RWA is a survey that can be done via e-mail, the Web, or interviews, depending on the sample size. It tells you whether particular parts of the organization need more attention.

How it Works

The RWA assessment produces both quantitative and qualitative data. Prepare for 30 to 50 quantitative statements that require responses on a scale of one to five, from "strongly disagree" to "strongly agree." The qualitative questions ask for written responses, which often produce great volumes of verbiage. Duck (2001) recommends limiting demographic questions to ensure confidentiality, but you do need to record the stakeholder group that the respondent belongs to. The following are examples of representative statements for an RWA assessment:

- Readiness to change (ingredient: knowledge):
  - The challenges we face over the next five years will require us to change dramatically.
  - Our organization is ready to undertake this SAP implementation.
  - I understand the benefits that this implementation will bring.
  - Changes within our organization are driven by business needs and not hidden agendas.
  - I agree that changes to my job are necessary.
- Willingness to change:
  - I understand the vision and the strategy behind the SAP implementation.
  - I understand how this vision will impact what I do and how I make decisions in my job.
  - I know what is expected of me and why.
  - I believe in the value and the efficiency of the change.
  - I will get more out of this change than I will leave behind.
- Ability to change:
  - We have the skills that are required to do the change.
  - I can count on my department/division to follow through and do what they say they will do.
  - The program communication is clear.

▶ The implementation team has the skills it requires to implement the change.

▶ The person I report to translates the program's vision into action for our group.

▶ I am confident that the program will be successful.

When the quantitative and qualitative observations are analyzed and reported, you are only halfway done. The quantitative data provides the headlines, and the verbiage provides the color and the emotion. It is useful to look at the results for each stakeholder group and see how their perceptions differ from one group to another. Figure 11.5 shows an example of an RWA assessment that has been split up into smaller segments of the RWA dimensions.

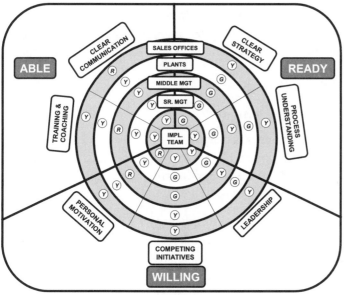

Ⓡ = RED LIGHT, SIGNIFICANTLY NEGATIVE PERCEPTION
Ⓨ = YELLOW LIGHT, NEUTRAL PERCEPTION
Ⓖ = GREEN LIGHT, SIGNIFICANTLY POSITIVE PERCEPTION

Figure 11.5 Example of RWA

Why it is Important

The value of the RWA assessment is that it shows you where the hot spots are and gives you an opportunity to proactively manage them. We recommend doing multiple RWA assessments over the lifecycle of the program, even starting earlier than the test phase. That way, the assessment serves as a fact-based feedback tool you can use to set priorities for organizational change management. There are two more reasons why RWA assessments are important:

▶ **RWA Assessments are Diagnostic Interventions**
This means that they not only help you to diagnose the perception throughout the organization; they also constitute an intervention of psychological safety. Acknowledging receipt of what people tell you and feeding them back what you have understood is an essential part of providing psychological safety. The other essential part is acting on the feedback (see the subsection *Preventing Survey Fatigue*).

▶ **RWA Assessments Prevent Project Cocooning**
They provide you with an objective mechanism for raising key issues because they present a picture of how is perceived across the organization.

As a final note on RWAs: you should always remember that the results represent a map of the organization at a given moment in time. Like any other map, it is useful to guide you in a certain direction. But don't fool yourself by thinking that the map is the territory.

11.4.2   Preventing Survey Fatigue

During large implementations, it is very difficult to keep an eye on what is cooking inside the organization and how people's perceptions of the upcoming change are evolving. Hence, surveys are commonly used to check this "change readiness."

The RWA assessments are not the only surveys you will conduct. For example, we encourage you to think of learning evaluations as surveys. Course evaluations should not be restricted to the course content but should inquire into all other aspects of the program that are visible for the user, such as data cleansing, communication about the program, and UAT.

Naomi Karten (2002) gives the following six recommendations for conducting surveys and preventing them from becoming a waste of time:

▶ **Set Survey Objectives**
Define those objectives before you start, or you will end up with a list of questions that are unanswered because they were never asked.

▶ **Keep Survey Length Under Control**
Avoid nice-to-know-but-so-what questions. A well-designed survey can be completed in less than 10 minutes.

▶ **Make the Survey Action-Oriented**
Surveys are often full of thermometer questions. For example, "Did this course match your expectations?" is a thermometer question. Responses may suggest the existence of a problem, but provide too little information for you to understand the problem or recommend changes. If, instead, you ask questions like "Are you now able to go back to your workplace and put what you have learned into practice?", "Which difficulties did you experience when making the exercises?", or "Which topics will require extra attention before using them in practice?", you can use the responses you receive to plan a course of action.

▶ **Balance open-ended and closed questions**
Closed questions ask respondents to select from a set of fixed responses. Respondents can answer these questions quickly, and responses can be tabulated, summarized, graphed, charted, analyzed, and reported. Open-ended questions, by contrast, ask respondents to answer in their own words. Responses take time to review and are subject to interpretation. However, open-ended questions frequently provide a level of insight into the customer perspective that is impossible to obtain from closed questions.

▶ **Ensure an adequate survey response**
To generate interest, set the stage by publicizing the importance of the survey in helping you improve your service effectiveness. Explain your objectives and note how quickly the survey can be completed. Marketing and branding the survey can dramatically influence the level and quality of the responses you will receive.

▶ **Tell stakeholders about your survey findings**
This is the most important and yet also the most forgotten element. Inform stakeholders of your findings and the changes you will make as a result of their feedback. When you implement suggested changes, announce that you're doing so because of their feedback. Don't overlook this essential element of providing feedback about their feedback to you.

11.4.3   Pace the Organization

More people become closely involved in the work of the program during the test phase. Users are invited for testing, and key users become primary communication partners.

You should be aware that this is also the first time that you cross the chasm we discussed in Chapter 6. Pragmatists hook into the details of the testing, and conservatives start to wonder what this is going to mean for them. As Figure 11.6 illustrates, at the end of the test phase you will notice that the big boulder of the program has reached a tipping point and is now rolling downhill.

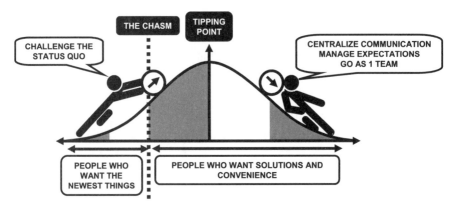

Figure 11.6 Pacing Communication

From now on, you will have to pace the majority of pragmatists and conservatives, who will be pressing you for concrete details. Therefore, it is important that you set the right expectations during your communication and that you do not over-promise with regard to delivering prototypes and demonstrating solutions.

It is painful to be applauded for the demonstration of a certain solution only to find out that you overlooked some important elements because you did not consult the implementation team at large. Your team is a big team by now, and you must align solutions internally first before making promises to the organization. Minor and major incidents in this area will make you aware that you will need to centralize communication as you are approaching the go-live.

11.5 The Learning Stream in This Phase

In this phase, training materials must be further prepared, fine-tuned, and validated. Let us gain an understanding of how this happens.

11.5.1 Trainer Materials

Trainer materials are the slideshows, posters, cards with specific exercise information, etc., that facilitate the courses. They are derived from the participant materials, and their primary goal is to enhance the delivery of the courses. They need to be created, so they take up time and budget.

11.5.2 Local Enhancements and Translations

The delivery of a course will not only be affected by language differences and cultural differences. On the level of business processes, you should be aware of the local legal requirements. As these will create extra work for the implementation team, these differences may cause extra work on the level of documentation.

The translation of courses to the local language is a positive thing for the users. However, there are some cons you have to take into account before deciding to translate the whole training catalog:

▶ Think about the consequences for later updates to the training materials.

▶ Qualitative translation takes time and outsourcing it to a third-party will not speed up the process unless that third-party is very familiar with the local organization and knows the specific language of SAP.

11.5.3 Pilot Training With Key Users

In our opinion, the validation of the participant materials should not be restricted to the functional team members. We see it as an opportunity to involve the key users early on. The sooner key users are involved in the learning stream, the sooner they will be able to take on the role of change agent. An additional advantage of pilot training with key users is that they will be better prepared for the UATs.

11.5.4 Keeping in Synch with Security Profiles

In this phase of the implementation, the UAT may call for changes in the security profiles and some processes. This may affect the way that roles are defined or the functioning of the system is described. In our experience, informing the learning stream responsible about the changed roles is the last thing on the testers' minds. As a result, the manager of the learning stream needs to proactively focus on any changes going on the security profiles.

11.6 The Performance Management Stream in This Phase

In Chapter 4, we mentioned that an old organization with a new system equals an expensive old organization. To prevent this, we underscore that you not only need to test the processes, but also measure this process testing.

11.6.1 Measuring Process Testing

As discussed in the organization process stream, it is essential to test the processes down to shop-floor level for a number of reasons. The performance dashboard in Figure 11.7 shows how the process steps of the logistics day from the previous example can be measured.

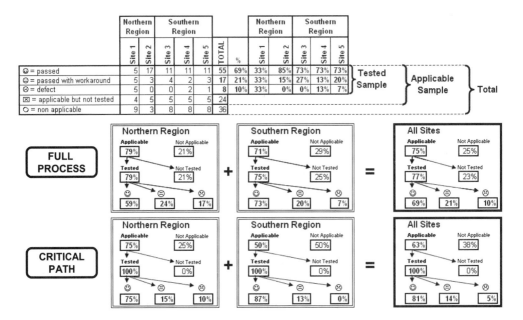

Figure 11.7 Performance Dashboard of Logistics Day Process Testing

The test results for each site are counted, regrouped into the regions they report to, and drilled down to the level of the tested sample only. In this example, we also made a distinction between the complete process and the process steps on the critical path. With regards to this critical path, you should pay close attention to the following points:

▶ Make sure that all of the steps on the critical path are part of the tested sample (indicator **tested** is at 100 %)

▶ You should be able to apply a zero tolerance on the steps of the critical path. In this example, the process performance rate of the critical path is at 95 % because defects are still at 5 %.

The advantage of testing and measuring the process in this way is that you can easily track down the performance ratios to the process steps, to the roles involved, and eventually to their learning profiles. This is exactly what we meant when we mentioned in the previous chapter that learning links strategy to performance.

11.7   Moments of Truth

We find following moments of truth in the test phase. Let's proceed with this section so you can get an idea of what they are.

11.7.1   Evaluation of Testing

The evaluation of the test results at each test round is a moment of truth: either it is confirmed to move forward, or it is confirmed that the prototype setup is not working properly.

11.7.2   Sign-Off of the Prototype

With sign-off of the prototype, the organization confirms that the tool functions according to requirements and that the organization is convinced that it will properly support the new ways of working.

11.7.3   Engaging Data-Compliance Auditors

Why on earth would you want to be involved in an auditing process at all during implementation? The point is that basic data needs to be checked not only by those at the top but by all users who will be affected. This means you are playing the game on two levels: involving the target users (which contributes to their motivation), and sending the signal that data accuracy is going to be of vital importance in the future.

If you package this last communication appropriately, it can really be a learning moment for the organization. Here are two examples to confirm this moment of truth:

- As the needs and the landscape of HR is evolving from payroll and personnel-administration automation to employee and manager self-service, many implementations have hiccups because of workflows and approval processes that are based on false organizational structures. As you may be aware, turning back workflows that start on the wrong foot is no fun. Therefore, you should prepare by involving all users in the cleansing of the organization structure and getting the data right before deploying a full suite of e-HR applications. A first go-live of a simple "Who's who" with an organizational structure linked to it is the key to not disappointing employees and managers.

- As the equipment is one of the most important data types in the plant-maintenance cycle and the asset-lifecycle management, you should get the mountain of equipment and organizational structures data cleansed beforehand.

This involves time and effort from the users, but consider what happens when you decline this opportunity for involvement: hours and hours of cleansing and turning back of workflows, and on top of that impatient and unhappy users. It's up to you.

11.7.4 Taming the "Local Pets"

Every country and every project has its specific elements, and every industry has its specific exceptions. We are referring to the processes that are not the core processes but the exceptions that people warn you about 80 % of the time. Examples of these local pets include the following:

- Imperial versus metric systems in US deployments of global programs.
- Nota Fiscal in Brazil.
- Luxury taxes in Indonesia.
- Post-dated checks in Taiwan.
- All kinds of industry specific pets like samples or returns.

The sensitive atmosphere hanging around local pets illustrates the need for psychological safety. Even though the program may have completed the 80 % of the processes that are business-critical, people won't place their trust in the program until you tame their local pet. It becomes a symbolic hurdle that you have to clear. Taming the local pet equals creating buy-in by investing all of your attention into these special processes. Make sure that you involve the local key players.

11.7.5 Course Invitations

You should be aware that course invitations are probably the first individualized communication that the users receive. Instead of restricting these to the usual invitation details ("be there at that date and time"), this is an opportunity for delivering the complete message, including the Know-why and Know-what. Now it's time to look at the deliverables for this phase.

11.8 Deliverables

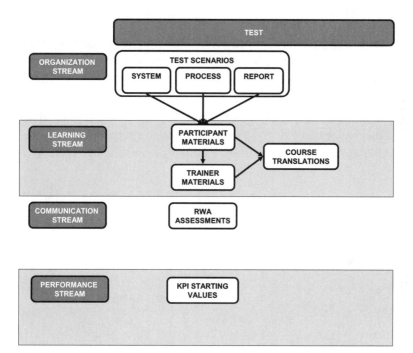

Figure 11.8 Organizational Change Deliverables of the Test Phase

The deliverables for this phase are as follows:

▶ Test scenarios:

- System

- Processes

- Reports

▶ Participant materials

▶ Trainer materials

- Course translations
- RWA assessments
- KPI starting values

Figure 11.8 outlines these deliverables per stream.

For the complete map of all deliverables during the program lifecycle, see Appendix C.

11.9 Conclusion

The test phase is a big moment of truth. It is nearly impossible to exaggerate how critical this phase is when it comes to user acceptance of the future solution. You have to make sure that there are enough iterations with the build phase. Many times, it is during testing that inefficiencies in the future ways of working and its supporting SAP environment are detected. But most of all, you should make sure that you don't restrict testing to system-testing. Implementing SAP is about processes, so not testing processes puts you in a serious danger.

In Chapter 12, we will cover the deployment phase. This is where you will bring the implementation to a point of no return.

In the deployment phase, the new organization, its ways of working, and the supporting SAP system are put on the rails. You are bringing the implementation to a point of no return. For this reason, the previous test phase needs a clear sign-off, and each of the steps you take must be carefully planned.

12 Deploy

12.1 Phase-Specific Characteristics and Needs

In this section we explain how you should use and read the soft-stuff and hard-stuff radars, taking into account the specific characteristics and needs of the deployment phase.

12.1.1 Soft-Stuff Radar

Deployment is when the soft-stuff radar (shown in Figure 12.1) tends to indicate some alarming levels, certainly if you omitted the involvement of stakeholders in previous phases. The boulder mentioned in Chapter 6 (see Figure 6.2) has now passed a tipping point and is rolling downhill. Stay calm and try to stay focused on the following radar readings:

▶ **Learning Relationship Radar**
This is the phase where the majority of the organization will be confronted with SAP. The organizational change all of a sudden becomes undeniable. As you will be deploying the system and the training according to a strict timetable and plan, the implementation sometimes resembles a military operation. The implementation team is in command and is issuing orders to the organization.

By now, the level of permission has increased to a level that the organization depends on the implementation team to go forward. Systems are prepared, users are trained, data cleansing is finished, etc. Your organization is getting ready for a new beginning (although you may be looking at go-live as a a conclusion).

▶ **Agent Radar**

It is often said that groups under pressure are the best-performing teams. The adrenalin of the situation will help you, provided that you offer the team a certain level of psychological safety. In the background, the infantry are working long hours to prepare the system, and on the front lines of the implementation UN peacekeeping troops are taking their positions as they are assigned to certain areas or departments of the organization to perform what we could call "pre-implementation coaching."

▶ **Target Radar**

Unavoidably, you run into the conservatives and the skeptics during this phase. Don't let their mood bring you down. Rather, look at is as a sign that you now have reached the furthest reaches of the organization. The resistance that you start to experience at the deploy phase will also be more explicit than before. User resistance will not be restricted to the classroom or the written responses to open survey questions. Some middle managers will be tempted to amplify user complaints. One more time: Approach this resistance with respect, and try to filter the feedback.

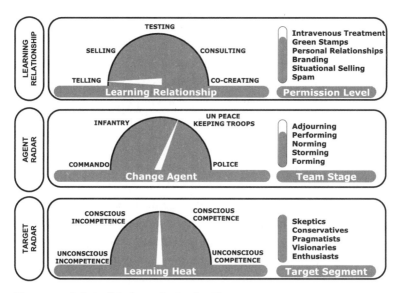

Figure 12.1 Soft-Stuff Radar at the Deploy Phase

12.1.2 Hard-Stuff Radar

In this phase, the danger zones on the hard-stuff radar, shown in Figure 12.2, are still valid, or even require more than usual attention.

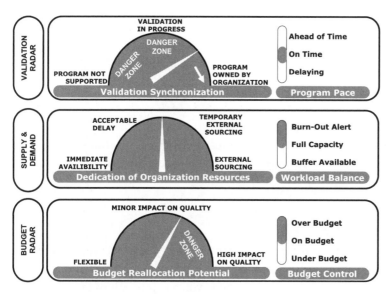

Figure 12.2 Hard-Stuff Radar at the Deploy Phase

▶ **Validation Radar**

Deployment is about delivering SAP to the whole of the organization. Buy-in is important here. All deliverables need sign-off without exception, a fact illustrated by an increased danger zone. Program pacing in this stage depends entirely on the supply-and-demand radar.

▶ **Supply-and-Demand Radar**

The supply-and-demand radar needs to be followed up very carefully for the people in the entities where you are doing the deployment but also for the implementation team. The latter may be moving from location to location on many overlapping deployments, so try to keep their workload in balance. On the other hand, we have removed the danger zone reading for this phase because some activities such as training and technical writing is often better done by external resources.

▶ **Budget Radar**

Being a budget manager in this phase is tough. In the deployment phase, it is typical that budget buffers are used. While rolling out a system, certain change requests pop up. Some of them might be necessary, and it is very difficult to take these into account at the end of the design phase. Close follow-up is required, especially the closer you get to the end of the deployment. The further you move toward the end of the program, the less flexibility you have in reassigning your budget resources.

Now, let's proceed to discover what occurs at the program level during this phase.

12.2 What Happens at the Level of the Program

In the deploy phase, the program must first focus completely on the go-live of the pilot. The roll-out approach must be defined carefully, taking into account geography and culture but also the business criticality of the entities to be covered.

12.2.1 Locking the Program

The choice of the pilot is important because the pilot group will be the first to go-live. They must understand the fact that they are the first and that they will face issues that others in the chain will not face. They must be more patient than the other entities. Also, they will have to deal with some typical malfunctions of a system that is brand new. Don't expect that the system will be perfect once it has been tested. Some things you will only discover when running live.

As illustrated in Figure 12.3, you should make sure that you lock the program into a period of about three months before and after a pilot or rollout. More specifically, this means:

- No other deployments
- No scope changes
- No other major business initiatives

Figure 12.3 The Program Lock

During this period, initial malfunctions can be eliminated and the system can stabilize. The locked period also allows you to slightly change your deployment approach based on the things you have learned.

We have learned that there is no magic recipe for successful deployments, apart from learning by doing. Each deployment that you do gives you more experience, and you learn the most from your mistakes.

12.2.2 Cultures and Geography

The key element to keep in the back of your mind is that, in the beginning, you need to learn. Don't make your life more difficult by first rolling out program entities in a part of the world that is culturally very different from the one you work in.

First plan to roll out the entities in the continent where your organization's headquarters is situated. By doing so, you avoid additional complexity and can concentrate on the essential issues in the beginning.

Geography is also an element that determines your roll-out sequence. If you plan your roll-outs in parallel in different parts of the world at the same time, you risk spending too much time traveling, losing time for more valuable activities, and increasing your costs unnecessarily.

12.2.3 Business Coverage and Criticality

Another criterion for defining the order of the roll-out is the percentage of total business that is realized in a certain entity or part of the world. The entities representing larger portions of the business should get higher priority.

You might run into situations where a number of entities urgently need this SAP system to be implemented, as they currently have no system at all or because current legacy systems' continuity is no longer guaranteed.

12.3 The Organization Stream in This Phase

In the deploy phase, it is all about making the change happen. This definitely applies to the organization stream.

12.3.1 The Deployment Team

Your deployment team is made up of people of the entity in which you are rolling out SAP, supported by people from the global core team.

You need the local team to make sure that the local entity is fully involved and that knowledge about the local business is available. You need the global implementation team because of their knowledge about the global SAP system and the SAP program, and for sharing the experience that they have gathered during other roll-outs. In this phase, you need to make sure that the whole team is working together at the deployment site.

12.3.2 The Deployment Cycle

For each roll-out, you follow a cycle that is comparable to the program cycle applicable for the entire SAP implementation: Unfreezing, Changing, Refreezing, as discussed here:

► **Step 1: Unfreezing: Project Setup**
Each deployment is treated as a project requiring a project charter, resources, and budget. Unfreeze the local organization by making sure that all is in place. The team is a combination of local and global members. You also need a local steering committee, project sponsor, project owner and project manager. You might consider—depending on your organization's way of working—also having shared budget responsibility locally and globally.

► **Step 2: Changing**
This is made up of the following four stages:

   ► **Design**
   The implementation starts with comparing the new ways of working with the current ones. A gap analysis is put together that may lead to change requests. Also, the need for interfaces is evaluated.

   ► **Build**
   The change requests result in additional configuration and development. Functional elements must be completed according to the needs of the local entity and master data must be cleansed. Data must be converted.

   ► **Test**
   Once the system is ready, it must be tested. This includes unit testing, integration testing, and acceptance testing. In this phase, you only test

the things that have changed with respect to localization. It is only localization that still needs to be accepted; the original prototype was accepted earlier.

▶ **Depoyment**
After that the system is set to go-live and the entity starts using it.

Step 3: Refreezing

For the refreeze activities, please refer to the discussion in Chapter 9. Then, read the upcoming subsections.

12.3.3   Cutover Approach

You must carefully plan how to move from the current ways of working and the use of the current system to the new ways of working and use of the new SAP system.

This plan must be as detailed as possible, describing all steps. The cutover plan does also include backup or roll-back scenarios for the sake of guaranteeing continuity. The cutover plan must be tested thoroughly.

12.3.4   Go-Live

The go-live date must be planned very carefully. The whole of the organization must be prepared. Go-live does not only mean starting to use the new SAP environment. It also means physically switching off the old systems.

Some organizations allow the use of the new system and the old system in parallel for a number of weeks. We firmly recommend that you resist the temptation to do something similar. It saves time, but it also keeps you from focusing on the future. It is as though you were divorcing from your partner while continuing to live together when your partner already has a new relationship with someone else.

We would also recommend planning a go-live on the first day of the week. If go-live is planned on the last day of the week, you take the risk that the users will be less focused and that the system will not be fully used on the first day. People tend to behave a bit different at the end of the week, when they are looking forward to the weekend.

12.3.5 Sign-Off

There are two major moments of sign-off in a local deployment. At the end of the test phase, there must be a sign-off allowing the program to move towards go-live. The go-live itself must be signed-off by the local steering committee and by the global program steering committee.

The most important sign-off is the one given by the global steering committee for the total rollout of the SAP system across the whole of the organization. This is a major milestone for the program.

12.3.6 Preparing External Stakeholders

As you are approaching the moment of cutover to another way of working, you need to take into consideration how things will change for external stakeholders and non-users. The most common forgotten stakeholders are:

▶ **Suppliers**
When switching over to a new procurement process, you need to involve your suppliers. By educating them about your purchase orders and how they need to change their work in order to continue to deliver succesfully.

▶ **Customers**
You may want to ask your customers to build up some extra stock as a means of preparing for a business risk. Accordingly, you will probably build up credit lines for these customers.

We are at the stage where we must examine the communication during this phase.

12.4   The Communication Stream in This Phase

At this moment the organization is under high pressure. You will tend to pay less attention to communication activities because there is work on the table. Nevertheless, it is now that communication matters the most.

12.4.1   Centralizing Communication

In this last phase before go-live, you will notice that the atmosphere is quite different than during the other phases and that the number of hours worked also shows some flexibility compared to the start of the program. A direct result of an increased pressure—be it positive or negative—is that the communication tends to be less organized and followed up.

Communication Gaps

The first audiences to fall victim to communication gaps are entities and users that are at wider geographical distances. However, you will note communication gaps appearing more often at closer distances as well, so there is a need in this stage to review the communication principles.

You will need to find out what works best for you, but our experience shows that centralizing all formal communication and assigning a spokesperson or communication office works best in this phase.

On the other hand, informal communication relies completely on the local coaches and their ability to measure the local temperature, to report back, and to share and recycle their lessons learned within the implementation team.

Managing the Communication Pipeline

In the last month before go-live, and until one month after go-live, we advise you to manage your communication pipeline of outgoing communication. This means that you will need to make an inventory of all outgoing messages, determine their release times, and analyze whether they can be bundled. You should bundle as many messages as you can into a maximum of three communications a week. Any higher frequency will blur the communication and make it less relevant in the eyes of the audience.

The example in Table 12.1 illustrates how you can use different communication channels according to the urgency of the communication need during this period.

Communication Need	Communication Type	Communication Channel
Nice to know	Pull	FAQ on website
Need to know	Push	SAP-Flash newsletter
Need to buy-into	Push & dialogue	Personal by coaches

Table 12.1 Example of Communication Matrix for Go-Live

Leveraging the Knowledge Portal

The knowledge portal mentioned earlier in this chapter needs to be the single most visited Website of the organization by now. Ideally, users are in the habit of regularly checking the site for updates.

Next in importance to making the training materials available, we recommend investing in several search mechanisms to facilitate browsing through the ocean of information you are making available. Searching training materials and FAQ's by transaction code or by functional role are very popular activities close to go-live.

12.4.2 Agreeing on Post-Go-Live Communication

You will need to communicate about your communication with every individual of the organization. The go-live communication plan needs to be on everybody's desk and in everybody's memory.

Figure 12.4 shows an example of a go-live communication plan. The grey arrows indicate the bottom-up communication and the black arrows the top-down feedback.

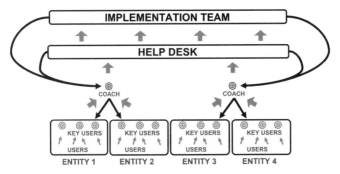

Figure 12.4 Go-Live Communication Plan Example

You need to make sure that every user understands and agrees to follow the steps indicated in Figure 12.4, namely:

▶ Report problems to key users, who will try to solve the problem.

▶ Have key users consult the coach about unresolved problems. The latter will try to solve the problems.

▶ The coach registers unresolved problems at the helpdesk. The helpdesk will try to solve the problem.

▶ The helpdesk consults the implementation team for unresolved problems.

This way, the implementation team only gets the questions that they alone are able to resolve, which saves precious time.

12.4.3 Preparing for Crisis Communication

Sometimes you need to communicate as a way of warding off disaster, whenever your ability to perform business as planned is at risk. We hope you will never need to make emergency communications, but if an emergency occurs you should be prepared.

Figure 12.5 illustrates how normal communications and emergency communications differ from each other. This is the relationship between reliability and paparazzi value. In emergency situations, faster communication still needs to be reliable. The best way to do this is to use priority senders (certain sponsors) and priority channels (face-to-face, phone, etc.)

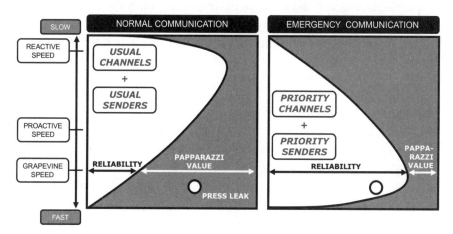

Figure 12.5 The Reliability of Normal and Emergency Communication

The point is that you be aware that urgent messages need a specific channel and a particular sender in order to be reliable in the eyes of a receiver.

12.5 The Learning Stream in This Phase

During the deployment phase, the learning stream is very active. This is where the training plan gets executed. You must be prepared to deal with resistance in a proper way.

12.5.1 Training the Users

There are different ways to train users and, as we mentioned higher, "the magic is in the blend." Depending on the combination of learning forms that you provide, ranging from trainer-controlled to self-paced, everyone has the opportunity to get to know something more about the user.

The delivery of training should not be restricted to the pure handover of knowledge. You should be aware that training is for most users the first real confrontation with the implementation. The perception of the training activities will influence to a large extent their (and their bosses') perception of the complete program. As trivial as it may seem, most users will decide whether they will trust the implementation based on the quality of the training delivery.

We want to emphasize that the success of training delivery depends on the emotional intelligence and the didactic devotion of the trainers and the technical writers. These qualities matter more than the competence of the best experts in the team (provided that you are running a stable training environment).

12.5.2 Resistance in the Classroom

In Chapter 2, we described resistance as the emotion that occurs when we experience an interruption of our expectations. For the majority of the users, the moment of training is their first real interruption of the world as they know it. As a result, you will probably be confronted with colorful expressions of resistance.

Identifying Resistance in the Classroom

In his years of travels around organizations, Robert Bramson (1981) found that the same kinds of difficult people appeared constantly. They appeared with such regularity that he was able to give them identifying names and descriptions. Bramson's widely cited cast of characters is listed in Table 12.2.

The Drama Triangle mentioned in Chapter 2 helps in identifying the underlying feelings. Not only will this approach provide information about the underlying needs, it also provides some direction as to how to respond. Figure 12.6 matches Bramson's difficult people with the insights gained from Chapter 2.

Characters	Characteristics
Sherman Tanks	▶ Attacking, accusing, intimidating ▶ They are always right ▶ Get irritated or angry if they sense resistance ▶ See tasks as clear and concrete ▶ Value assertiveness ▶ Value confidence
Snipers	▶ Use teasing and innuendo ▶ Often very witty ▶ Share Sherman Tank's strong sense of how others should act, but are often unrealistic ▶ Can turn into a Tank if exposed
Exploders	▶ Adult tantrum ▶ May cry, be silently enraged, or yell/scream ▶ Anger often moves to suspicion and blaming ▶ Creates resentment
Bulldozers	▶ Low tolerance for correction and contradiction ▶ Condescending ▶ Don't wait for others to catch up ▶ Highly productive and accurate thinkers ▶ Believe facts and knowledge provide stability
Think-they-know-it-alls	▶ Seek admiration and respect of others by trying to act like experts when they are not ▶ Don't always know they are not experts ▶ Curious people; like to learn a little about a lot of things
Super-Agreeables	▶ Want to be liked and loved ▶ Make others feel liked and approved ▶ Tell you things that are satisfying to hear ▶ Say "Yes" to everything ▶ Can secretly be resentful
Indecisives	▶ Put off making important decisions ▶ They don't want to hurt anyone ▶ Strive to help people ▶ Stall until the decision is made
Unresponsives	▶ Close down, even when asked direct questions ▶ Clam up when you need a response or expect conversation ▶ Difficult to determine why they are silent

Table 12.2 Ten Common Difficult Behaviors in the Classroom (Bramson, 1981)

Characters	Characteristics
Complainers	▶ Find fault with everything ▶ Feel someone should be doing something, but feel helpless to take action ▶ Have distinct idea of what should be done ▶ Usually there is some truth to their complaints
Negativists	▶ Feel defeated and dispirited as though they have little power over their lives ▶ Pessimistic, more bitter than complainers ▶ Bring others down quickly

Table 12.2 Ten Common Difficult Behaviors in the Classroom (Bramson, 1981) (cont.)

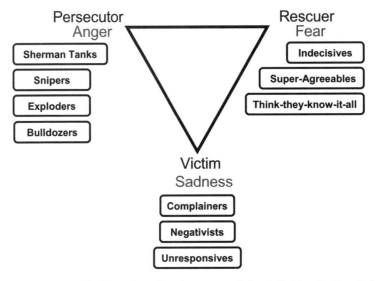

Figure 12.6 Difficult People in the Classroom and the Underlying Feelings (adapted from Callahan, 2004; Bramson, 1981; and Karpman, 1968)

Dealing With Resistance in the Classroom

When confronted with difficult behavior in the classroom, your goal is not to solve the person's problems. Your only goal is to make sure that all participants are getting the full benefit of the session. Remember the following:

▶ You can't change someone's behavior, only give them good reasons to change it.

▶ You need to determine if the situation is really causing a problem for the group's learning, and, if it's not, to let it go.

In Table 12.3, we suggest how you can deal with these types of difficult people.

Type	Persecutor	Rescuer	Victim
Underlying Feeling	Anger	Fear	Sadness
Information Value	Clarity	Possibilities and Threats	Relationships
Don'ts during the session	Take it personally	Take their fears as the reality and respond to their individual fears	Rescue them by responding to their individual complaints at the expense of the other participants
Do's during the session	Involve them and leverage their expertise for the group	Clarify the information they provide through examples and providing the right context	Summarize their communication and stay clear on the facts and the goals
Do's after the session	Consider recruiting them as Key Users	Use their insights to check for risks and possibilities you may not have thought about	Use their insights to check for relationships with stakeholders who may need some extra time

Table 12.3 Basic Dos and Don'ts for Difficult Behavior in the Classroom

Experienced trainers know many tricks and tools for preventing most of the situations from getting out of hand. These range from the setting of ground rules to the use of a parking lot (a place to hold items for a later, more appropriate time). Unfortunately, for some severe cases you will be forced to ask the participant to leave the room. Always keep in mind that the learning of the participants takes priority.

12.5.3 Training Helpdesk Personnel

Often forgotten but nevertheless of vital importance are the helpdesk personnel. Our advice is to invest enough time in training them on all levels: know-how, know-what, and know-why.

Keep in mind that helpdesk people should be trained as agents of change. Every incident they receive is a moment of truth. The way they talk about the implementation and how comfortable they are with it will determine how convincing they are in conveying their message.

When thinking about their contribution to the success of the implementation, keep in mind that:

- They are continuously in contact with the users. Therefore they deserve the same level of attention as the key users.
- The user incidents that they log provide a major input to the implementation team with regard to:
  - Technical failures
  - Training needs
  - Process understanding
- The helpdesk is a communication channel for providing specific knowledge to the users when they most need it (i.e., when their time-to-ask equals zero). As a consequence, they should be able to navigate through the learning deliverables. In other words, look at the helpdesk person as a "knowledge sales person" and provide them with updates first-hand.

12.5.4 Evaluating Learning

Training evaluation—if properly set-up—can serve as an early warning system and allow you to make corrections as you go. The sample evaluation matrix in Figure 12.7 will help you to gain clarity about what you will be measuring and how to gather the data.

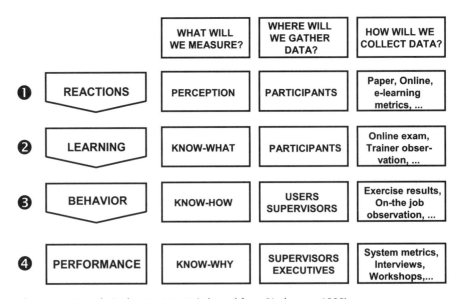

	WHAT WILL WE MEASURE?	WHERE WILL WE GATHER DATA?	HOW WILL WE COLLECT DATA?
❶ REACTIONS	PERCEPTION	PARTICIPANTS	Paper, Online, e-learning metrics, ...
❷ LEARNING	KNOW-WHAT	PARTICIPANTS	Online exam, Trainer observation, ...
❸ BEHAVIOR	KNOW-HOW	USERS SUPERVISORS	Exercise results, On-the job observation, ...
❹ PERFORMANCE	KNOW-WHY	SUPERVISORS EXECUTIVES	System metrics, Interviews, Workshops,...

Figure 12.7 Sample Evaluation Matrix (adapted from Birnbrauer, 1998)

In many organizations, feedback gathering is viewed as an isolated activity. They gather feedback but do nothing with the information they've obtained. This failure to take action is mostly a major step backwards in building trust because, having been asked for their feedback, stakeholders then watch for changes to take place as a result of their input.

Gathering feedback and taking no action based on the findings is worse than not gathering feedback to begin with (Karten, 2002). Remember the emotional bank account that we mentioned earlier when we explained the importance of branding? Gathering feedback and not taking action results in a withdrawal of trust from that bank account. Once again: Trust is the currency of change.

12.5.5 Integrating Materials in Work Environment

We are learning all the time. Contrary to what we may think, people chatting in the coffee room or the person having an "A-ha!" revelation of how to solve a vexing problem might well be doing the most important work of all.

Learning by doing predominates, as methods such as simulation, performance support, and augmented reality become the norm rather than the exception. We have known for a long time that people learn best by doing.

The way we can put this learning in real-time to best use is by putting the learning objects where they are needed: in practice and in the system's help files. This is the point of having a knowledge portal.

Now let's see how we can manage performance during this phase.

12.6 The Performance Management Stream in This Phase

During the deployment phase the KPIs are put in practice. This is at the same time also a learning process.

12.6.1 Install KPIs Locally

If you want the KPIs to be fully operational after go-live, you should start installing and measuring them locally in this phase. Preferably about two months before go-live start communicating and measuring them. The example in Figure 12.8 illustrates KPIs that can be used for Supply Chain.

Supply Chain KPI's	Friday	Saturday	Sunday	Monday	Tuesday	Wednesday	Thursday	Friday	Saturday	Sunday	Monday	Tuesday	Wednesday	Thursday	Weekly total	Role
Number of Sales Orders received after 12AM	0							2							2	Local Logistics Coordinator
Total Number of Sales Orders	39			40	40	36	41	30			37	48	22	33	366	Local Logistics Coordinator
Number of Transport Plans received before 2PM	1			1	1	1	1	1			1	1	1	1	10	Local Logistics Coordinator
Total Number of Transport Plans	1			1	1	1	1	1			1	1	1	1	10	Local Logistics Coordinator
Number of Delivery Notes Confirmed the Same Day	0			0	0	0	0	0			0	0	0	0	0	Local Logistics Coordinator
Total Number of Delivery Notes	47			47	51	38	55	36			42	40	46	47	449	Local Logistics Coordinator
Number of Trucks checked at departure + at return	0			0	0	0	0	0			0	0	0	0	0	Local Logistics Coordinator & Drivers
Total number of Trucks on the road today	6			4	4	6	6	3			7	6	4	4	50	Drivers
Number Final Products Scanned				206		101					158		254		719	Production Supervisor
Number Final Products Produced				219		101					172		268		760	Production Worker

Figure 12.8 Supply Chain Local KPIs on Site Level

As noted in example of Figure 12.8, not all KPIs are measured on a daily basis; some are measured weekly, and others on an every-other-day basis. However, they are consolidated bi-weekly. This table allows you to take the following actions:

- Link back to the roles whose holders are in charge of these performance levels and eventually to their learning curriculum.

- Make a bi-weekly evolution report for the site, and follow up the progress.

- Compare sites to one another with regard to performance readiness.

As shown in Figure 12.8, you will notice problems with the confirmation of delivery notes and the checking of trucks at departure and return. When diagnosing this performance, you need to link back to the nine fields of the performance matrix we mentioned earlier. The following questions can help you to diagnose this particular example:

- On the level of motivation (goals):
  - **Organization goals:** Is the importance of the program clear?
  - **Process goals:** Are the targets of the supply-chain process known by holders of all involved roles?
  - **Role goals:** Are all individuals aware of what is expected of them in their particular roles?
- On the level of knowledge (structure):
  - **Organization structure:** Does the overall supply-chain organization allow for this task to be accomplished?
  - **Process structure:** Is the supply-chain process designed in order to allow truck checking and delivery note confirmation? (Note: for this

aspect, you may find that the KPI is applicable but that you are unable to confirm delivery notes before go-live).

- **Role structure:** Does the role description include delivery-note confirmation and truck checking, and is the workload for this role balanced enough to perform this task (for example, the local logistics coordinator may have to do another task at the moment of truck departure and arrival)?

▶ On the level of management (skills):

- **Organization management:** Do all the players in the organization have the skills to facilitate checking trucks and confirming delivery notes?

- **Process management:** Do all the players in the process have the skills to make sure that trucks can be checked on departure and return and that delivery notes can be confirmed the same day?

- **Role management:** Do the local logistics coordinator and the drivers posses the skills to accomplish this performance?

12.6.2 Local KPI Setting is a Two-Way Learning Process

The best way to fail in the performance stream is to enforce KPIs locally and have people comply with them without their involvement. Take for instance procurement KPIs that need to be installed locally. The example in Figure 12.9 demonstrates the project-cocooning effect: KPIs that look trivial for the implementation team members are pushed down to the local level, on the assumption that they are easy to understand and simple to measure.

The context of the implementation in this example is one where local sites had their own procurement rules with a lot of local purchasing power and substantial paperwork and signatures. The future procurement process was going to be a workflow-based, centralized process based on an organization-wide approval matrix.

Therefore the creation and validation of purchase orders was a necessary habit that needed to be learned in advance. The implementation team determined three KPIs to make sure that this was going to happen:

▶ The purchase order-invoice ratio.

▶ The purchase order validation ratio.

▶ The number of incorrect invoices.

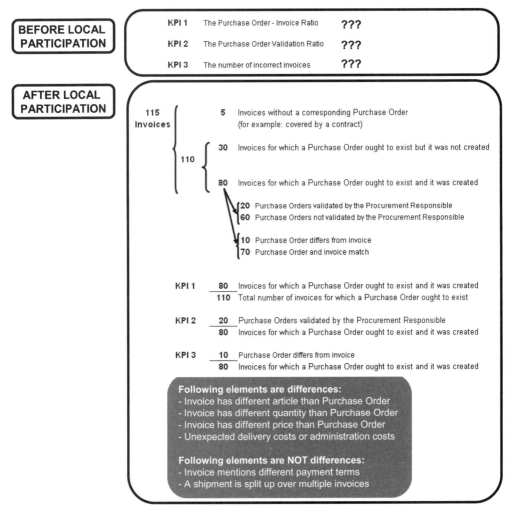

Figure 12.9 Performance Dashboard Before and After Local Participation

However, after some discussion between the coach, the key users, and the users it became clear that nobody understood the KPIs (know-what) and that nobody saw the use of installing KPIs (know-why). As a result, we needed to spend time explaining what it was all about and why it is important to them. But that was enough. As the lower part in Figure 12.9 shows, the top-down KPI setting still contained a lot of vagueness and ambiguity. It was only after local participation of the procurement managers that these KPIs were adjusted, refined, and put to practice.

It is the coaches' job to consolidate all the learning with regards to the KPIs at the program level and then to re-communicate the adjusted and workable KPIs that will be set for all of the involved sites. As mentioned in Chapter 3, managing organizational change means managing three basic ingredients. The same is true for the KPIs from our example that were adjusted after local participation. They ran successfully because people understood them (knowledge), they knew how to measure them (skills and they saw the use of measuring them (motivation).

12.7 Moments of Truth

We find the following moments of truth in the deployment phase. We have found them to be quite useful and hope that you do as well.

12.7.1 Pilot Go-Live

The pilot's go-live is probably one of the most important moments of truth within an SAP implementation. At this moment the new ways of working and the new system become a fact. If the pilot go-live fails, the program loses a lot of credibility. Pilot success makes further deployments much easier, as it helps us to reduce resistance.

12.7.2 Further Go-Lives

Each go-live is an important moment of truth. One single failure can affect the rest of the deployment.

12.7.3 Final Sign-Off

Sign-off of the SAP implementation by the steering committee is the confirmation that the program has been a success so far. It means that the organization is in the process of adapting to the new ways of working, and it confirms that the system is accepted by the user community.

12.7.4 Discovering Hidden Communication Channels

Most communication departments will start designing their content according to the channels they are comfortable with. This almost never includes learning occasions or the use of learning media as a communication channel. There are two main communication channels to consider:

- Training sessions, invitations and every single learning deliverable that is intended for users or key users are often forgotten as an opportunity for branding, know-why, and receiving feedback.

- Helpdesk calls are mostly not recorded in such a way that we can track patterns in user learning. If you want to have meaningful feedback during and after the go-live, then now is the time to tell the helpdesk people what to look for and how to record incidents.

12.7.5 Learning Moments of Truth

- Put into place support resources that are related to topical and IT issues and are available for individuals throughout the entire learning cycle.

- Keep executives involved by regularly reporting on learning activities.

- How successful are you at dealing with resistance in the classroom? In fact, effectively dealing with resistance is what sets experienced trainers apart from inexperienced trainers, regardless of their subject expertise.

- For e-learning, the extent to which middle managers and supervisors take care of the course organization internally will determine its success.

- Continuous course evaluation reporting allows you to take corrective actions of any kind as you go. Remember that feedback on results is the number-one motivator for trainers to improve what they are doing.

- A set of basic principles for learning has been validated, including:

  - No SAP access without training.

  - Everyone should follow the base course.

12.8 Deliverables

Deliverables for this phase are the following:

- Deployment plan
- Training evaluations
  - Reactions
  - Learning
  - Behavior
- Integrated learning materials
- Go-live communication plan

- Emergency communication plan
- Locally refined KPIs

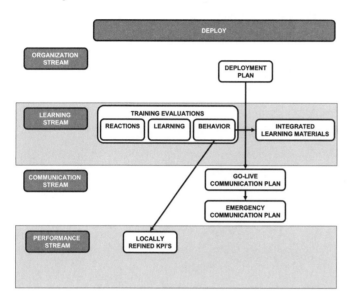

Figure 12.10 Organizational Change Deliverables of the Deploy Phase

Figure 12.10 shows the interaction of these deliverables. For the complete map of all organizational change deliverables during the program lifecycle, see Appendix C.

12.9 Conclusion

In the deployment phase, the planned changes become real. In this phase, the organization is under a lot of pressure as it strives to make the change happen now.

At this phase, all the entities are prepared to adopt the change, each in its own time. Therefore, it is important that you stick to the timetable if you don't want to negatively impact the motivation and with that the acceptance of the change that is implemented. The users need a lot of attention and guidance. In between the long working hours that are a typical characteristic of this phase, you should stay aware that all of the organizational change streams are critical streams during the deployment.

In Chapter 13, we will address post-implementation activities, ranging from damage control to leveraging success.

PART IV
Refreezing

With the post-implementation phase, the refreezing of the organization is announced. Post-implementation work is much more than two to four weeks of go-live support. This is because your purpose should not only be to stabilize the systems, but also to make sure the new ways of working are sustained.

13   Post-Implementation

13.1   Phase-Specific Characteristics and Needs

This section explains how you should use and read the soft-stuff and hard-stuff radars, taking into account the specific characteristics and needs of the post-implementation phase.

13.1.1   Soft-Stuff Radar

In this phase, the soft-stuff radar should indicate that the implementation team and the organization are working toward the same goal:

▶ **Learning Relationship Radar**
The implementation team has no secrets any more in this phase, and its boundaries now also include many people of the organization who are not formally dedicated to the program. Any solution that comes out of the implementation team is created in close relationship with the organization, because people are now increasingly able to see what is needed to make the program work.

The permission-level meter indicates that the organization now totally depends on the program team's efforts as a patient depends on an intravenous treatment. As strange as it may seem, this is a positive indicator at this point, as it shows that you have successfully switched off any other system or working method that may shortcut the program's goals (e.g., parallel legacy systems or a parallel paper track).

▶ **Agent Radar**
Ownership is the key word that characterizes this radar. The UN peace-keeping troops should now adapt their methodology to prepare the local

police (i.e., line managers of the organization) to take over their leading role. To use less warlike terminology: Like a midwife, the implementation team has delivered the organization's program; like a first-time-mother, it is now up to the organization to learn to take care of the program.

Most probably, the implementation team is now rapidly adjourning, so you should make sure that knowledge does not disappear along with the people who developed it. Effective knowledge transfer within the implementation team and between the team and the organization is essential at this point.

▶ **Target Radar**
Keep a close eye on the learning that occurs and allow people enough time to adopt new habits. As stated in Chapter 4, this is the radar that indicates whether your organization is ready for the second wave of refinement. As long as people are still in the phase of conscious competence, they will not be able to distinguish a minor issue from a business-critical issue. A sign of unconscious competence is that skeptics start telling you which enhancements would add more value. This may take longer than expected.

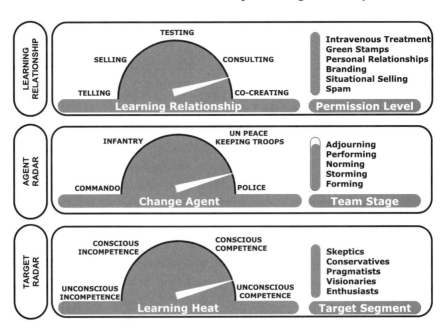

Figure 13.1 Soft-Stuff Radar in the Post-Implementation Phase

13.1.2   Hard-Stuff Radar

Because the go-live of the SAP program is not the end of the program, it is still necessary to keep an eye on time, head count, and money (see Figure 13.2).

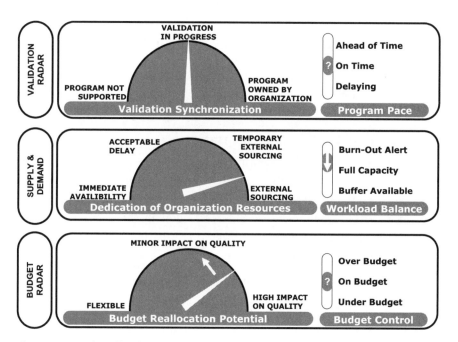

Figure 13.2 Hard-Stuff Radar of the Post-Implementation Phase

▶ **Validation Radar**

In this phase of the program, all your deliverables should have been signed off. However, the proof of the pudding is in the eating; in this phase it is important to get final sign off of the biggest deliverable of the SAP implementation: the rollout across the organization. Whether your implementation is on schedule is hard to tell, but if you successfully jumped the testing hurdle the answer is probably affirmative.

▶ **Supply-and-Demand Radar**

Make sure that you don't get surprised by this radar. People have been postponing their holidays, saving up overtime, and piling up their less urgent stuff. As a result, you will need more people right after go-live to keep everyone out of the alert zone of burnout.

▶ **Budget Radar**

Call yourself lucky when your reallocation potential did not impact major elements of the program by the time you go-live. However, if the next budget check shows serious deficits, you should not suddenly restrict refreezing projects. Instead, a new business case must be developed showing the need for some refreezing activities, so budget can be made available.

13.2 What Happens at the Level of the Program

Program management must secure that the SAP implementation is validated by the organization. Outstanding issues must be identified and listed.

13.2.1 Validate the SAP Implementation

It is important to get official sign-off from each entity where SAP has been implemented. This validation is the official confirmation that the new ways of working and the implementation of SAP are happening within scope and with the expected quality that was agreed upon in the program charter. There are several questions to be answered as a basis for the evaluation to sign-off on the implementation, as listed here:

▶ Has the scope of the implementation been maintained?

▶ Has the appropriate quality level been reached?

▶ Are there any critical outstanding issues?

Wherever there are gaps between the requirements described in the program charter and the delivery, they must be examined in detail. We must specify which specific actions will be taken to solve the issue and identify the owner of the action.

13.2.2 Plan for Solving Outstanding Issues

The focus must be on solving the outstanding issues that block final sign-off. Requirements listed in the program charter and not delivered at moment of go-live must be described and a decision made whether they still make sense at this point in time.

If so, a plan must be presented showing how they will be solved in a second-wave improvement period. The purpose of such a plan is to allow the program to be validated and to get clarity and a budget for the work that is still ahead of you. And now, let's go on to the organization stream.

13.3 The Organization Stream in This Phase

At the post-implementation phase, the activities of the organization stream focus on refreezing the organization.

13.3.1 Gradual Shift in Program Ownership

The program phases out. The ownership of the new organization, its ways of working and the SAP system must be handed over to the operational organization gradually.

Handover Ownership

Handover of local maintenance and support responsibilities from the program team to the organization happens a few weeks after each entity's go-live. However, the final handover of all responsibilities only happens at the moment that all entities are live. To secure a qualitative handover, take into account the following elements:

- Clear understanding of how the support organization will function.
- List of all remaining issues and identification of responsible to solve.
- Intense training of support people.

The success of this handover is determined by how well you have involved the organization during the previous phases of the program. Don't expect your support team to support the organization if they have not been involved throughout the whole program from the start.

Make it Work

It is up to the program team and the support organization to set up the ways the support organization will work and to define the performance requirements. All this is documented in a service-level agreement (SLA) signed by the support organization (IS/IT) and the business. The SLA must describe in detail the required level of service provided by the support organization to the business.

This SLA is the continuation of the program charter, and likewise it should not only contain service elements such as service hours, availability, reliability, support, and response times, but also management elements such as:

- How deliverables and milestones will be validated.
- How information about the system will be reported and addressed.
- How disagreements will be resolved.
- How and under which circumstances the IS/IT representatives and the process owners will review and revise the SLA.

The objectives of this operational SLA should be reflected in the targets of the support organization and the business organization at all appropriate levels.

13.3.2 Audit Old and New Habits

People are people, so soon after go-live, some of them tend to go back to their old ways of working as much as they can. As a result, they will try to find ways to make the system function according to their old ways of working. Remember the equation that we used earlier: $OO + NT = EOO$ (Old Organization + New Technology = Expensive Old Organization). The purpose of post-implementation audits is to prevent this from happening

Clearly, this puts at risk the realization of the program's benefits in the long term and the quality of the data that is entered into the system in the short term. The way to deal with this is to execute audits on the use of the system. In this delicate process, we recommend the approach shown in Figure 13.3.

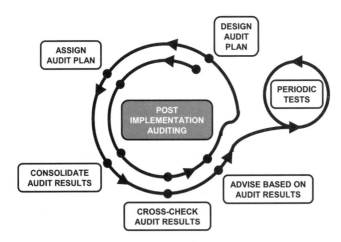

Figure 13.3 Post-Implementation Auditing

- **Design Audit Plan**
  Carefully design an audit plan that provides you the information to evaluate the use of the SAP system according to the new ways of working. Con-

cretely, this means that you mainly evaluate whether the system is used to enhance quality. This is where the audit plan differs from KPI follow-up. When following up KPIs, we measure how well the job/role performance, the process performance, and the organizational performance are contributing to the realization of the strategic objectives.

▶ **Assign Audit Plan**
Send the plan to entities, explain the purpose of the audit, and give them time to execute the plan themselves so that they can take mitigating initiatives themselves. Giving users and key users the ownership of this step is extremely important for the following reasons:

  ▶ It prevents them from thinking that big brother is watching them while showing you are serious about the proper use of the system and the processes.

  ▶ It shows that they—and not you—are responsible for applying the new ways of working properly; it enables taking of ownership.

  ▶ It acknowledges that it is not easy to adapt to the changes, and it gives them time to organize themselves and to take self-correcting actions.

▶ **Consolidate Audit Results**
Ask the users to provide you with feedback on the results of the audit, and to inform you about the actions that were taken or will be taken to make sure that the system is properly used and that the processes are applied properly. Consolidate the feedback and communicate the overall results to the entire organization so that one can learn from the other.

▶ **Cross-check Audit Results**
After a reasonable time frame (about four to six weeks), inform the users that the audit will also be executed at headquarters' level to stress again that executive management is serious about refreezing the changed organization. The objective is to check that the organization has really taken action where it was required. Send out the results to the entities, asking clarification on the items where you have found that the system is not properly used. While doing so, you encourage them again to take up their responsibility to comply with the new ways of working.

▶ **Advise Based on Audit Results**
Help the entities to start using the system properly across all areas, focusing on the areas that are indicated as problem areas by the audit results.

Additionally, we recommend the following steps:

- **Second Round**
  After a number of weeks, execute the audit again, and inform entities about the result. Have executive management intervene if necessary.

- **Periodic Tests**
  Once the system is being used properly, execute sample tests at random to ensure that the ways of working are refrozen and to communicate to the organization that controls are still in place.

The initiation and monitoring of this complete audit process is the responsibility of the process owners because they need to continuously improve the ways of working.

13.3.3 Plan Careers for Program Team Members

One of the bigger HR challenges of an organization is to re-integrate the program team members into the organization. For people who have been promised a career move and have lived up to expectations, that won't be a problem. However, there will always be people whose positions were backfilled for the continuity of the organization's operations.

Our experience has taught us that some of the team members joined the program to gather SAP experience with the idea of boosting their careers, inside or outside the organization. Some of them may have discovered that they like project work much more than their previous jobs in the organization. You should negotiate at that point whether there are long-term positions for these people within the program organization or whether they want to continue their careers elsewhere.

Let's see how communication should work during this phase.

13.4 The Communication Stream in This Phase

In the post-implementation phase, the communication stream focuses on dealing with the remaining resistance. You should also evaluate the effectiveness of your communication during the former phases of the SAP implementation program.

13.4.1 Structure Escalation Communication

People have a natural tendency to emphasize the point they are making in order to receive immediate attention, and in the process to exaggerate the information they use. You should not neglect these kinds of exaggerations, but instead try to get to the facts.

If a sales representative tells you that half of last month's deliveries were wrong, there is probably some truth in there. There is no other way than to get into the details of the customer orders that were wrong to discover how much truth there is to the sales rep's story. For you both to avoid wasting time discussing who is right and who is wrong, you should provide the sales rep with a standard structure for indicating the details of the problem and possible causes.

After some time, you will even be able to categorize the problems you receive. Before you know it, you will have brought this conversation back to the facts and created a useful categorization for your organization's service desk.

13.4.2 Transfer Program Intelligence

We have suggested maintaining two databases during the program lifecycle: the *stakeholder database*, and the *knowledge platform*. As soon as the program is live, they both risk being abandoned without owners. The next thing you know, there will be a gap between records and reality and you will have lost control over both. You should avoid this at all cost by doing the following:

▶ Involving HR in advance in taking over the ownership of the stakeholder database. This includes deciding which parameters are still useful after go-live and which ones can be abandoned.

▶ Involving IS/IT in advance in taking over the ownership of the knowledge portal and making sure that it gets integrated into whatever exists on the corporate intranet. This may include melding the branding of the program into the corporate branding.

13.4.3 Communication Evaluation

If you have been conducting ready-willing-able (RWA) assessments and temperature readings over the previous phases, you should consider doing one more after go-live. Stick to the questions you have been using until now (provided that they still make sense at this time) so you have a point of reference with regards to the perception of the program.

But this is not the only way to evaluate past communication. A far more direct manner is to check for the facts. Here you should be using the power of what we have called *hidden communication channels* (training sessions, helpdesk calls, etc.) higher on. Consider the following questions:

▶ What did people do as a result of direct communications to targeted stakeholders (last-minute instructions, coaching, newsflashes, e-mails, visits of implementation team members, etc.)?

▶ Are people willing to walk the lines that you set out with the program, or do you get direct and indirect complaints?

▶ Are people aware of the rationale behind the program, or can you derive from the type of questions they ask that they did not really get it?

13.4.4 Make Sense of Small Victories

In his 1996 bestseller, *Leading Change*, John Kotter lists eight reasons why transformation efforts fail. Two out of these eight reasons refer directly to making sense of the results you achieve during the post-implementation phase.

Kotter's advice is to create short-term wins (Kotter's sixth rule). Most people won't go on a long march for change unless they begin to see compelling evidence that their efforts are bearing fruit. Therefore, you need to plan and achieve some short-term gains which people will be able to see and celebrate. This provides proof to the organization that its efforts are working, and adds to the motivation to keep the effort going.

However, as you are declaring small victories, you should definitely hold off from declaring the big final victory. In his seventh rule, Kotter warns us not to declare victory too soon. A premature declaration of victory kills momentum, allowing the powerful forces of tradition to regain ground.

Rather, you should use the credibility afforded by short-term wins to tackle the bigger outstanding problems.

13.5 The Learning Stream in This Phase

The learning stream has a major role in the post-implementation phase, ensuring that the change is sustained in the organization.

13.5.1 Review Roles

Within the first few months after go-live, there is a reasonable chance that roles and security profiles will be refined and new ones created. Within the learning stream, it is important to keep track of those changes and to refresh the role-course matrix accordingly. Additionally, some people may need to be retrained.

In this phase of the program, you also should take care to hand the role-course matrix over to the organization. Again, as the role-course matrix is a joint effort of IS (security profiles) and HR (functional roles) this is typically a responsibility that risks winding up with no owner at all.

13.5.2 Review Blend

The learning blend and the intensity of the training that was needed to get the whole organization past the go-live is different than the ongoing maintenance effort that you will need to instill from now on.

Reviewing the blend implies that you measured what worked in your organization and what didn't. The best way to find out is just by asking people. As an example, Figure 13.4 shows the results of a small survey we held about one month after the implementation for approximately 2,000 users divided among about 50 production units. We simply asked them which learning means were most popular after go-live. The major findings for this specific organization were as follows:

▶ Traditional aids, like course books, were still quite popular.

▶ E-learning was most often used as an additional information source, but never as the one and only source.

▶ We also found out that each user had personally assembled his or her own blend, that everybody uses more than one means, but that none of the users were using all the learning means at their disposal.

Once you learn what the preferred means of learning are best for your organization, you can redesign the way you make knowledge available and better target your future learning investments.

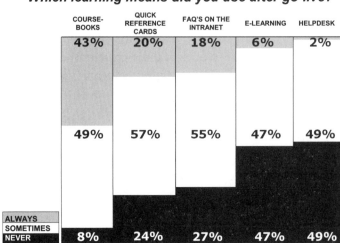

Figure 13.4 Example of Measuring the Use of Your Learning Blend

13.5.3 Make Support Materials

Creating support materials is a task that is ideally started before the go-live. There are two kinds of support materials: those that can be made right after key users and users completed the training, and those that are integrated into the system by means of help files. These include the following:

▶ Quick reference cards, posters and other written job-aids should be created and owned by the key users and the users. Occasionally, you may help them by providing templates and by giving examples, but as an implementation team member you are by no means able to edit these materials at the level of the receiver. Your job is rather to make sure that these materials travel freely from one user to another, for example, by simply picking them up and promoting them on your knowledge portal. Remember that the assignment for users and key users to draw up quick reference cards is an extra exercise, forcing them to translate what they have learned into practice.

▶ Use support materials that you integrate into the working environment of the user, such as enhanced help files.

▶ An additional third category of support materials are the standard operating procedures (SOP). These are drawn up within a few weeks after go-live and they are a joint responsibility of the coach, who makes sure that all requirements are in there, and the users, who make sure that the procedure makes sense in practice. Solid SOPs are one of the foundations for linking strategy to performance, so taking the time to reach agreement between coach and user is not a waste of time (although to some executives it may seem so at first sight).

Although all of these support materials should be made with the 100% involvement of users and key users, it is important that they be written by a technical writer or a coach with technical-writing skills.

13.5.4 Train New Users

As an organization is not a static thing, new roles are created, newcomers are assigned to roles, and people change jobs. For all these occasions, all the materials need to be kept up-to date, and people need to be able to access all of the updated materials.

In real life, new users don't come in classes of 12, ready to be trained at the same time. Rather, they come one by one, and you often discover that they are using the system before they come and ask for training. Preparing and conducting class-based courses in this case is not cost-effective. Hence the importance of having high-quality participant materials and an up-to-date knowledge platform.

13.5.5 Numbers

An important element in keeping the commitment of the sponsors is making sure that they get evidence on learning in numbers and percentages. What is even more important is you don't wait until they ask you for evidence, but that you provide these numbers regularly; and that you indicate the evolution.

For example, once the courses started, on a monthly basis you can give an update on the following dimensions:

▸ Course statistics:
  ▹ Total number of participants for a course
  ▹ Number of participants that followed the course
▸ Level 1 evaluation statistics (Reactions):
  ▹ Learner's quotation on the content
  ▹ Learner's quotation on the trainer
  ▹ Learner's quotation on the training conditions
  ▹ Learner's quotation on e-learning

▶ Level 2 evaluation statistics (learning):

  ▶ Number of participants who passed the test

  ▶ Number of participants who failed the test the first time

  ▶ Number of participants who passed the test a second time

Some of the dimensions in this list may seem silly as you read them here. However, in the light of approaching a go-live deadline, statements such as "50 % of the users in department A have already worked through the e-learning modules, but department B is only at 7 %" can really inspire the department leaders to take action.

What's more, once you have captured the executives' attention with the hard numbers, they will be more receptive to your arguments concerning underlying causes. You should be able to underpin these numbers with qualitative data. As an illustration, Table 13.1 shows for each department of this example you can add qualitative data to indicate a possible underlying cause. This kind of survey is typically a five-minute, 10-question effort for the participants.

Question	Agree	Partially Agree	Partially Disagree	Disagree
I have an overview at all times during the sessions				
I can easily navigate through the learning modules				
I can combine e-learning with my daily job				
I get the required time for e-learning				
The response times of the e-learning system are good				
The e-learning system is always available				
I can solve the test if I attentively followed the modules				
The instructions for e-learning are clear				
I have access to the key-user of my department for support				
The indicated time corresponds with the time it took me.				

Table 13.1 Sample Qualitative Questionnaire to Monitor E-Learning

The level 3 (behavior) and level 4 (performance) evaluations of learning are discussed under the next topic: *performance management*.

13.6   The Performance Management Stream in This Phase

Performance management becomes fully operational now. The achievements of the intended benefits must be monitored.

In Chapter 12, we mentioned that the intended benefits must be translated into KPIs. This is necessary to follow up on the realization of the organization's strategy through new ways of working, and as a result of this, the underlying benefits. Ward & Daniel (2006) make the distinction between the following benefit types:

▸ **Financial Benefits**
By applying a cost/price or other valid financial formula to a quantifiable benefit a financial value can be calculated. For instance: reduction of the days of sales outstanding (DSO) with five days, multiplied by the turnover, multiplied by the interest rates for overdrafts.

▸ **Quantifiable Benefits**
You have enough data to forecast how much improvement/benefit should result from the changes. For example: reduce the financial closing period to three days from a current total of eight days.

▸ **Measurable Benefits**
These are performance criteria for which it is not possible to estimate how much performance will improve when the changes are complete. For example: reduction of lead time order-to-delivery.

▸ **Observable Benefits**
Achievement of the benefit is evaluated by an individual or a group of individuals on the basis of agreed-upon criteria. For example: the degree to which the organization has changed from functional thinking to process thinking and is operating in new structures.

For every benefit that was not realized, appropriate action must be taken to catch up on the realization of these benefits.

13.7 Moments of Truth

We find following moments of truth in the post-implementation phase.

13.7.1 Keep the Program Locked

As mentioned in Chapter 12, you should maintain a lock on the program for a period of three months before and after go-live. In the locked period after go-live, the system is used, but no changes are allowed except in the case of bug fixes or critical support issues.

However, during this period you must allow users to log change requests for things that they would like to see changed, in processes as well as systems. People are only able to see what works for them once they are using the process and system day-to-day. Even with the best training, testing, and simulations, users will still find inefficiencies. However, it is only after they have grown into the new habits (i.e., unconscious competence) that they will be able to distinguish a minor issue from a business-critical issue.

13.7.2 Redefining the Coaches' 80/20 Rule

You need to be aware of the difference between the formal role description of a local coach on paper and what being a coach looks like in practice. About 80 % of the topics in the formal role description will take up 20 % of their time, which may lead you question the return on investment in local coaching. However, the other 80 % of their job is what brings the return on the coaching investment. The only problem here is that this part is not quantifiable because it is not about executing actions and making things work technically. Rather, it is about being there physically, shutting up and listening, understanding people's points of view, and helping them to make sense of the changes. In short, the biggest part of the coach's job is to build the learning relationship between the program and the organization down to the most affected level: operations.

13.7.3 Developing a Sixth Sense

On the surface nobody will ever talk about their resistance, their lack of change-readiness, or how they hate to give up the status quo (would you?). Rather, an organizational change problem will come to the surface as "a technical issue" or "a shortcoming of the process." This is when you need to have built a learning relationship with the users and the operators so you can track the problem down to its root cause. In time, you will develop a sixth sense based on your understanding that an escalated issue always looks different on the surface than it does at its source.

13.8   Deliverables

Deliverables for this phase include:

▸ Planning of open issues

▸ Operations SLA

▸ Post-implementation audit

▸ Standard operating procedures (SOPs)

▸ Revised roles

▸ Revised learning blend

▸ Support materials

▸ Learning statistics

▸ Structured communication

▸ RWA assessment

▸ Benefits mapping

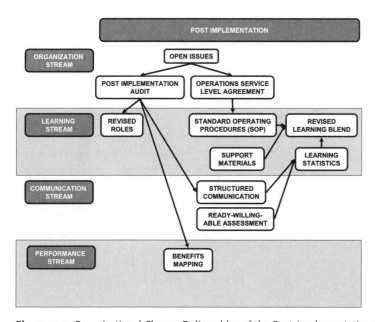

Figure 13.5 Organizational Change Deliverables of the Post-Implementation Phase

For the complete map of all organizational change deliverables during the program lifecycle, see Appendix C.

13.9 Conclusion

Post-implementation is much more than a few weeks of intensive user support. During the post-implementation phase activities must not only focus on stabilizing the organization, but also on sustaining the effort so the changes really become effective and that the intended benefits are achieved. A goal of post-implementation is to keep the organization from falling back into old habits, applying former ways of working while using the new SAP system.

In the final chapter, Chapter 14, we will discuss life after SAP, underscoring what you can do to sustain the change in the long run and to prepare for a second wave.

The SAP implementation and the organizational change effort are not finished when the system is running production. The program does not stop until the benefits are realized. The challenge you will face is that your implementation team has adjourned and you have to rely on your new organization to sustain what its members have learned.

14 Life After SAP

14.1 What Happens at the Level of the Program

The program does not stop completely once the system is running in production. There are still some activities to pay attention to.

14.1.1 Writing a White Book

We have found it valuable to write a white book about the SAP implementation program that documents in detail the lessons learned; you could call it a biography of SAP implementation. The purpose is to make sure that all experiences are described so that they can be re-used as and when needed. This white book must be a learning document. In our opinion, the white book should include:

▶ Critical moments in the program, how they were caused, how it was dealt with and a comment on how you would handle it in a next time.

▶ What you would definitely do the same in the future and an explanation on the reason why.

▶ What you would do differently in the future and an explanation on the reason why.

▶ Issues that were identified and description of how they were solved.

▶ Risks that were identified and how they were mitigated.

14.1.2 Restructuring the Program

The program setup must be restructured in function of the remaining activities. This includes the following:

▶ Program organizational setup, including the position of the program manager.

▶ Resource allocation.

▶ Budget confirmation.

▶ Identification and preparation of remaining projects required to refreeze the organization.

14.2 The Organization Stream in This Phase

The activities in the organization stream focus on further refreezing the change in the organization by improving the implemented ways of working and by improving the supporting SAP system.

14.2.1 Launching a Second Wave

We believe you need to take into account a period of at least 6 months and up to 12 months to implement second-wave improvements. During the testing, during the deployment, and during the program lock period (i.e. go-live plus and minus three months), you will find out that a number of improvements should happen to the system and to the ways of working. There are four kinds of improvement projects as seen here:

▶ **Process Improvements**
For instance, a procurement workflow that proves unrealistic in practice and that should be redesigned.

▶ **System Improvements**
Such as system performance.

▶ **Usability Improvements**
Such as making it easier for production workers to confirm production orders (e.g., less screens, easier search, less complex interface, etc.).

▶ **Training Projects**
Some change requests, upon further investigation, may turn out to be training issues. For instance, you may need more on-site support for a third-party distributor operating your systems.

Out of the requests that were logged, you need to select the ones that are important. For each of them, you have to make a detailed description that contains the following:

▶ Scope

▶ Reason why it should be done

▶ Estimated cost and effort

The list of selections should be presented to the steering committee, which confirms it.

14.2.2 Enabling Business Intelligence

The implementation of SAP Business Warehouse (SAP BW) should, in our experience, be the subject of a second-wave project and not be part of the initial SAP implementation stream. There are several arguments that justify making this statement, as follows:

▶ SAP BW is fed by information coming from other SAP modules and optionally also from non-SAP systems. To ensure that the information in the business warehouse is qualitative, the other SAP environments must first be in a mature state in which they are properly used.

▶ During the build phase, there is an overlap with the design phase. A number of change requests that get approved may have an influence on the design of SAP BW.

▶ When testing SAP BW, you must have relevant information available. If SAP is not live yet, there is not enough qualitative business-representative information available.

14.2.3 Anchoring Process Thinking

Remember that an SAP implementation triggers your organization to shift from functional thinking to process-oriented thinking. Your organizational structure must support that.

Process Owners Enter the Organization

Now that your organization is live with SAP and shifted—or still shifting—from a functional thinking approach to a process approach, you need to continue paying attention to the process thinking within your organization.

The way to do this is to establish an additional unit within your organization that unites the process owner of the SAP program. The role of the process owner within the operational organization would be to continuously improve the processes for which it is responsible. This group follows up on the realization of the key performance indicators (KPIs) and continuously identifies areas for improvement.

Transferring Process Methodology

Successful process owners bring with them the business process management skills they learned at the program. They are the ambassadors of process thinking and should make sure that the organization's processes are properly documented to the same level of detail using the same tools as in the design phase.

14.2.4 Creating a Program Management Office

We recommend installing a program office that provides a structure to centralize and prioritize projects and to manage a program portfolio. That way, the organization can consciously improve its operations in line with the strategy by executing projects.

The program office ensures that a proper project initiation and selection process is in place. The selection of projects must be subject to a decision taking process that reflects the culture, the structure, and the ways of working of the organization in function of the strategic objectives.

14.3 The Communication Stream in This Phase

From a user's point of view, handing over of the system to the organization should happen gradually and should be done by local coaches. We referred to those coaches as the UN peacekeeping troops to stress the fact that their goal is to handover the complete governance to the local police force. Coaches need to be there to prevent simple things from going wrong and to help people make their first small victories in SAP.

You may wonder how a coach divides his or her time with the team he or she has been assigned to. The easiest anchor point for coaches is found in two of the three ingredients of change. To know the optimal frequency, you need to examine the combination of the ingredients know-how and know-why.

The so-called Skill-Will Matrix (Landsberg, 1998) in Figure 14.1 can be used to this end. This matrix is often used to estimate the frequency of coaching. The model is based on four combinations, each with a different follow-up.

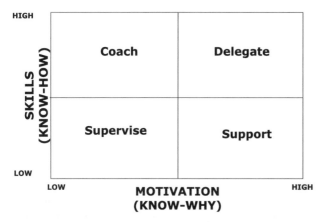

Figure 14.1 The Skill-Will Matrix (Landsberg, 1998)

These four combinations are described as follows:

▶ **Supervising**
The coach clearly defines the roles and tasks and supervises their execution. Decisions are made by the coach and communication is unidirectional.

▶ **Coaching**
The coach still determines the tasks and roles, but also asks the coached person for suggestions. Decisions are made by the coach, but communications are dialogue-based.

▶ **Support**
The coached person accepts the decisions and executes against them. The coach facilitates decision-making, but is no longer in the driver's seat.

▶ **Delegating**
The coach is still involved in problem-solving, but the coached person is in the driver's seat. The coached person decides when and how the coach is involved.

After a day or two of walking around and helping out people, you should be able to map the people on the Skill-Will Matrix. However, in practice we often find that coaches use this matrix to confirm their prejudices. Supervision for instance, will not inspire people to take responsibility and to work independently. The skill-will balance of a person is not a constant given; it evolves as time goes by. Nevertheless, it is a good guideline for estimating your timekeeping as a coach, especially when coaching an entire team.

14.4   The Learning Stream in This Phase

The cost of coaching on the job is one of the most difficult parts to budget. According to most executives: "If people can operate the system, the training has accomplished its goals." However true this statement may be, it will only get you as far as getting it right at the level of know-how.

The cost of coaching on the job is worth the investment. As Figure 14.2 illustrates, the purpose of coaching is to make sure that all three performance ingredients can be reached on all organizational levels (role, process, organization).

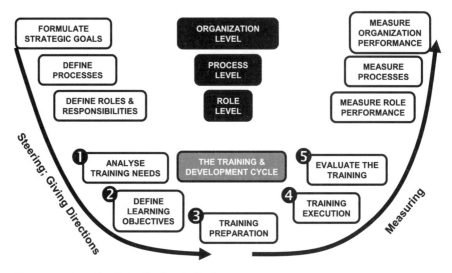

Figure 14.2 Coaching Links Strategy to Performance

Let's examine these ingredients:

▸ The first ingredient, know-how, relates to the realization of outcomes. Coaching on this ingredient is limited to hand-holding and making sure that people can operate the system.

▸ Know-what relates to features and structures. Coaching here means making sure that the structures and procedures are in place the way they should be, for instance by making standard operating procedures (SOPs).

▸ Know-why relates to the benefits of the program. Coaching on this ingredient predominantly involves making people aware of the goals, measuring against these goals, giving feedback, and making corrections where necessary.

14.5   The Performance Management Stream in This Phase

Performance monitoring is a very important activity in the long run. The KPIs must have an owner, and the performance model must continuously be fine tuned to the circumstances.

14.5.1   Focusing the Performance Model

The best performance model in an organization is not the one providing as much information as possible about the performance of the organization. It is the one that provides the right information at the right time in the right format to the right people.

People can only absorb a certain amount of information. Therefore, it is important that once the organization is live with SAP, executive management decides on which key performance indicators are the most important ones or the ones most efficient at following up on the realization of the corporate strategic objectives. It's best to follow up on no more than 30 KPIs.

When you zoom in on the learning perspective of Figure 14.3, it gives you a hint on how these 30 KPIs could be divided among different levels. As mentioned in Chapter 8, there are three types of KPIs to follow up on: do new things, do things better, and stop doing things. Accordingly, there are nine possible evaluation fields to spread the major KPIs:

1. **Evaluate New Organization**
   Examples include the efficiency of the new cross-departmental processes.

2. **Evaluate New Process**
   For instance, the efficiency of a proactive receivables collection process.

3. **Evaluate New Role**
   For example, the process owners.

4. **Evaluate Improved Organization**
   For instance, the redesigned business units.

5. **Evaluate Improved Process**
   The sales order to delivery process for example.

6. **Evaluate Improved Role**
   For instance, the enhanced role of a role holder responsible for procurement.

7. **Evaluate Old Organization**
   For example, the step-by-step evolution of closing down in-house application development.

8. **Evaluate Old Process**

Time saved by stopping accounting reconciliation processes, for instance.

9. **Evaluate Old Role**

Time saved by eliminating tasks that have become unnecessary, for example.

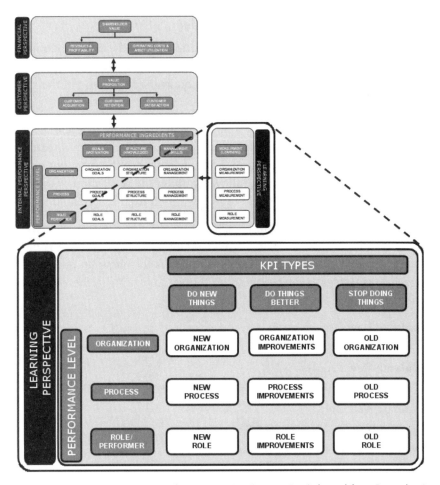

Figure 14.3 Generic Strategy Map from a Learning Perspective (adapted from Rummler & Brache, 1990, and Kaplan & Norton, 2000)

14.5.2 KPI Ownership

The efficiency of a performance approach is directly linked to the degree of the penetration of the approach throughout the organization. We believe that it is not sufficient to set objectives for the organization, its processes, and related roles or functions.

The organization must be made responsible for the realization of the KPIs. This can be done by making the responsible persons accountable for the result, detailed here:

▶ For the organizational objectives: executive management.

▶ For the process objectives: senior and middle management, process owners.

▶ For the objectives at job/role level: each individual.

This means that the objectives must be included in the objectives of individual persons or groups of persons, and that evaluation processes and determination of remuneration (bonus or penalty systems) must be put in place in consistent ways.

14.6   Conclusion

The program is not finished when the system is productive and stable. After go-live and after post-implementation, there are still a number of other activities to do. Don't expect that the system will be perfect from the beginning. It won't. Therefore, you should expect from the very start of the program that you need second-wave activities.

You need to ensure that the organization sustains the change that was introduced. This can only be achieved by making sure that the performance- management model supports the new ways of working and by following up on the achievement of the intended benefits.

14.7   Moving Forward

There is no such thing as the *simple truth* when it comes to managing organizational change. The only certainty is that your organization will have to change when you decide to implement SAP. In summarizing this book, we list elements that you need to keep in mind:

▶ New technology in an old organization equals an expensive old organization.

▶ An SAP implementation triggers your organization to shift from functional thinking to process-oriented thinking.

▶ Using program-management approaches facilitates change.

▶ You should focus on and manage the delivery of benefits.

▶ The bad news is that organizational change involves a great deal of emotion.

▶ The good news is that there are patterns (unfreezing, changing refreezing) and a fixed set of ingredients (know-how, know-what and know-why) behind organizational change.

▶ You can cut the work into four manageable streams, which are:

  ▶ Organization

  ▶ Communication

  ▶ Learning

  ▶ Performance management

▶ Applying a customer relationship management approach to your SAP program helps to manage the relationship and the expectations between the program and the organization.

▶ Refreezing takes more than providing extended support during a few weeks after go-live.

▶ Implementation matters, no matter what the plan may promise.

The insights and advice in this book should be applied in the context of your own organization. This will take some translation work from your side. Above all, you should be suspicious when you catch yourself saying: "We are different, so this stuff does not apply to us."

Writing this book was a big learning experience for us. Our families and friends were witness to our lively discussions and lengthy phone calls and email threads. The main thing we learned while writing this book is that it is very difficult to integrate the hard-side and the soft-side of organizational change into a good marriage.

We definitely want to continue our learning process, and at the same time we realize that we cannot take the next step alone. It will require your experiences and your own application of the contents of this book. We are convinced that the enhancements in the next edition of this book need to come from you.

We wish you all success with your current and future SAP projects, and we invite you to take part in this learning experience.

Appendix

A   Bibliography

Argyris C.; Schön D: Organizational Learning II: Theory, Method and Practice, Addison Wesley (1996).

Ashby, W.R.: An Introduction to Cybernetics, Chapman and Hall, (1956).

Birnbrauer H.: Evaluation Techniques that Work. From: Kirkpatrick D. L.: Another Look at Evaluating Training Programs., ASTD (1998).

Block, P.: Flawless Consulting: A Guide to Getting Your Expertise Used, University Associates (1981).

Block, P.: The Empowered Manager: Positive Political Skills at Work, John E. Wiley & Sons (1987).

Bramson, R.: Coping With Difficult People, Anchor (1981).

Brennan, M.: Blended Learning and Business Change: Key Findings, IDC White Paper June (2003).

Bruner, J.: The Process of Education, Harvard University Press (1960).

Callahan, C.: Abenteuer Denken, Genius Verlag (2004).

Carnegie Mellon SEI (Paulk, M., Curtis, B., Chrissis, M.& Weber C.): Capability Maturity Model[SM] for Software, Version 1.1, Software Engineering Institute, Carnegie Mellon University (http://www.sei.cmu.edu/pub/documents/93.reports/pdf/tr24.93.pdf) (1996).

Chilton Pearce, J.: The Magical Child: Rediscovering Nature's Plan For Our Children, Bantam (1977).

Christensen, C.: Making Strategy: Learning By Doing, Harvard Business Review (1997).

Clampitt, P. G., DeKoch; R. J. & Cashman T.: A Strategy for Communicating About Uncertainty, Academy of Management Executive, Vol. 14, No. 4, pp. 41–57 (2000).

Clark K., Wheelwright S.: Organizing and Leading "Heavyweight" Development Teams. California Management Review, Vol. 34, No. 3. (1992).

Connor, D.: Managing at the Speed of Change, John Wiley and Sons (1992).

Covey, S.: The 7 Habits of Highly Effective People, Free Press (1990).

Cringely, R.: Accidental Empires: How the Boys of Silicon Valley Make Their Millions, Battle Foreign Competition, and Still Can't Get a Date, HarperCollins (1993).

Duck, J. D.: The Change Monster, The Human Forces that Fuel or Foil Corporate Transformation and Change, Crown Business (2001).

Gladwell, M.: The Tipping Point. How Little Things Can Make a Big Difference, Little Brown (2000).

Glasser, William: Choice Theory, A New Psychology Of Personal Freedom. Harper Perennial (1998).

Godin, S.: Permission Marketing. Simon & Schuster (1999).

Goss, T., Pascale; R. & Athos, A.: The Reinvention Roller Coaster: Risking the Present for a Powerful Future, Harvard Business Review November–December (1993.).

Gourville, J.: Eager Sellers, Stony Buyers, Harvard Business Review, June (2006).

Hammer, M.: Succeeding with SAP, video, Hammer Videos (1998).

Hammer, M.: SAP and the Power of Process, unpublished notes of a seminar in New York (2005).

IMA: Accelerating Change: A Practical Guide to Implementation, Implementation Management Associates, Inc. (1997).

Ind, N.: Beyond Branding: How the New Values of Transparency and Integrity Are Changing the World of Brands, Kogan Page (2003).

Jensen, Bill: The Search for a Simpler Way, The Jensen Group; Northern Illinois University College of Business (1997). www.simplerwork.com

Jensen, Bill: The Simplicity Survival Handbook, Perseus Books (2004).

Johnson, S.: Who Moved My Cheese?, Vermilion (1998).

Kaplan, R.; Norton, D.: Having Trouble with your Strategy? Then Map It, Harvard Business Review, January-February (2001).

Karpman, S. : Fairy Tales and Script Drama Analysis, Transactional Analysis Bulletin, Vol. 7, No. 26, pp. 39–43, (1968).

Karten, N.: Communication Gaps and How to Close Them, Dorset House Publishing (2002).

Kirkpatrick D. L.: Evaluating Training Programs. The Four Levels, Berrett-Koehler Publishers, (1998).

Kotler, P.; Armstrong, G.; Wong, V.: Principles of Marketing, Prentice Hall (2005).

Kotter, J.: Leading Change, Why Transformation Efforts Fail, Harvard Business Review (1996).

Kubler-Ross, E.: On Death and Dying. Macmillan, (1969).

Landsberg, Max: The Tao of Coaching, Knowledge Exchange (1998).

Levy, J. D.: Corporate Wisdom: Using e-Learning and Knowledge Management for Competitive Advantage, South African e-Learning Conference, September 1–2, (2003).

Lewin, Kurt: Frontiers in Group Dynamics: Concept, Method and Reality in Social Science; Social Equilibra and Social Change, Human Relations, No. 1, pp. 5–41, 1974

McKaskey, M. B.: The Executive Challenge: Managing Change and Ambiguity, Pitman (1982).

Mitroff, I.: Stakeholders of the Organizational Mind: Toward a New View of Organizational Policy Making, Jossey-Bass (1987).

Moore, G. A.: Crossing the Chasm: Marketing and Selling High-Tech Products to Mainstream Customers, HarperBusiness (1999).

Morgan, G.: Images of Organization, Sage (1998).

Normann, Richard: Service Management: Strategy and Leadership in Service Businesses, John Wiley (2001).

Peppers, D.; Rogers, M.: Managing Customer Relationships: A Strategic Framework, John Wiley & Sons 2004

Piaget, J.: Piaget's theory, from P. Mussen (ed) Handbook of Child Psychology, Vol. 1, John Wiley & Sons (1983).

Reiss, G.; Leigh, G.: One Project Too Many, Project Management Today (2004).

Reiss, G.: Project Management Demystified, Chapman Hall (1992).

Rogers, E.: Diffusion of Innovations, Free Press(1962).

Rummler, G.; Brache, A.: Improving Performance: How to manage the White Space in the Organizational Chart, Jossey Bass Wiley (1990).

Schein, E.: Organizational Psychology, Prentice Hall (1980).

Schein, E.: Models and Tools for Stability and Change in Human Systems, Reflections, Volume 4, Number 2, Society for Organizational Learning and the Massachusetts Institute of Technology (2002).

Schein, E.: Process Consultation Revisited, Addison-Wesley (1999).

Seely Brown, J.; Duguid, P.: Balancing Act: How to Capture Knowledge Without Killing It, Harvard Business Review May-June (2000.).

Seely Brown, J.; Duguid, P.: The Social Life of Information, Harvard Business School Press. (2000).

Seely Brown, J.: Growing Up Digital, Change March-April (2000). www.johnseelybrown.com

Senge, P.; Kleiner A.; Roberts, C.; Ross, R.; Smith, B.: The Fifth Discipline Fieldbook: Strategies and Tools for Building a Learning Organization, Doubleday (1994).

Sisson K.; Storey J.: Managing Human Resources and Industrial Relations, McGraw-Hill (1995).

Stewart, I.; Joines, V.: TA Today, A New introduction to Transactional Analysis, Russell Press Ltd. (1987).

Tichy, Noel M.; Fombrun, Charels J.;Devanna, Mary A.: Strategic Human Resource Management, Sloan Management Review, 23(2), 47–61 (1982).

Trompenaars, F.; Hampden-Turner, C.: Riding the Waves of Culture, McGraw-Hill (1995).

Tuckman, B.: Development Sequences in Small Groups, Psychological Bulletin, No. 63, pp. 384–99, (1965).

Ward, J.; Daniel, E.: Benefits Management, Delivering Value from IS & IT Investments, John Wiley & Sons (2006).

Weick, K.: Sensemaking in Organizations, Thousand Oaks: Sage Pubications (1995).

Weick, Sutcliffe and Obstfeld: Organizing and the Process of Sensemaking, in Organization Science 16(4), pp. 409–421, (2005).

B   Activity Examples

To help you keep a holistic view, we have grouped all activities that must be executed per stream during the different phases of the lifecycle into a single chart per activity example. This appendix includes information about all activities that must be executed per stream. We have provided you with snapshot views of these figures in the following subsections. However, you can get a more detailed look at each of these figures if you visit the page devoted to this book on *www.sap-press.com* or at *www.sap-press.de*.

B.1 Organization Stream Example

Figure B.1 gives you a quick look at an example of activities you may take into account for the organization stream.

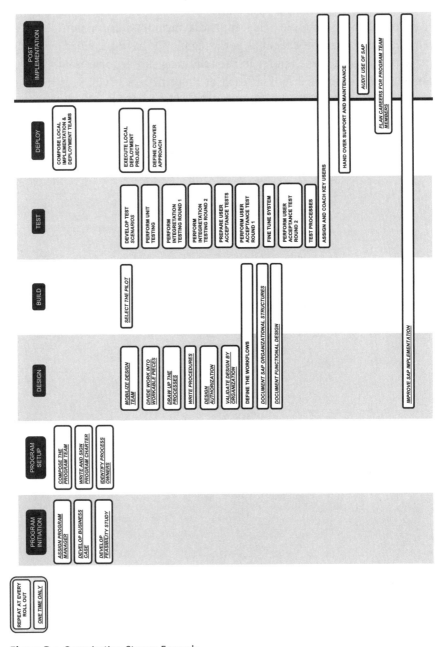

Figure B.1 Organization Stream Example

B.2 Communication Stream Example

Figure B.2 provides a quick overview of the activities that are part of the communication stream.

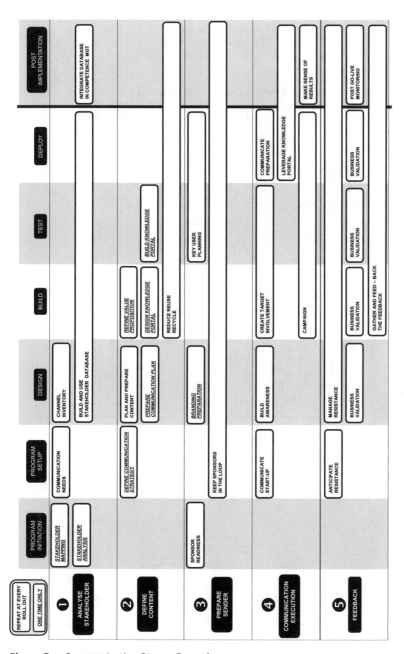

Figure B.2 Communication Stream Example

B.3   Learning Stream Example

Figure B.3 gives an you overview of the learning stream activities.

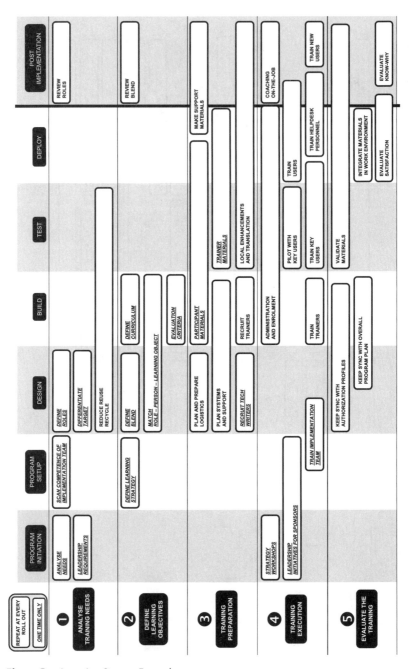

Figure B.3 Learning Stream Example

B.4 Performance Stream Example

Figure B.4 gives you a quick glimpse of the performance stream activities.

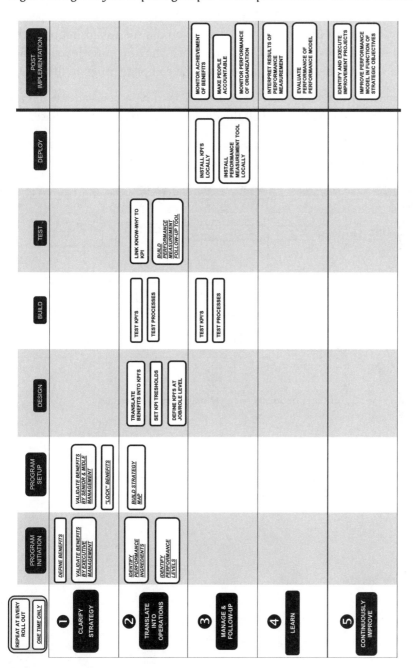

Figure B.4 Performance Stream Example

C   The Map of Deliverables

Near the ends of Chapters 7–13 we listed all deliverables for that specific phase of the project lifecycle. In Figure C.1, you can see a snapshot of all the mapped deliverables combined into one chart, showing interdependencies between all of the deliverables throughout the complete program lifecycle.

The purpose of this map, seen in Figure C.1 is to help you gain awareness about the interdependencies of all the deliverables from phase to phase.

To see Figure C.1 in more detail, please visit the page dedicated to this book at *www.sap-press.com* or *www.sap-press.de*.

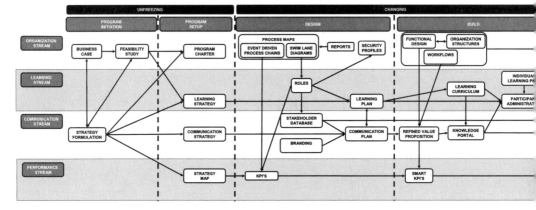

Figure C.1 The Map of Organizational Change Management Deliverables

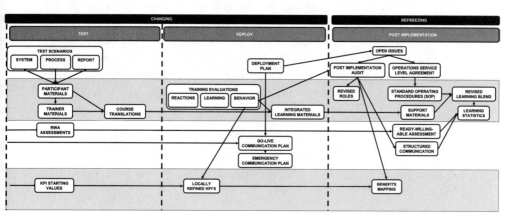

D   HR's Roadmap

In Chapter 1, we stated that HR is not an agent of change but an agent of stability. This means that HR has a specific role to play during the program lifecycle. In Table D.1 you will find the major actions that we recommend from HR during each phase. The columns represent key HR process (Tichy et al., 1982).

HR Process	Recruiting and Selection	Training and Development	Performance Management and Appraisal	Compensation and Benefits	Work Organization and Communication Systems
Goals	Employment continuity	Knowledge and skills continuity	Performance continuity	Stability in personnel costs	Social stability
Unfreezing					
Program Initiation	▶ Assign a program manager ▶ Recruit the commando team	▶ Set up leadership initiatives ▶ Facilitate strategy Formulation	▶ Offer a career perspective to recruited people		▶ Manage backfilling of internal recruitment actions
Program Setup	▶ Implementation team recruitment ▶ Recruitment of process owners	▶ Participate in formulation of learning strategy ▶ Train implementation team	▶ Offer a career perspective to recruited people		▶ Manage backfilling of internal recruitment actions
Changing					
Design	▶ Recruit technical writers	▶ Heavily participate in learning plan ▶ E-learning platform setup ▶ Training logistics	▶ Manage career perspectives of team members: motivation and retention	▶ Budget for impact on personnel costs ▶ Define KPIs at job-role level	▶ Plan and manage reorganization efforts and industrial relations ▶ Communication channel inventory ▶ Be involved in set-up of stakeholder database

Table D.1 Major HR Action Recommendations During Each Phase

HR Process	Recruiting and Selection	Training and Development	Performance Management and Appraisal	Compensation and Benefits	Work Organization and Communication Systems
Build	▶ Recruit Trainers	▶ Define the curriculum ▶ Design evaluations ▶ Training administration		▶ KPI target setting	▶ Be involved in set-up of knowledge portal
Testing			▶ Get involved in RWA assessments		
Deployment		▶ Support training delivery ▶ Evaluate Learning		▶ Link performance KPIs to pay	
Refreezing					
Post-Implementation		▶ Review learning blend ▶ Train new users ▶ Learning statistics	▶ Take ownership of roles and link to competence management system		▶ Take ownership of stakeholder database
Life After SAP	▶ Redefine selection criteria in function of process thinking.	▶ Take ownership of all learning deliverables	▶ Focus the performance model	▶ Redefine the compensation and benefits strategy in accordance with new performance criteria	

Table D.1 Major HR Action Recommendations During Each Phase (cont.)

E   IS/IT's Roadmap

In Chapter 1, we stated that IS/IT is not an agent of change. But IS/IT does have a specific role during the program lifecycle. In Table E.1 you will find the major actions that we recommend from IS/IT during each phase. The columns represent key IS/IT responsibilities.

IS/IT Responsibility	Prepare IS/IT Department	Infrastructure Setup	Implementation Support	Functional and Technical Support	Maintenance
Goals	Ensure that the IS/IT organization is ready for the SAP implementation	Ensure availability of required IS/IT infrastructure	Support implementation track	Provide support to the user community	Maintain the technical SAP environment and the SAP application
Unfreezing					
Program Initiation	▶ Build SAP competence ▶ Clean up outstanding issues and organize properly				
Program Setup			▶ Delegate people to SAP program		
Changing					
Design	▶ Design IS/IT landscape ▶ Set up transport procedures ▶ Set up technical change request procedures	▶ IS/IT landscape ▶ Transport procedures ▶ Technical change request procedures	▶ Support technical design ▶ Design interfaces	▶ Design support procedures ▶ Design support organization ▶ Design support SLA in collaboration with business	
Build		▶ Set up infrastructure	▶ Execute transport requests ▶ Monitor system performance ▶ Install interfaces	▶ Install support organization ▶ Install supporting tools for support organization	

Table E.1 Major Actions Recommended for IT

IS/IT Responsibility	Prepare IS/IT Department	Infrastructure Setup	Implementation Support	Functional and Technical Support	Maintenance
Testing		▶ Test performance of infrastructure ▶ Set up test environment	▶ Support test team ▶ Secure continuous availability of test environment ▶ Test interfaces	▶ Test supporting tools	▶ Maintain technical environments ▶ Install SAP notes where necessary
Deployment		▶ Enable use of infrastructure locally	▶ Set up user access ▶ Develop additional interfaces ▶ Install interfaces	▶ Support entities that have gone live	▶ Install upgrades or SAP notes where necessary ▶ Switch off replaced systems
Refreezing					
Post-Implementation		▶ Monitor system performance	▶ Delegate people to SAP program for supporting improvement projects	▶ Take over full support from program team	▶ Maintain software
Life After SAP		▶ Monitor system performance		▶ Provide support following SLA ▶ Go for continuous improvement of support delivery; create synergies ▶ Identify improvement areas	▶ Execute upgrades ▶ Identify improvement areas

Table E.1 Major Actions Recommended for IT (cont.)

The Authors

 Luc Galoppin is managing director of Reply Management Consulting, a consultancy specializing in organizational change. He picked up his organizational change skills on SAP programs of different scopes and user communities as well as in interim management assignments. His customers are based in the chemicals, gas, and cosmetics industries. He also trains in-house and lectures at several business schools on the topics of organizational change and communication. Mr. Galoppin holds a Master's degree in applied economics from KU Leuven and a Master's degree in European industrial relations from Warwick Business School.

 Siegfried Caems is managing director of Leading Edge Management Consultants, a consultancy specializing in management of large change programs. As a global program manager in multinational organizations, he has successfully managed organizational change during the implementation of large-scale application packages such as SAP. His customers are based in the financial, automotive, service, utilities, and cosmetics industries. Siegfried is a guest lecturer at the Universiteit Antwerpen Management School. Siegfried holds a Master's degree in applied economic sciences from the Universiteit Antwerpen. He is SAP certified at the SAP Academy in London.

Index

Detailed guidance on RFC programming

Object-oriented access with BAPIs, Active X, and JCo

Advanced techniques: tRFC, qRFC, and parallel processing

379 pp., 2004, 69,95 Euro / US$ 69,95
ISBN 978-1-59229-034-5

SAP Interface Programming

www.sap-press.com

J. Meiners, W. Nüßer

SAP Interface Programming

A comprehensive reference for RFC, BAPI, and JCo programming

With a strong focus on the RFC Library, this book gives beginners a first-hand introduction to basic concepts, and highlights key tools in the ABAP Workbench. Actual programming examples help to illustrate client-server architecture, and show you how to assess the appropriate tools for error diagnosis, troubleshooting and more. Experienced SAP developers can dive right into comprehensive chapters on programming the RFC interface, and advanced techniques such as tRFC, qRFC, and parallel processing. Extensive coverage of BAPIs, ActiveX, JCo and highly-detailed programming examples serve to round out this exceptional resource.

zing and Availability of Platform,
Storage, Memory, and Network
Infrastructure

Adaptive Infrastructures and SAP
Adaptive Computing Controller

Service Level Agreements, IT
Service Management, and TCO

534 pp., 2005, 79,95 Euro / US$ 79,95
ISBN 978-1-59229-035-2

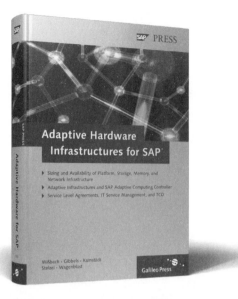

Adaptive Hardware
Infrastructures for SAP
www.sap-press.com

M. Missbach, P. Gibbels, J. Karnstädt, J. Stelzel, T.
Wagenblast

Adaptive Hardware Infrastructures for SAP

Constantly changing business processes pose a
critical challenge for today´s hardware. In order to
conquer this challenge, companies must respond
quickly and in a cost-effective manner, without
risking the future safety of their infrastructure. This
unique new book helps you to understand the most
important factors for determining what hardware you
´ll need to support flexible software systems in the
months and years ahead. Plus, discover the ins and
outs of exactly how SAP systems support your
business processes. In addition, you'll benefit from
highly-detailed insights, essential for helping you
calculate your true Total Cost of Ownership (TCO).

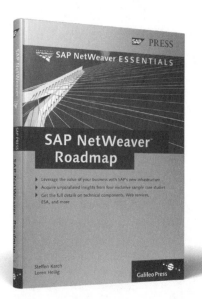

SAP NetWeaver Roadmap

S. Karch, L. Heilig, C. Bernhardt, A. Hardt, F. Heidfeld, R. Pfennig

SAP NetWeaver Roadmap

This book helps you understand each of SAP NetWeaver's components and illustrates, using practical examples, how SAP NetWeaver, and its levels of integration, can be leveraged by a wide range of organizations.

Readers benefit from in-depth analysis featuring four actual case studies from various industries, which describe in detail how integration with SAP NetWeaver can contribute to the optimization of a variety of essential business processes and how the implementation works. Finally, detailed coverage of SAP NetWeaver technology gives you the complete picture in terms of architecture and functionality of each component.

Comprehensive details on the new capabilities of mySAP ERP

Expert insights and best practices to ensure a successful upgrade

In-depth analysis of the technical infrastructure of SAP NetWeaver and ESA

293 pp., 2006, 59,95 Euro / US$ 59.95
ISBN 978-1-59229-071-0

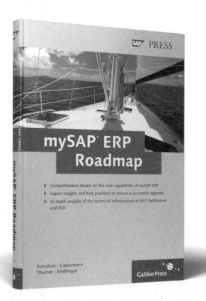

mySAP ERP Roadmap

www.sap-press.com

F. Forndron, T. Liebermann, M. Thurner,
P. Widmayer

mySAP ERP Roadmap

Business Processes, Capabilities, and Complete
Upgrade Strategy

Finally, a book that delivers detailed coverage of the
functionality and technology of mySAP ERP, and
provides you with a clear, simple and comprehensive
path to your upgrade. This book introduces you to
the business processes supported by mySAP ERP and
helps you understand the evolution from SAP R/3 to
mySAP ERP. You get exclusive insights into the
technical infrastructure of SAP NetWeaver and the
Enterprise Services Architecture, all designed to help
you hit the ground running. Through clear decision
criteria, practical examples, and Transition Road-
maps, readers will uncover the optimal path from
SAP R/3 to mySAP ERP. This book is an invaluable
resource to support your upgrade decision.

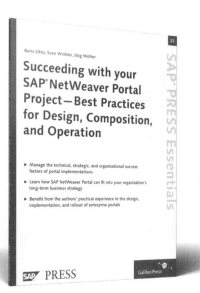

**The benchmark work
for release 4.0**

500 pp.,2006, 69,95 Euro / US$ 69,95
ISBN 978-1-59229-091-8

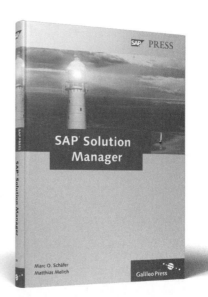

SAP Solution Manager

www.sap-press.com

M.O. Schäfer, M. Melich

SAP Solution Manager

This unique book helps administrators and IT
managers to quickly understand the full functionality
of SAP Solution Manager, release 4.0. Readers get a
thorough introduction in the areas of Implementation and Operations, especially in the scenarios
Project Management, Service Desk, Change Request
Management, and the brand new function
Diagnostics (root cause analysis).
The integration capabilities with third-party tools
from the areas of Help Desk and Modelling, as well
as the relation between the functionality and ITIL
Application Management are also dealt with in
detail.

Expert insights on local SAP
scheduling facilities such as
CCMS, BI and Mass Activities

echniques to maximize the full
capabilities of SAP central job
scheduling by Redwood

312 pp., 2006, 69,95 Euro / US$ 69.95
ISBN 1-59229-093-0

Job Scheduling for SAP

www.sap-press.com

K. Verruijt, A. Roebers, A. de Heus

Job Scheduling for SAP

With this book, you'll learn the ins and outs of job
scheduling with "SAP Central Job Scheduling by
Redwood" and "Redwood Cronacle." Uncover critical
details on the architecture, plus exclusive technical
insights that cannot be found elsewhere. The authors
cover both decentralized and centralized SAP job
scheduling and provide you with practical advice to
drastically bolster standard installation and configuration guides. Special attention is paid to both
individual CCMS and SAP BI jobs as well as to
integration methods for these enterprise-level job
chains. Best Practices from real-world case studies
ensure that this book leaves no stone unturned.

Rapid ROI by use of efficient systems

Optimization of architecture, business processes and support

Including first-hand information on NetWeaver system landscapes

223 pp., 2004, 79,95 Euro / US$ 79,95
ISBN 978-1-59229-026-0

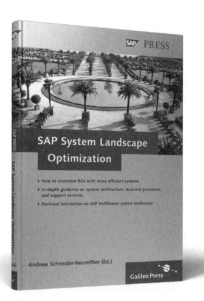

SAP System Landscape Optimization

www.sap-press.com

A. Schneider-Neureither (Ed.)

SAP System Landscape Optimization

This reference book serves as an essential collection of insights, procedures, processes and tools that help you unlock the full potential of your SAP systems. First, hit the ground running with a detailed introduction to SAP NetWeaver and the mySAP Business Suite. Then, elevate your mastery of key concepts such as system architecture, security, Change and Transport Management, to name just a few. All of the practical advice and detailed information provided is with a clear focus on helping you guide your team to achieve a faster return on investment.

Thoroughly revised and extended edition!

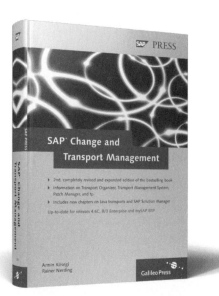

744 pp., 2. edition 2006, 99,95 Euro / US$ 99,95
ISBN 978-1-59229-059-8

SAP Change and Transport Management

www.sap-press.com

A. Koesegi, R. Nerding

SAP Change and Transport Management

This bestseller focuses on concepts and strategies related to the system landscape, making it an indispensable reference for project leaders, consultants and system administrators.
You learn everything needed to record customizing and development changes to an SAP system SAP R/3 as well as SAP ECC (mySAP ERP), so you can transport your changes to testing and production environments. You'll help SAP keep pace with your organization's evolving business needs, promoting greater efficiency and flexibility. This brand new edition has been completely revised and significantly extended, with the addition of new chapters on Java transports, Solution Manager, maintenance, and release upgrades.

**A practical guide
to implementing and using
SAP xApp Analytics**

**Easily deploy, configure, and
combine analytic applications
to customize SAP xApp
Analytics for your needs**

408 pp., 2006, 69,95 Euro / US$ 69.95
ISBN 978-1-59229-102-1

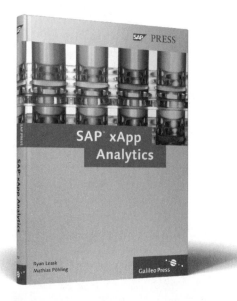

SAP xApp Analytics

www.sap-press.com

Ryan Leask, Mathias Pöhling, Ryan Leask,
Mathias Pöhling

SAP xApp Analytics

A practical guide to implementing and using
SAP xApp Analytics

This book fulfills two goals. First, it gives readers a
look at the technology behind building Analytic
Applications within SAP. Second, it gives a business
perspective as to why xApp Analytics are beneficial.
It addresses how SAP meets industry-specific
challenges with various pre-packaged Analytic
applications. Practical examples and the authors'
experiences while working with Analytics are
valuable resources for readers. Readers will also
obtain insight into the future of xApp Analytics.
Other topics include installation, administration,
transporting, and coverage of the Visual Composer.